Class, Capital and Social Policy

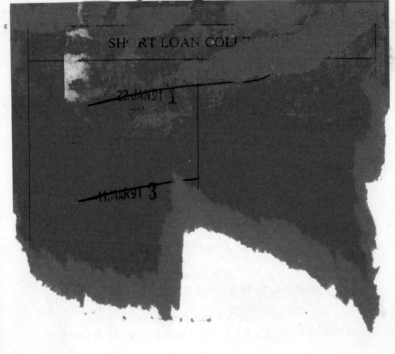

Critical Texts in Social Work and the
Welfare State

General Editor: Peter Leonard

Published

Pete Alcock and Phil Harris
WELFARE LAW AND ORDER: A CRITICAL
INTRODUCTION TO LAW FOR
SOCIAL WORKERS

Steve Bolger, Paul Corrigan, Jan Docking and Nick Frost
TOWARDS SOCIALIST WELFARE WORK:
WORKING IN THE STATE

Paul Corrigan and Peter Leonard
SOCIAL WORK PRACTICE UNDER CAPITALISM:
A MARXIST APPROACH

Norman Ginsburg
CLASS, CAPITAL AND SOCIAL POLICY

Ian Gough
THE POLITICAL ECONOMY OF THE WELFARE STATE

Chris Jones
STATE SOCIAL WORK AND THE WORKING CLASS

Chris Phillipson
CAPITALISM AND THE CONSTRUCTION OF OLD AGE

Forthcoming

Lena Dominelli and Eileen McLeod
FEMINISM AND WELFARE:
SOCIAL ACTION AND SOCIAL WORK

Peter Leonard
PERSONALITY AND IDEOLOGY:
TOWARDS A MATERIALIST UNDERSTANDING
OF THE INDIVIDUAL

Geoffrey Pearson
IDEOLOGICAL CRISIS IN SOCIAL WORK

Class, Capital and Social Policy

Norman Ginsburg

MACMILLAN PRESS
LONDON

4607
Pascall

© Norman Ginsburg 1979

First edition 1979
Reprinted 1981, 1983

Published by
THE MACMILLAN PRESS LTD
London and Basingstoke
Associated companies throughout the world

ISBN 0 333 21600 8 (paper cover)

Typeset by Santype International Ltd, Salisbury, Wilts

Printed in Hong Kong

cc

Contents

Acknowledgements   vii

Editor's Introduction   ix

Notes to the Editor's Introduction   xv

1 Introduction: Class Power and the Welfare State   1
2 Some Basic Concepts and Assumptions   20
3 Social Security, Class Struggle and the Reproduction of
   Capital   46
4 Social Security and the Questions of Women and Bureaucratic Power   79
5 Private Housing, the State and the Working Class   108
6 Council Housing   138

Notes and References   169

Index   187

Acknowledgements

I should like to acknowledge the assistance of the innumerable people with whom I have discussed the questions covered in this book, notably colleagues and students at Warwick University, welfare activists in Coventry and elsewhere and members of various discussion groups within the Conference of Socialist Economists.

In particular I am grateful to Simon Clarke, Lena Dominelli, Simon Frith, Tim Godfrey, Ian Gough, Peter Leonard and Jane Taylor, who made painstaking comments on various drafts of the manuscript. I would also like to acknowledge the general support and encouragement which I have received from Veronica Beechey, Simon Clarke, Paul Corrigan, Simon Frith, Peter Leonard, Heather Macrae, Dave Smith and Jane Taylor. Finally I must thank Pat Ludgate and Lydia Thorpe for their assistance in typing sections of the final manuscript.

N. G.

Coventry
November 1978

Editor's Introduction

The welfare state in Britain is in a condition of profound crisis; this can no longer seriously be questioned. Although the precise nature of this crisis is subject to much debate, its effects are recognised everywhere, but especially among those working within the apparatus of the welfare state at central and local level, and those most dependent on certain welfare services – the poor, the deprived and the most exploited, including women, the black population and the unemployed.

EXPLANATION OF THE CRISIS

But although the material effects of the crisis on services are increasingly evident, its ideological and political repercussions are also becoming clearer and, to some at least, almost equally disturbing. Thus, at one level, resistance to welfare cuts is sometimes associated with political subversion and the debate moved from the substance of the cuts to the issue of seeking out those who are attempting to infiltrate the 'democratic processes'. At another level, the failure of crude models of individual pathology to explain continued poverty has led to the invention of an apparently more sophisticated response – the idea of 'transmitted deprivation'. As an explanation of the 'cycle of poverty', it performs an invaluable ideological function in directing attention towards those experiencing poverty and away from the broader structural questions which might be raised about the effects of fundamental features and contradictions of an advanced capitalist economy. At yet a further level, attacks on 'welfare scroungers' reflect explanations of the crisis which reveal a deeply reactionary ideological response which may eventually work its way through into more overt political strategies.

Despite the impact of the powerful apparatus of the mass media and education which frequently support these and other self-justifying explanations of the crisis, those who work in welfare frequently experience a disturbing degree of cognitive dissonance between the dominant explanations and their knowledge of the material reality of their work. A realisation that the crisis in welfare reflects more fundamental crises also leads to increasing demands, especially among students in the social sciences, in social administration and in social work, that more structurally informed explanations should be developed. Within social work, for example, the crisis raises in an inescapable form the dilemma which faces practitioners in struggling with their roles as agents of the state. In assessing their clients and in delivering services, social workers are undertaking a profoundly ideological task on behalf of the established structures; at the same time they are often trying to help clients resist the most oppressive and discriminatory features of the welfare system. How are social workers to understand this conflict in their practice?

Those who have studied or lived through the social legislation of the 1960s and early 1970s are bound, as the crisis deepens, to ask themselves on what assumptions this legislation was based and whether it had any relevance to the most crucial problems involved in developing welfare within a specific kind of economy at a particular historical juncture. The slogans of that era – community care, participation, family-oriented services, prevention, consumer rights – pervaded the government reports, the legislation and much of the writing and discussion which took place in the fields of planning, housing, mental health, child care and personal social services generally. These slogans, and the policies and practices which were initiated to reflect them, based their ideological justification on the liberal democratic assertion that humane, universalist and non-stigmatising services could be developed within the existing structure of British capitalism. The essence of this assertion is captured in the following passage from the Seebohm Report, published in 1968:

> we see our proposals not simply in terms of organisation but as embodying a wider conception of social service, directed to the well-being of the whole of the community and not only of social casualties, and seeing the community it serves as the basis of its authority, resources and effectiveness. Such a conception

spells, we hope, the death-knell of the Poor Law legacy and the socially divisive attitudes and practices which stemmed from it.[1]

To read such a passage now provokes an acute awareness of how far the British welfare state has moved into a different situation in the intervening years, and how necessary it is to re-examine the historical antecedents, ideological underpinning and economic context of the present services in the welfare state.

THEORY AND PRACTICE

One main function of this series of 'Critical Texts in Social Work and the Welfare State' is to address itself to explanations of the crisis which relate to the immediate material reality experienced by state workers in the welfare field and to link this to the economic, political, ideological and historical context within which the crisis occurs. Some of the volumes in the series therefore focus primarily on *explanation*. Others also place emphasis on sketching the beginnings of alternative forms of *practice* which some workers within the welfare state might test out against the realities and possibilities of day-to-day activity. Prescriptions for practice, however tentative, are bound to be received with justifiable scepticism among those, such as students and practitioners in social work, who have a bitter experience of the gap between theory and practice revealed in most of the textbooks they have tried to use. A frequent complaint is that many of these books hardly reflect the desperate pressures of present-day practice – the lack of resources, the bureaucratic oppression, the despair and fatalism which often come from struggling against problems which are totally unresponsive to social-work intervention.

In general terms the series approaches the theory–practice relationship from two starting-points. One starting-point is to reflect systematically on practice and develop theory from it. Gramsci[2] writes that 'one can construct, on a specific practice, a theory which, by coinciding and identifying itself with the decisive elements of the practice, can accelerate the historical process that is going on, rendering practice more homogeneous, more coherent, more efficient in all its elements'. The task here is to select those areas of practice within the welfare state which seem most promising as points of departure in developing critical, 'progressive' strategies and which deserve theoretical attention.

Alternatively, Gramsci continues, 'given a certain theoretical position, one can organize the practical element which is essential for the theory to be realized'. In this second process, ideas actually become a material force. Here, the series draws primarily, but not exclusively, on Marxist theory as a basis for its efforts to contribute to the development of practice.

The emphasis on practice in this series stems in part from the importance which is attached to the difficult struggle involved in developing knowledge and in the need to change reality in order to understand it. Mao Tse-tung, in a seminal paper, writes:

> If you want to know a certain thing or class of things directly, you must personally participate in the practical struggle to change reality, to change that thing or class of things, for only thus can you come into contact with them as phenomena.[3]

Because the series takes a stand severely critical of dominant forms of theory and practice in the welfare field, it would be valuable to sketch in the ideological context within which it attempts to make an intervention. It is not possible, however, to give a full account of this context – we shall instead simply indicate one feature of the surrounding landscape: prevailing accounts of social policy development.

ACCOUNTS OF SOCIAL POLICY

We have argued that students and practitioners in the social welfare field have found that the dominant accounts of the crisis in the welfare state are unsatisfactory in that they neither relate to experienced reality nor link to the wider structural features of society and the economy. This is especially true of the *ad hoc*, low-level explanations of social problems and social policy which have dominated much of the work undertaken in the study of social administration in Britain. Even accounts of social policy development which operate at a more theoretically sophisticated level nevertheless are based upon consensual and pluralist theories of the state and society which are ill equipped to handle, for example, the phenomenon of increased class conflict or the relationship between community problems and international capital.

At the peak of Fabian optimism in social policy, two simultaneous developments took place which have since been seen, in their different ways, to fail to live up to the expectation which surrounded them at their birth. They will serve as examples of both the limitations and the ideological functions of dominant forms of explanation in the social policy field. They are the reorganisation of local authority welfare services with the setting up of a unified social service department, and the establishment of government-sponsored Community Development Projects.

In the case of the new social service departments, the unification which was so welcomed by social workers and social administrators at the time of the Seebohm Report in 1968 was implemented in legislation in 1970. Since that time the promise of a destigmatised, community-based and easily accessible service has not materialised. Explanations of the reason for this failure include lack of resources, bureaucratic growth, weak professionalism, and local political and professional resistance to community participation. In addition, some would argue that the transformation of social workers into agents of outdoor relief to the poor has struck a nearly fatal blow at the more traditional, humane, therapeutic roles of social workers.[4] Whilst all of these points have a certain validity they are usually made without reference to their relationship to more fundamental questions; they remain at a symptomatic level. Dominant accounts of social policy fail to use a class analysis which would highlight the role of personal social services in deflecting attention from structural failures by focusing on individual or community 'pathology'. They fail to see how professionalism can, in effect, be allied with bureaucracy against the interests of the welfare client. They see bureaucracy as a dysfunction of organisation rather than a form of organisation which merely reflects the dominant political and economic imperative to control the welfare system in the interests of the state.

In the case of the Community Development Projects, the picture which emerges is one where the unintended consequences of government policy at the ideological and political level lead to a retreat to safer ground. The Community Development Projects were begun in 1970 on the basis of a conception of community pathology central to the ideology of the consensual and pluralist policy-makers in government. As in the case of the Educational Priority Areas, special resources and knowledge were to be pumped into certain selected communities which exhibited a high level of pathology in terms of delinquency, deprivation, mental disorder and other associated indices. The experiment was ostensibly designed to show whether more resources, better co-ordination and more effective connection to community needs could contribute to ameliorating the extent and depth of individual and community problems in the selected areas. The end result, in most cases, was that the workers came to reject the assumptions upon which projects were established and to see individual and community problems as inextricably related to the class structure and the exploitive nature of the capitalist economy. Such alternative explanations, however, are ill fitted to take their place beside those which emphasise community apathy and the need for more effective corporate management in local government. The consequence, however, is that the monopoly of consensual and pluralist explanations of social policy has at least been broken in the fields of community action, housing and planning.

CLASS, CAPITAL AND SOCIAL POLICY

The way in which consensual and pluralist explanations of social policy have been challenged can be seen in this present volume in the series. In it, Norman Ginsburg develops an impressive analysis of the relationship between social policy developments and the imperatives of the capitalist economy. Whilst a previous volume in the series, Ian Gough's *The Political Economy of the Welfare State*,[5] provided an overview of the state's response to the functional needs of capital and to the pressures of class struggle, Ginsburg deepens the historical and political analysis by selecting two areas of welfare: social security and housing.

The most important feature of this book lies in its detailed account of the way in which the administration of particular sectors of the welfare state can be shown to reflect, in precise ways, the balance of class forces within the society as a whole. In particular, Ginsburg is able to produce compelling evidence that whilst organised working-class power has definitely influenced the administration of some aspects of welfare at the local level, this has been continuously counteracted by the growth of state bureaucracy. Concentration on the issue of bureaucratic power is most significant here, and the book shows how a Marxist analysis of this phenomenon can cut through what

Alvin Gouldner referred to as the 'metaphysical pathos' of many writers on bureaucracy. Ginsburg shows us that the characteristics of modern state bureaucracy, scientific management, professionalisation, corporate planning and the rest, can only be understood as *specifically* related to the demands of and crisis in capitalist development. Far from being 'inevitably' the result of organisational growth *per se*, bureaucratic development has to be located precisely within specific historical processes reflecting the stage which the capitalist mode of production has reached.

This book is quite clearly, then, a most important contribution to that development of a political economy of welfare to which this series is committed. But it not only raises theoretical questions of great significance but also provides an analysis of value to those who are working within the state apparatus itself. Ginsburg's work on welfare administration reveals itself as especially powerful when he discusses the position of women in relation to social security. The oppression of women is nowhere more clearly demonstrated than in the exercise of state power, economically and ideologically, in the field of social security. The penetration of Ginsburg's analysis at this point will do much to clarify the nature of the struggles to be engaged in here.

PETER LEONARD

NOTES TO THE EDITOR'S INTRODUCTION

1. *Report of the Committee on Local Authority and Allied Personal Social Services*, Cmnd. 3703 (1968) para. 474.
2. A. Gramsci, *Prison Notebooks* (Lawrence and Wishart, 1971) p. 365.
3. Mao Tse-tung, 'On Practice', *Selected Readings* (Foreign Languages Press, Peking, 1971) p. 71.
4. See B. Jordan, *Poor Parents* (Routledge & Kegan Paul, 1974).
5. I. Gough, *The Political Economy of the Welfare State* (Macmillan, 1979).

1

Introduction: Class Power and the Welfare State

This book examines the development of state policy and administration in two areas of social welfare in Britain, housing and social security. In both these areas it is suggested that, on the one hand, a quite specific historical and theoretical analysis is required and that, on the other hand, state policy has been directly formed by the exigencies of the continual crises of capitalist development and their political consequences. Hence we shall try to draw out the relations between the apparently discrete questions of housing and social security, and the broader development of the capitalist social formation. Neither a unitary theory of the welfare state nor even a theory of the state is the end in view here, but rather to begin to locate the development of particular welfare policies within the broader political economy. In these opening chapters some of the conceptual and theoretical questions concerning the general analysis of the welfare state within a Marxist perspective are aired briefly.

In any critical consideration of the welfare state, one must distance oneself from the barrage of ideological assumptions surrounding it, as it is continually reinforced by politicians, the media and the academic literature as well as by the agencies of the state themselves. The dominant view or ideology promotes the appearance of the state as neutral, representing a coalition of all classes and pursuing the common interest or 'the national interest'. This is particularly true of the welfare state, and it is a view shared in slightly different forms by a wide range of ideologues of social welfare, ranging from the anti-collectivist right to many socialists. It is a widespread belief, even amongst socialists, that the welfare state is essentially administered in the interests of its working-class consumers and is even to some extent 'under the control of' working-class politicians, and therefore capable of further reforms to satisfy the needs of the working class.

It is true that specific reforms have come about as the result of pressure from the organised working class, though the enlightened bourgeoisie and the threat of the unorganised working class have also been important sources of pressure. It is also true that the welfare state is a response to the democratically expressed aspirations of the working class. Nevertheless, it will be argued here that a detailed examination of the functioning and management of state welfare suggests that it remains part of a *capitalist* state which is fundamentally concerned with the maintenance and reproduction of capitalist social relations. It requires only the briefest acquaintance with Britain's social and labour history to discover how consistently and how effectively working-class struggle and demands for better living conditions and welfare have been thwarted and repressed.

Thus the welfare state is not considered here as an untrammelled achievement of the working class in struggle, an oasis of socialism and hence a series of concessions by the bourgeoisie. Nor is it viewed as an institution shaped largely by the demands and requirements of the capitalist economy. The welfare state has been formed around the contradictions and conflicts of capitalist development in specific historical contexts. From the working-class point of view it is a response to their continual struggle to improve and secure their conditions of existence or standard of living. From the capitalist point of view state welfare has contributed to the continual struggle to accumulate capital by materially assisting in bringing labour and capital together profitably and containing the inevitable resistance and revolutionary potential of the working class. Hence it is suggested here that the social security system is concerned with reproducing a reserve army of labour, the patriarchal family and the disciplining of the labour force. Only secondarily and contingently does it function as a means of mitigating poverty or providing 'income maintenance'. It is similarly argued that housing policy is directed towards regulating the consumption of a vital commodity for the reproduction of the labour force, and only secondarily and contingently as an attempt at providing secure and adequate accommodation for the working class. Thus the possibility of securing a fundamental shift in the structure of class inequality in favour of the working class through administrative and policy reform or working-class political struggle within the state apparatus is severely constrained by the essential form and functions of the state as a capitalist state, which boil down to the reproduction of the relationship between capital and labour.

The term 'welfare state' is used here as a shorthand for the state's role in education, health, housing, poor relief, social insurance and other social services. This role is paradoxically both wider and narrower than is commonly appreciated. It is narrower because the liberal capitalist state's room for manoeuvre within its own ideology is clearly circumscribed by its lack of direct control over capital and the production and consumption of welfare. For example, council housing is largely built by private firms on land bought in the private market with money borrowed in the finance markets. The government merely acts as an intermediary entrepreneur in the process of production and consumption. Similarly the social security system is geared to the apparent needs of the labour market and the private patriarchal family. Here governments respond to crises, such as unemployment or desertion, in which they claim little responsibility or directive role. In areas such as industrial relations, occupational welfare, preventive medicine, owner-occupation and so on, state bodies take on an advisory, watchdog role with a preference for self-regulation by the parties involved. The state's role in welfare is also wider than is commonly appreciated because it is not just involved in the provision of services through its agencies. It is crucially involved in the regulation of private provision and consumption of welfare as a major employer, the taxation authority and general overseer and maker of ground-rules for the private markets in such services. One of the major features of the post-war period in Britain has been the expansion of occupational welfare, particularly superannuation schemes, and owner-occupation for the upper echelons of the working class. This trend has been increasingly encouraged and orchestrated by state policy measures.

The welfare state is not therefore adequately conceived as simply a collection of policies and agencies. The idea of the welfare state has been a very powerful ideological force within post-war British society. It has emerged as a generic term to describe the expansion of government activity on many fronts – such as industrial, employment and incomes policies – as well as what are usually referred to as welfare policies. The phrase 'welfare state' conveys the benevolent and responsive appearance from which many liberal, capitalist governments derive substantial legitimacy. In post-war Britain the working class has regarded the contemporary welfare state, particularly the National Health Service, as perhaps the most profound and significant outcome of the struggles of the inter-war years and during the Second

World War. We are not of course suggesting that the positive perception of state welfare by working-class people is illusory or ill founded. On the contrary it has obviously contributed very substantially to the improvement of working-class conditions of existence during the post-war boom. The significance of the strong working-class commitment to the welfare state has been made clear during the successive economic crises since the end of the post-war boom in the 1960s. Governments have tried to cut back on welfare spending in order to redirect money capital towards industrial investment and thereby restore profitability. The success of such strategies has been partial for a variety of reasons, not the least of which has been the political difficulty of cutting welfare spending. In the struggle over the conditions of the International Monetary Fund loan in 1976, many members of the Labour cabinet genuinely feared that further cuts in welfare spending would destroy the Labour Party, and they successfully resisted proposed cuts in social security benefits, though massive cuts in the housing programme survived. Although the cuts have contributed to the deterioration of welfare services in the 1970s, at the moment the dismantling of the National Health Service or substantial cuts in social security benefits remain politically unacceptable to the British working class, and it is hard to envisage such policies without an unprecedented defeat for the working-class movement.

The specific cuts in welfare spending have generated a fairly fragmentary and localised movement to defend the welfare state, which has understandably been confined in most cases to the protection of employment rather than a questioning of the control or the function of the services defended. Nevertheless, there is widespread working-class ambivalence towards the welfare state which consists of disillusion and suspicion created by negative individual and collective experiences. This ambivalence on the part of welfare state employees and consumers alike is generated, on the one hand, by its appearance of class neutrality, benevolence and subjection to democratic controls and, on the other hand, by the frequent experience of the very opposite.

Obvious negative aspects of welfare state management as experienced by its employees and consumers are bureaucratism, remoteness and lack of effective democratic control through Parliament, trade unions and local councils. It is argued in this book that these are not incidental or accidental features of the welfare state that can be eliminated by further administrative reform. On the contrary, they play a central role in fulfilling some of the essential functions of capitalist welfare, rationing benefits and services according to ideological criteria of deservingness, and containing individual and collective pressure for change. The discussion of social security and housing administration in later chapters suggests that administrative discretion and bureaucratism are essential to the smooth functioning of the welfare state. The growth of bureaucratism has been enhanced by the centralisation of government agencies and the ineffectiveness of political controls. This is reflected in the experience of remoteness from the decision-making process by employees and consumers, and the increasingly obvious helplessness of members of Parliament and local councillors in challenging the state apparatus on their behalf. There has occurred a manifest centralisation of control over state activity, a prime example of which has been the relentless stripping away of local authority functions and increased control of local authority finance and administration by central government.

There has also been the removal of state decision-making from the democratic political arenas into relatively autonomous state bodies – autonomous, that is, from Parliament and local councils. Even within the less autonomous areas of government, such as local government departments, the power of management and chief officers appears to have grown at the expense of the power of elected members, and the whole structure of local government has of course recently been centralised and concentrated by reorganisation. This continuing restructuring of the state apparatus no doubt reflects the centralisation and concentration of capital itself, but it is also a response to the increasing power of the working class through trade union organisation, pressure and action groups, Parliament and local councils. This working-class power has gathered strength slowly but surely since the late nineteenth century. It has not only forced the pace as far as the expansion of welfare expenditures is concerned, but it has paradoxically forced the gradual removal of the potential for democratic control which to some extent existed in previous structures. The rest of this chapter is devoted to examining some of the problems concerning working-class power and the welfare state within various socialist perspectives.

THE WORKING CLASS AND THE WELFARE STATE

The view that the welfare state represents a victory for socialism and working-class values which must be cherished and improved from within is very widespread in the labour movement. It has never been better expressed than in a short article by Dorothy Thompson written over 20 years ago, but still relevant today. She argues that a whole range of welfare benefits and services are now provided

> purely on the basis of *need* and not of cash payment, or even of any abstract conception of *social value*. This conception is a profoundly anti-capitalist one . . . The real significance of the welfare services, and of the legality of Trade Unions and other working class organisations, is that these are, objectively, victories for working class values within capitalist society.[1]

Taking first the point concerning the importance of free or subsidised services, clearly these are of great benefit to the working class. State welfare takes the provision of certain use-values out of the private market, generating wider and more secure access to them and depriving capital of some opportunities for the appropriation of value (in the form of profit, interest, etc.) in their production and consumption. In the case of council housing this undoubtedly reduces the direct cost to some tenants. At the same time the 'provision' of these use-values by the state has opened up new opportunities for capital accumulation – for example, in the pharmaceutical industry and the construction industry. When direct private provision of these use-values to the working class becomes profitable, the government may begin to withdraw into a more regulative role.

Secondly, there is the question of benefits and services being made available 'purely on the basis of need'. Certainly, in terms of the ideological principles of the welfare state, provision is made on the basis of individual need, but how is individual need established? It is certainly not established by collective and democratically determined criteria of working-class welfare needs, except in the most general terms. Within the British welfare state 'need' is defined in reality in at least three different ways. Firstly, it is registered by individual consumer demand filtered by bureaucratic procedure and rationing – for example, by the use of waiting lists. Secondly, need is defined by professionals and administrators within the particular services who, in the absence of effective and specific mandates from consumers, exercise technical and professional expertise within broad parameters set by the government. Thirdly, there are the taken-for-granted parameters to the definition of need formed by the functional requirements for the maintenance of the labour force, such as the 'need' to get sick workers back to work as soon as possible or the need to provide cheap housing close to centres of employment. In other words, the welfare state is in many ways geared to the needs of capital in its requirements of the labour force, but this by no means accords with the needs of the working class in a broader context.

To what extent the welfare state is primarily geared to meeting and articulating the true needs of the working class is a moot point, since the definition of need appears, at present, to be largely imposed 'from above'. While undoubtedly the existence of state welfare has proved to be a gain for the working class and must be defended as such, it must also be recognised that 'there is nothing about any of the particular bits of social welfare legislation which is specifically or "essentially" socialist'.[2] The identification with socialism suggests that a part of the state apparatus has been created and administered by the working class in its own interests. Such misrepresentation remains an important element of the anti-collectivist rhetoric of the right wing, and is a product of the late Victorian era, when reactionary ideologues identified collectivism, that is state intervention, as a form of socialism threatening the full-blooded competitive capitalism of a bygone era, though in fact it was a progression of capitalist development.

Perspectives which suggest that the welfare state is an oasis of socialism mistakenly imply that the working class has been the prime mover in not only prompting welfare reform, but in shaping and administering it. It is true that the support of the organised working class has been crucial to almost all progressive reforms, but one cannot argue that the welfare state is the product of a consistent, mass campaign by the working-class movement. The labour movement has never in fact developed and promoted a programme of state welfare measures. The working class has maintained a healthy suspicion of legislation in general, including many aspects of welfare reform. Nevertheless, one must recognise the emergence at the local level of programmes for municipal socialism initiated by the Social Democratic Federation (SDF) from 1887 onwards, covering a wide variety of welfare measures.[3] Many of these proposals were subsequently adapted as piecemeal welfare reforms implemented by Liberal and Labour councils. Certainly, also, both before and after the First World War, the labour movement declared itself on particular issues, such as support for the abolition of the poor law, universal non-contributory pensions for old age and the nationalisation of the hospitals.[4] So developed the pragmatic and loosely defined principles of welfare Labourism, whose relationship to socialism remained tortuous to say the least. In 1918 the Labour Party adopted its new constitution and the policy statement *Labour and the New Social Order*, which 'insisted on the State's responsibility for the provision to every citizen of a minimum standard of health, education, leisure and subsistence'.[5] The new constitution consolidated the power of the trade unions at the expense of the left, while the policy statement was 'an explicit affirmation by the Labour Party of its belief that piecemeal collectivism within a predominantly capitalist society was the key to more welfare, higher efficiency and greater social justice'.[6] It hardly constituted a programme of wholesale welfare reform even along the Fabian lines advocated, for example, by the Webbs in the 1909 Minority Report to the Royal Commission on the Poor Laws. Neither the welfare programme nor the structure of the Labour Party have changed fundamentally since 1918. The 1924 and 1929-31 Labour governments were largely incapable of significant shifts in welfare policy, with the possible exception of their more energetic public housing programme.

Turning to the period since 1940, it becomes even more difficult to distinguish the contribution of the organised Labour movement to welfare policy-making, since the leadership of the movement now becomes closely integrated into the state apparatus, combined with the continued absence of a distinct and comprehensive socialist welfare programme. Since TUC pressure initiated the Beveridge committee by its renewed advocacy of a comprehensive National Health Service in 1941, and since also the post-Beveridge reforms of the social security and health services were implemented by a Labour government, one could argue that the Labour movement was the vital force in not only pushing for the post-1945 welfare state, but in actually creating it. Indeed the post-1945 welfare state is widely believed to embody the essence of the social democratic achievement or even revolution, sometimes misleadingly labelled socialist. A crucial distinction must, however, be made between, on the one hand, working-class pressure and aspirations for vastly improved welfare and social conditions filtering through to the TUC and Labour Party leaders, and enhanced and developed by the demands of the war; and, on the other hand, the active participation of the working class in shaping the post-war reforms as they were implemented. Clearly the latter did not take place – the planning and implementation of the reforms were left to individuals and groups largely outside the Labour movement and the working class. Labour party and trade union members did of course discuss the reforms, but they were delivered 'from above' in the form of government reports and so on, and the Labour movement gratefully accepted that deliverance in the absence of their own programme and in the concomitant rejection of more fundamental, socialist proposals for change.

This is not to argue, along functionalist lines, that whatever political party had been in power in 1945–51, the outcome would have been the same. A Conservative government might have tried to shelve Beveridge in favour of something closer to the American welfare system, with greater emphasis on occupational, fiscal and private welfare for the working class regulated by the state. American finance capital and American governments have applied pressure on British governments in this direction during the economic crises of the post-war period, beginning in 1947. The policies of the 1945–51 Labour government reflected the state of party thinking on welfare before the war – a fragmentary collection of notions such as 'the national minimum', 'universal benefits', anti-landlordism, pro-council housing, anti-means testing and so on. Some of these principles could be incorporated into the post-1940 reforms, but only in this vague sense can it be said that the reforms were shaped by working–class values. The principal architects of the post-1940 reforms were in fact the progressive, liberal bourgeois who had become committed to Keynesianism and the interventionist state in the crises of the 1930s.[7] The interpretation and implementation of the post-war legislation, as well as its design, were left in the hands of civil servants and professionals, whose class bias, particularly in the upper echelons, remained unshaken.

The direct influence of the Labour movement over welfare policy since the early 1950s also appears to have been small, with one or two notable exceptions, such as the advocacy of earnings–related pensions in the mid-1950s and the struggles over the Housing Finance Act in the early 1970s. Crossman's diaries reveal the vacuity and weakness of Labour's plans in the 1960s for housing and social security. In relation to social security one political scientist has concluded that 'neither [Labour] party functionaries nor organisational structures have been prominent in the creation of specific new policy departures',[8] while the TUC 'has rarely played anything approaching a creative role in the development of policies'.[9] The fragmentary principles of welfare Labourism *were* consolidated at the municipal level in the shape of Labour councils who generally supported council housing and direct works departments, resisted means tests and pursued comprehensive education, often hampered by central government. Yet even some of these principles seem to have been eroded by the rise of owner-occupation and the effects of expanded working-class private consumerism. Thus, at both national and local levels of government, it is often difficult now to distinguish the *welfare* policies of the two major political parties, particularly since the election of the October 1974 Labour government. Welfare policy (inasmuch as it can be distinguished from cuts in welfare spending), aside from the issues raised by the women's movement, would be almost a non-political and non-controversial matter in contemporary mainstream politics, were it not for the revival of radical anti-collectivist ideology within the heart of the Conservative party.

We must conclude that the working class through the organs of the trade union movement and the Labour Party has exerted very little 'real' as opposed to 'formal' control over the shape of welfare policy and administration, and we hope that this is confirmed by the following analysis of the development of social security and housing policy. A political space has developed in the area of welfare in which pressure groups and interest groups of a great variety of social and political complexions bargain over small-scale reforms and parochial, although for them important, issues. The resultant of these pressures, which in most cases reflect the continuing and developing welfare needs of the working class and the failure of the welfare state to meet them, has hastened the restructuring of the state apparatus, designed to resist these demands with bureaucratism and closer control of the welfare professions.

While the working class has exerted little 'real' control over welfare policy and administration, it is equally true that the welfare state is a response to the presence of the working class, and the continuing plight of either some or all of its members in inadequate or insecure living conditions. This presence comes to the attention of governments and the bourgeoisie in any number of ways, apart from Labour movement pressure and pressure from other groups. Important examples in Britain might include the cholera epidemics of the mid-nineteenth century, the West End riots of the 1880s, the strikes and revolutionary agitation before and after the First World War, the hunger marches and rent strikes of the inter-war period, unofficial strikes in the 1960s, delinquency, squatting, family breakdown and so on. While none of these phenomena have represented an organised threat to the state, they forcibly bring home to the bourgeoisie the existence of a class or fragments of it which either rejects or is rejected by bourgeois values and whose needs must to some extent be accommodated or repressed to ensure the survival of capitalist social relations. It was in such a historical context that in 1885 Joseph Chamberlain, a leading Liberal figure, advocated a state welfare programme. He began with the question 'what ransom will property pay for the security which it enjoys?'[10] and later observed that 'the foundations of property are made more secure when no real grievance is felt by the poor against the rich'.[11]

In many examples of welfare reform, therefore, the conscious initiative has been made by the bourgeoisie in order to forestall and contain the potential or veiled threat to capital, politically articulated or otherwise, which the working class inevitably represents. Historians are sometimes surprised by the discovery of working-class resistance to and capitalist support for welfare reform. Indeed the working class has often been extremely suspicious of capitalist state welfare precisely because its members would rather maintain a healthy independence from the state apparatus, over which it exerts so little real control and which is not fundamentally designed with its interests in mind. The Labour movement was decidedly ambivalent about the Liberal welfare legislation of the Edwardian era, particularly national insurance, for a whole variety of reasons, ranging from the use of labour exchanges to recruit blacklegs to the threat to the tradition of working-class cooperative welfare exemplified by the friendly societies. It is a commonplace of social administration that the friendly societies were virtually bastions of reaction, preventing the emergence of social insurance, but, as Pat Thane has suggested, this rests upon a misinterpretation of the relationship between the working class and state welfare:

> The ideology of the Friendly Societies cannot simply be interpreted as exemplifying working class internalisation of middle class values . . . members identified themselves as part of a class whose interests were antagonistic to those of other classes and . . . they claimed a class identification with the poor outside the Friendly Societies.[12]

Like the friendly societies, all working-class organisations have been faced with an acute dilemma in the face of advancing state welfare as to whether welfare and other provisions on terms dictated by a capitalist state should be pressed for and accepted as a short-term gain, or whether the working class should retain independence from the state, concentrating its energies on improving the welfare of workers through struggle over wages and conditions, or working towards the achievement of real working-class control of the state apparatus.

In the end of course the working class has had to accept capitalist welfare as an immediate amelioration of its conditions of existence, though it has resisted the terms on which it has been offered, and opposed means-testing, work relief and fair rents, etc. But this accept-ance has been predicated on the hope that the working class would be able to impose its own values on the welfare state through Parlia-mentary channels. It is argued here that this has only occurred in a strictly limited fashion and only when it presents no threat to capital in its various forms, as was the case until recently with council housing. The broad acceptance of the welfare state by the working class just before the First World War reflected 'the realities of a situation in which a powerful capitalist government was using a highly successful reform strategy to undermine socialist support'.[13]

One may argue that state welfare represents a *quid pro quo* or a 'bribe' offered to the working class in exchange for political quies-cence and industrial peace. This was certainly Bismarck's view of his social insurance schemes, Lenin's view of Lloyd George's welfare legislation and a common interpretation of the reforms initiated by the Beveridge report. It captures the political importance of capitalist state welfare, which is correctly considered by working-class con-sumers as a 'piece of the cake' sacrificed by capital to secure their wider cooperation. The welfare state indeed exerts an important cush-ioning effect on working-class experience, actively diverting attention from the real relations of appropriation and the structure of class inequality. In this sense state welfare is a *quid pro quo* but it is not an equal exchange, for the 'piece of the cake' is not offered without important strings, functional to capital accumulation, and it is certainly not allowed to threaten capitalist social relations. On the contrary, it is essential in its detailed functioning to asserting the command of capital over labour and in its general ideological existence to securing the loyalty to the state of the working class. Hence in our discussion of housing and social security policy we shall concentrate on particular aspects that are directly functional to capital accumulation, as well as the ways in which the form of state administration processes and redefines the welfare rights of citizenship in such a way that the *overall* appearance of a democratic welfare state is preserved, while in practice remaining illusory as experienced by individual consumers.

STATE POWER

So far we have suggested that while the welfare state is a response to the presence and the pressures created by the working class which obviously goes some way towards meeting basic needs, it does not represent a victory for socialism nor, as we shall try to document in detail, is it a realm of the state over which the working class has established real control. For Marxists the question of class power within the welfare state immediately brings into view the general relationship between the working class and the state, and the means for the advancement of working-class power. Within the Marxist currents in the working-class movement the centrality of the attack on the state apparatus is not in doubt, but two distinct positions may be distinguished concerning the transformation of the state apparatus including the welfare state. On the one hand, there is the view that power should be sought within the state apparatus as presently constituted, consolidating the power of the organised working class in order to stifle state bureaucratism and bring about progressive and large-scale reform of both its functions and administration. On the other hand, there is the view that only a revolutionary break from the stranglehold of the capital-labour relation and the present form of the state can lead to fundamental change in the relationships of class power in favour of the working class, including above all an entire reconstruction of the state apparatus on a new democratic basis.

The former view suggests that the transformation of the state apparatus must take the form of a 'war of position' or a war of attrition prosecuted by the working class and its allies, using the democratic channels of the capitalist state apparatus itself. The theoretical origins of this position can be traced to the writings of Kautsky and Gramsci, both of whom attempted to come to terms with the specificity of the political situation facing the working-class movement in Western Europe in the twentieth century, as distinct from the situation in Russia, which invited an insurrectionary strategy or 'war of maneouvre'. Marxism was trying to come to terms with the emergence of the organised working class and the welfare state. Thus in 1910 for Kautsky 'the nub of this strategy of attrition were successive electoral campaigns'[14] precisely because in Western Europe the working class had been granted political citizenship and the rights to organise politically and in trade unions, while the state apparatus was also highly organised and apparently well equipped to stifle extra-parliamentary struggle. The very success of Bismarck's welfarism thus prompted a strategy of Parliamentarism in which the defensive strength of working-class organisations could eventually guarantee the imposition of the will of the 'people's representatives' on the state apparatus. The final rupture with capitalism was not rejected, but relegated to a future whose relationship to the present strategy was left unclear.

In the 1930s Gramsci, reacting like Kautsky to left adventurism, described a similar revolutionary strategy of a war of position, in which emphasis was laid on the importance of undermining bourgeois cultural and ideological domination or hegemony in the sphere of civil society beyond the state, concomitant with or even prior to the struggle for working class political hegemony within the state. Many contemporary Marxists have interpreted Gramsci as suggesting that socialists must develop working-class hegemony within the institutions of civil society and the state, hence bringing about 'the progressive capture of the terrain of bourgeois hegemony, breaking down the apparatus of consent, forcing the gradual isolation of the ruling class, creating an ever clearer and more convincing image of the working people as the true "saviours of society"'.[15] The task of revolutionary socialists and their organisations is therefore, according to the neo-Gramscians, to implant socialist ideas into bourgeois culture, ideology and administration, ideas which will eventually discredit the latter and secure the allegiance of a broad coalition of forces behind the workers' movement.

Such a position clearly fails to take into account the role of the repressive state apparatuses (the armed forces, the police and so on), which are inevitably brought into the forefront if a serious threat to capital is posed. But with respect to the welfare state, it must be said against this position that the successful and exemplary implantation of socialist ideology within the state apparatus is severely constrained and deformed by the essential form and function of state policy and administration, which is not relatively autonomous from the capital–labour relation in its actual functioning, despite its appearance. The social security system is founded on and embedded within the exigencies of the capital–labour relation and the former cannot be transformed fundamentally without the supersession of the latter. The production and management of council housing testifies as much to the success of state entrepreneurialism in alliance with finance and construction capital and the limitations as opposed to the success of socialist ideology implanted within the capitalist state. It is essential that the active involvement of and pressure from workers and socialists within the participatory outgrowth of the welfare state be pursued, precisely because it can serve to puncture the illusions of the benevolent and neutral state, as well as necessitating the development of *independent* consumer and employee organisation. It is also essential to press for a democratisation of the welfare state, but these avenues of struggle cannot lead in themselves to the permanent implantation of socialist ideals within the welfare state, as is amply demonstrated by the history of the post-war welfare state in Britain.

A central feature of neo-Gramscian Marxism is a particular interpretation of the united front strategy – that is the necessity of winning mass support for a socialist programme. This is said to require 'building the widest possible mass movement . . . discerning the progressive potential in all expressions of rebellion and dissent',[16] and is therefore likely to bring in many who would not see themselves as socialists. This seems to suggest that either socialists must bury or disguise their views for the sake of the broad alliance or that the socialist movement can accommodate almost all pressure and interest groups, apart from those representing big capital or monopoly capital. In relation to the transformation of the welfare state, clearly the organisation of state welfare workers and consumers is vital, but within these organisations socialists must continually point to the limitations of particularistic struggles within the state apparatus, as well as promoting socialist demands posing a rupture with capitalism. This draws clear limits to the kinds of accommodation that can be made with the state apparatus and members of the broad alliance.

This brings us to the second position on the transformation of the state apparatus, which posits a rupture with capital and the capitalist state and the building of an entirely new structure, a socialist state, as the instrument of working-class power under a deeper and wider form of democratic control. It shares with the neo-Gramscians the emphasis on the need to undermine bourgeois hegemony and working-class consent, but it is argued that this cannot be achieved solely within bourgeois or reformist institutions. It also shares the concern to build a mass movement drawing in a wide range of working-class interests, but not such as may submerge revolutionary ideology. This position cannot simply be equated with the model of the Russian revolution, nor the adventurist insurrectionism to which Kautsky and Gramsci were reacting, but it may be conveniently labelled Leninist. For while Lenin emphasised the importance of participation and struggle within the Parliamentary framework of the western bourgeois democracies, he also insisted that this would be insufficient to transform the state apparatus into a socialist state. The working class, according to Lenin, must develop its own democratic institutions of popular power *independent* of the state apparatus – that is workers' and soldiers' councils and what amount to working-class interest and pressure groups and independent trade unions, which in a revolutionary crisis provide the organisational basis for the new workers' state. The tragedy of the Russian revolution was that these embryonic institutions of workers' democracy soon became integrated into the state apparatus itself. The Leninist position is articulated in the theory of the soviets and the model of dual power articulated by Lenin in *State and Revolution*, thus described by Lucio Colletti:

> Marxist literature since Marx knows nothing that could even remotely compete with the seriousness of the critique of parliament contained in *State and Revolution*; nor at the same time, anything pervaded with such a profound democratic inspiration as that which animates Lenin's text from beginning to end. The 'imperative mandate', the permanent and constant revocability of representatives by those they represent, the demand for a legislative power which would be 'a working, *not* a parliamentary body, executive and legislative at the same time' and in which, hence, the representatives 'have to work, have to execute their own laws, have themselves to test their results in real life, and to account directly to their constituents'.[17]

It is therefore assumed that the capitalist system will continue to be gripped by deep socio-economic and political crises in which more overtly coercive and undemocratic forms of government will emerge, making a pre-emptive seizure of state power the only means of preserving the working-class movement. This is therefore an 'insurrectionary' and opportunistic strategy in the sense that it is mindful of the sudden, mercurial and vibrant nature of revolutionary situations, and the need to anticipate and build upon them.

While the Leninist position may appear somewhat utopian in the context of Britain in the 1980s, and has been subject to widespread Marxist criticism, its importance is precisely that it continually poses within the working-class movement the limits to social reform, and the revolutionary alternative – a break with the capitalist system, and *thence* the creation of a state apparatus under the control of democratic mass organisations of the working class. In relation to housing, social security and the welfare state, this position suggests that while the capital–labour relation continues to exist, the form and functions of policy cannot be altered in their fundamentals; social security will continue to reproduce the labour reserve army at a level below wages, impose labour discipline and support the patriarchal family; and the production and consumption of working-class housing will remain an area largely reserved for private capital accumulation and appropriation, since the expropriation of the construction and housing finance industries is hardly likely except in the midst of a truly revolutionary crisis.

Possibly the crucial difference between the neo-Gramscian and Leninist positions is their respective conceptions of state power. Both take cognisance of Marx's observation that 'the working class cannot simply lay hold of the ready-made state machinery and wield it for its own purposes',[18] but the neo-Gramscians appear to argue that the working class can lay hold on the already-made capitalist state machine and turn it around, using a combination of various conventional sources of pressure within and upon the state. This suggests that the seizure of state power, peacefully and constitutionally, may be accomplished without the destruction and reconstruction of the state. The state is therefore conceived as an institution relatively autonomous from the capital–labour relation, which can be rescued by and for the working class. The fetishised form of the state, inherent in the separation of the 'economic' and the 'political' spheres, is therefore compounded and implicitly left untouched. The state is conceived as a vehicle currently occupied and driven by the representatives of the capitalist class, who, under an electoral mandate and the pressure of the broad alliance, will surrender the driving seat to the representatives of the working class and its allies, and they will then steer the ship of state in the direction of socialism. In some versions the occupiers of the driving seat are more narrowly conceived as the representatives of a small number of monopoly capitalists, so that the broad alliance may even include non-monopoly capitalists. This is inherent in the theory of state monopoly capitalism, which for some neo-Gramscians underemphasises the importance of hegemony in engineering consent and suggests a simple elite theory of power. More often than not, however, the two approaches are compatibly integrated precisely because they share the conception of the state apparatus as a neutral instrument at present dominated by the interests of either 'big capital' or monopoly capital.

Unfortunately, the form of the state is more deeply embedded in the capital–labour relation, and the class struggle cannot be refined into a struggle against one particular concrete form of capital's existence, whether it be monopoly capital or finance capital, or capitalist ideology in its various forms. Capital is here therefore conceived in more structural terms as the general form of production involving surplus value appropriation and the inevitable struggle between labour and capital in general, while the capitalist state organises the domination of capital over the working class, without necessarily representing the interests of individual capitalists or fractions of capital. We shall attempt very briefly to elucidate these concepts in the following chapter, but we can conclude here that, within the Leninist framework, state power is the power of capital organised outside the immediate point of production and it cannot be gradually transformed into a socialist state without the expropriation of capital and the supersession of capitalist relations of production.

In a modern liberal democracy, of course, state power is enforced by the electoral consent of the working class as individual voters, which maintains the illusion that they control the state, at least as much as every other individual. This consent is nourished and secured by the central element of state power in Britain today, which consists of a 'dense and complex structure of institutions and practices, many of them external to the state apparatus itself', such as the media and 'independent' research and advisory bodies 'through which the needs and demands of the masses are processed'.[19] Some of the most important of these institutions and practices are those concerned with the social welfare of the working class. Norman Geras has described the dual character of capitalist state power as it faces the working class:

On the one hand, it does provide the workers' movement with the organisational and political means for opposing the more blatant forms of exploitation and oppression, for defending the workers' most immediate interests, and for winning material gains on their behalf. This provision is the source of bourgeois democracy's self-legitimating power . . . On the other hand, this structure largely succeeds in sublimating and neutralising or sabotaging such genuinely anti-capitalist demands and initiatives as do emerge, by taking them through its many 'competent' and 'specialised' channels ie. away from the masses, out of their direct control and sight.[20]

This dual character of the state is nowhere more apparent than in the area of state welfare, where the demands of the working class have produced important material gains; but those demands have been processed and responded to in such a form that, far from posing a threat to capital, they have deepened its acceptance and extended its survival.

2

Some Basic Concepts and Assumptions

In this chapter we attempt to elucidate some of the theoretical assumptions and concepts which inform the following chapters. Unfortunately there is insufficient space here either to enter into the underlying debates or to draw out many of the general implications for the analysis of social welfare. The reader may find it hard going. It may be easier to return to it after reading the rest of the book or following up some of the exegetical accounts of Marx's mature work[1] and other references.

Marx's starting point for the analysis of capitalist social relations is the contradictory nature of commodity production, as the production of use-values, that is useful, marketable things, and as the production of *value*, that is the abstract application and appropriation of socially necessary labour time inherent in the labour–capital relation. All commodities are the products of human labour, and the value of a commodity is commensurate with the average socially necessary labour time required for its production. For the purposes of theoretical discussion at the level of capital in general, it is sufficient to assume that commodities exchange at their value, though in reality they exchange at prices that fluctuate around their value, which is an abstract average. The capacity of the worker to create use-values is itself a unique commodity, since its use-value is the production of other use-values. This productive potential or power to labour is the commodity, labour power, which is offered in exchange for the wage and, hence, the means of subsistence. The commodity, labour power, under capitalism is the only commodity which the immediate producer can sell in order to subsist, since the product of his/her labour immediately becomes the property of the owner of capital, and other avenues of producing the means of subsistence (e.g., smallholdings) are largely blocked off. This apparently free exchange of labour power for the wage is a feature of the capitalist mode of production, and distinguishes it from other modes of production in which surplus labour is extracted under more explicit social relations of brute force. Marx shows, however, that in the capitalist mode of production the worker is forced to sell his/her labour power because he/she has no substantial savings or independent access to the means of production, the wherewithal of subsistence. Hence the relations of production are enforced through the institution of the labour market, although capitalist social relations were often formed on the basis of the forcible expropriation of the peasantry from their independent access to the means of subsistence. The capitalist provides the tools and raw materials, the previously created value, to which the worker adds further value in order to eventually create a commodity suitable for exchange.

The worker, however, does not receive wages equal to the value of the commodities he/she has produced. A part of his/her labour time is not paid for by the capitalist and a surplus product is appropriated as surplus value. Thence the commodities produced enter the sphere of exchange and consumption in which the capitalist attempts to realise money capital in exchange for the use-value of the commodities. Money is a commodity which is the repository of previously created value and acts as the medium for exchange of other commodities. The capitalist begins with a certain amount of money capital, which he/she exchanges for such use-values as labour power, raw materials, tools, machinery and so on. Out of the production process or labour process in which labour adds value to the raw materials through the use of machinery, a more valuable commodity is created, and then exchanged for an increased amount of money capital. The whole purpose of the exercise from the capitalist's point of view is to achieve an increase in the amount of money capital originally advanced. This is the process of capital accumulation in its barest essentials.

The force of competition between capitals generates continual pressure to expand the total value created and hence the mass of profit. The mass of value created may be increased by expanding the scale, intensity and efficiency of production and reducing the socially necessary labour time taken in the production of a given commodity. This need not necessarily lead to an increased rate of exploitation or the shedding of labour, since wages may rise as fast as the surplus value extracted and the expansion of production may be sufficient to absorb or even increase the labour force. On the other hand, the tendency to expand the mass of value produced is clearly limited by the rate of technological advance, the supply of money capital (credit) and the danger of overproduction. In the long run the capitalist employs relatively more machinery and less labour in order to expand production and maintain a competitive rate of profit. It can be shown that, given various assumptions of Marx's value analysis, there is a long-run tendency for the rate of profit to fall, which spurs the capitalist on to further rationalisations of the production and exchange processes. It must be emphasised that this is merely a *tendency* for the rate of profit to fall under conditions created by competition and the class struggle. The value relationships established by Marx are sometimes referred to as the 'law of value' or the 'law of the falling rate of profit'. The term 'law' in this context is not used in a determinist sense; such 'laws' are merely the theoretical expressions of the tendencies and counter-tendencies inherent in the capitalist mode of production, which is predicated on the existence of two opposing classes, the class of producers and the capitalist class who are in continual struggle over the rate of exploitation, the form of the labour process, the shedding of labour and in political struggle through the form of the state. The tendency of the rate of profit to fall is 'merely the economic expression of a process of class struggle – a process inherent in, and structured by, the form of capital'.[2]

THE VALUE OF LABOUR POWER

There are a variety of strategies which the hypothetical capitalist can employ to counteract the tendency of the rate of profit to fall, and these form the foci of the class struggle.[3] One of the most fundamental strategies is the capitalist's attempts to maintain or increase the rate of exploitation by containing the price and value of that commodity labour power. On the other side the workers will struggle to maintain and improve their standard of living by seeking increases in the price and value of their labour power. The value of labour power is a critical concept in moving towards a theoretical analysis of the class struggle over the 'welfare' of the working class. At a particular point in history the value of labour power is equivalent to the socially necessary labour time required in the production of the commodity – labour power, in other words, equivalent to the value of the commodities necessary for the production or reproduction of labour power. Hence changes in the means of producing food or housing, for example, directly affect the value of labour power.[4]

The value of labour power must also be considered as a quantity which changes over time as the social definition of the necessaries for subsistence changes. Marx suggests that the value of labour power 'can be resolved into the value of a definite quantity of the means of subsistence' but 'in contrast . . . with the case of other commodities, the determination of the value of labour power contains an historical and moral element'.[5] In other words, the socially accepted requirements of the worker and his/her family will vary according to particular physical and historical conditions. Marx notes that 'in particular they depend on the conditions in which and consequently on the habits and expectations with which the class of free workers has been formed'.[6] Thus the value of labour power is to a considerable degree established by the struggle of the working class to further their standard of living.

The average price of labour power or average wages bears a close relationship to the value of labour power, and a significant long-term change in the average level of wages will eventually lead to a change in the composition of the bundle of use-values which make up the value of labour power, historically and morally determined. When the mass of value created is expanding and the working class is sufficiently organised, increases in real wages and hence the value of labour power are more than possible, and 'the working class can succeed in incorporating new needs . . . into the value of labour power'.[7] The notion that Marx suggests the gradual immiseration of the working class is completely false. Indeed satisfaction of these new needs can create new opportunities for the realisation of profit for capital. When, however, the rate or mass of profit is tending to fall and the working class is in a weak position, the lowering of the value of labour power may act as a powerful countertendency to the falling rate of profit and 'capital can successfully lower the value of labour power by annihilating a series of worker's historical or social achievements, i.e., by partially eliminating commodities which cover their needs from the "standard of life" regarded as normal'.[8] Marx notes the crucial importance of trade union organisation in the determination of the value of labour power:

. . . the value of labour power constitutes the conscious and explicit foundation of the trade unions, whose importance for the English working class can scarcely be overestimated. The trade unions aim at nothing less than to prevent the reduction of wages below the level that is traditionally maintained in the various branches of industry. That is to say, they wish to prevent the price of labour power from falling below its value.[9]

There is a distinct mechanism for mitigating the upward pressure on the price and value of labour power exerted through the wages struggle. This depends on the expansion of the reserve army of labour, which often accompanies attempts to counteract the tendency for the rate of profit to fall through the replacement of living labour by machinery. The expansion of the reserve army of the unemployed exacerbates competition amongst potential workers to sell their labour power and also acts as a discouragement to the employed in pressing for wage increases; thus the price and eventually the value of labour power falls. In periods of a shortage of labour power, or in branches of production suffering a shortage of labour power, capital digs deeper into the reserves of labour power such as migrants and married women, who are usually forced to accept below average wages. This too will act as a brake on any rise in the average price of labour power in such circumstances.

Amongst the necessaries for the production of labour power which Marx explicitly mentions are 'the means necessary for the worker's replacements i.e., his children'.[10] Marx assumes that the male worker's wage covers the maintenance of both him and his family, though in practice of course it often has not. It follows that any analysis of the value of labour power and its production must include the questions of child rearing, family relationships and domestic labour, and the welfare state. Unpaid domestic labour and the provisions of state welfare clearly contribute very significantly to the production of labour power, although they are not themselves exchange values or commodities. Hence 'the value of labour power is not synonymous with the labour time embodied in the reproduction and maintenance of labour power',[11] but the value of labour power *is* critically affected by the extent of unpaid domestic labour (largely performed by women) and the provision of state welfare.

With the development of capitalism 'the burden of the reproduction of the labour force has shifted proportionally from the family to capital and the state'.[12] There has occurred a 'replacement (and at the same time a transformation) of the work done in the home by goods and services produced for the market or provided by the state: laundries and prepared foods, education and health care'.[13] This reflects the continual development of the functional requirements for the production of labour power and the growing proportion of married women in wage work as well as the direct working-class pressure for state welfare. Private capital and the state have entered increasingly into the process of production of labour power through the provision of goods and services which may be described as welfare goods and services. The expansion of the requirements of the production of labour power, i.e. the changing bundle of use-values constituting the value of labour power, is related to both the struggle of the producing class to improve its standard of living and to the development of the mode of production itself – the increase in the intensity of the labour process generates expanded physiological and mental requirements of the worker, and the concentration of the means of production increases the journey time between home and work and hence the requirement of workers' transport. The producing class of course often has to struggle to ensure that the socially accepted standard of living keeps pace with these tendencies inherent in development of the mode of production. Married women or single mothers who enter wage labour must take home a wage sufficient to cover the cost of acquiring the use-values (in commodity form or from the state) previously met by domestic labour (plus the male wage in the case of separated women). Otherwise the family must suffer a reduction in its standard of living and/or an intensification of domestic labour.

The provision of welfare goods and services as commodities by capital is merely an extension of capitalist production and exchange, but the role of the state is more problematic, for the activities of the state are not directly subject to the law of value and state workers (outside the nationalised industries) do not take part in the production of exchange values. Nevertheless, the production of welfare goods and services by the state clearly influences the price and value of labour power, though it is only very tentatively here that we try to draw out some of the elements of this relationship. It is widely assumed that the working class itself largely pays for state welfare through income tax, but the application of value analysis suggests that in fact capital bears the direct burden of financing the welfare state. Recalling the simple capital accumulation process, it is obvious that by no means all the surplus value produced returns to the capitalist for reinvestment or private consumption. Some of it goes to merchant's capital, finance capital and landlords who appropriate surplus value in fulfilling various roles in the process of realisation of profit and the supply of land and credit. A further proportion of the total surplus value produced finds its way into the coffers of the state through the various forms of taxation and appropriation in exchange for the services provided by the state, which it is unprofitable and/or inappropriate for capital to provide directly. This taxation includes income tax on workers' wages, for, according to value analysis, the wage or price of labour power is the net wage after such 'stoppages'. The worker has no control over that part of the gross wage which he/she never sees, and it cannot therefore be considered part of the exchange between capital and labour – the exchange of the commodity labour power for the wage. The ultimate cost of state expenditures falls therefore solely on capital.

It is true that changes in the level of workers' personal taxation will have immediate effects on the level of net wages, and may even become a bargaining counter in wages struggle. Governments on behalf of capital may effect through tax increases an immediate reduction in the price of labour power and an increase in the rate of exploitation, but this can only lead to a reduction in the value of labour power if the working class is unable to restore the price to the level of the established value of labour power through wages struggle. Governments may use the extra revenue to provide use-values which were previously consumed in commodity form by the worker as part of the necessaries of life. In this case the overall bundle of use-values which form the workers' living standard may be unchanged, while the actual value of labour power is still reduced. Under certain conditions, therefore, governments can, through taxation adjustments, reduce or increase the value of labour power and also, what is not necessarily the same thing, the socially accepted standard of living for workers. The expanded state provision of welfare in late capitalism corresponds to the increase in the use-values required for the reproduction of labour power demanded both by the working class and the developing conditions of production. The provision of these use-values is not something that has already been paid for by workers through income tax. It is a tax on capital, which is a drain on the total surplus value produced, whose form and extent are shaped by the uneasy resolution of the political struggle of the working class and the functional requirements of capital.[14]

THE STATE

The role of the state in the reproduction of labour power and in marshalling the counter-tendencies to the falling rate of profit has already entered the discussion. It is assumed here that the state has not been formed by the capitalist class, the working class or any class fraction; nor is it simply the resultant of a struggle of class forces. Such approaches err towards overemphasising the political autonomy of the state and the importance of particular sociological aspects of state personnel and state apparatuses. Neither are the state apparatuses and state expenditures the immediate product of economic forces and determined laws of motion. In such an analysis the state becomes a mere manifestation of the logic of capital, and the contradictions of the political and ideological relations of the state are obscure and taken as unproblematic.[15]

The conceptualisation of the relationship between capital and the state has been advanced recently by the work of a school of German theorists. Recognising the problems mentioned above, they have struggled with the question of how to derive the form of the state (i.e. the most general relation of the capitalist state to civil society, capital and the working class) and the more specific functions of the state from the theory of capital. The mainstream of the German school argues that the form of the state derives from the requirement to regulate and stabilise the consequences of the existence of capital as individual capitals or units of capital. Hence the state essentially forms and develops the interest of 'capital in general'. The latter is not to be confused with a group of individuals identifiable as *the* capitalist class (not individual units of capital). One cannot allow for a simple interpretation of Marx and Engels' famous remark in the *Communist Manifesto* that 'the modern state is but a committee for managing the common affairs of the whole bourgeoisie'. The state expresses the average interest of capital in general, running alongside the force of competition, which hold apart the various individual units of capital. There arise certain functions which individual capitals are unable to assume for a variety of economic and political reasons in different historical circumstances. Accordingly, as Altvater has suggested,

> ... capital cannot itself produce through the actions of the many individual capitals the inherent social nature of its existence; it requires at its base a special institution which is not subject to its limitations as capital, one whose transactions are not determined by the necessity of producing surplus value, one which is *in this sense*, a special institution 'alongside and outside bourgeois society', and one which at the same time provides, on the undisputed basis of capital itself, the immanent necessities that capital neglects ... The state cannot be grasped therefore merely as a political instrument, nor as an institution set up by capital, but only as a special form of establishment of the social existence of capital alongside and outside competition, as an essential moment in the social reproduction process of capital.[16]

Hence the capitalist state is neither a relatively autonomous political institution, as bourgeois ideology suggests, nor is it merely the economic resultant of the actions of individual or many capitals. The capitalist state produces and reproduces the conditions for capital accumulation to occur, and at different periods, and in different economic and political contexts, there emerge quite different kinds of state activity. Specifically in relation to the welfare state Müller and Neusüss conclude that the historical process of class struggle and the development of the capital mode of production forces upon the state certain policy requirements. This process, 'mediated by catastrophes and conflicts, victories and defeats, establishes the "welfare state", the "interventionist state" etc., as a particular coercive power in which capital externally confronts itself'.[17] The existence of the welfare state is thus essential to the survival of capitalist society, not least because it ultimately prevents the exhaustion and destruction of the labour force by capitalist competition.

In a different approach Hirsch[18] suggests that the form of the state (as opposed to its functions) cannot be derived from *a priori* assumptions about the existence of the interests of capital in general. He derives the form of the state as establishing the necessary preconditions for the existence of capitalist social relations, in particular as the institution which forcibly establishes the 'freedom' of the worker to sell his/her labour power and excludes him/her from any alternative access to the means of subsistence. As guarantor of the rules of equal exchange and commodity circulation, the form of the state constitutes individual political citizenship and regulates the freedoms of civil society as spheres separated from and disguising the unequal relations of appropriation in the sphere of production. According to Hirsch 'the function of the bourgeois state can never be more than the creation of the "external" conditions for the social reproduction process',[19] that is ensuring that the ground rules for free exchange are enforced. Beyond these basic guarantor functions, for Hirsch it is the historically specific demands of the law of value and the laws of motion of capital which give rise to the particular activities and functions of the state.

It is suggested here that welfare policy has reinforced the form of the capitalist state as described by Hirsch. The social security system has clearly contributed to the separation of the worker from direct access to the means of subsistence, and the maintenance of the necessity of wage labour. Welfare policy as a whole is predicated on the notion of apparently equal and individualised relations of consumption and citizenship in the sphere of civil society. The general form of the capitalist state has been strengthened rather than altered by its development into a welfare state, and we shall therefore put considerable emphasis on the relatively unchanging form of welfare policy. On the other hand, within particular historical periods it is also possible to talk of state policy pursuing functions, on behalf of capital in general, going beyond the general form of the state and the immediate demands of the law of value.

PERIODISATION

In order to get to grips with the changing functions of the state we have distinguished four historical periods in the development of capitalism in Britain. This is a crude orientating device, which at least makes it possible to draw out some simple relationships between the minutiae of policy development and the broad sweep of qualitative changes in the labour process, class structure and the state. The four periods are:

1. Primitive accumulation: early 1400s to early 1800s
2. Competitive capitalism: early 1800s to 1880s

3. Classical imperialism: 1880s to 1930s
4. Advanced/monopoly capitalism: 1930s to present day

In the rest of this book little or nothing will be said about the historical period before the nineteenth century. Yet the history of the state as both a welfare state and as a form of the capital relation goes back of course to the genesis of capitalism from within the feudal mode of production. Marx describes this period as the era of primitive accumulation, because it was only haltingly, amidst great conflict and crisis, that by the expropriation and development of land, means of production and labour that considerable masses of capital and labour power began to be brought together productively by the late eighteenth century. For Marx the *sine qua non* of primitive accumulation is 'nothing else than the historical process of divorcing the producer from the means of production'.[20]

This separation of production and consumption and the creation of landless wage labour was nourished by the state in a number of ways. Firstly, the law sanctioned the expropriation of the peasant population and the genesis of the capitalist farmer through the forced dissolution of feudal labour and enclosure, particularly in the latter part of this period. The law and the definition of 'crime' became designed to punish offences against private property, as opposed to offences between men, and 'as, in the 18th century, labour became more and more free, so labour's product came to be seen as something totally "distinct", the property of landowner or employer and to be defended by the threat of the gallows'.[21] Secondly, the state became increasingly responsible for the landless and wage-less population which these processes thrust upon the world, and which could not be immediately absorbed into wage work, particularly following the changes from pasturage to tillage in the late fifteenth century, the depression of the early seventeenth century and the enclosures of the late eighteenth century. The creation of a whole army of vagabonds, beggars, robbers and paupers called forth 'bloody legislation', not only to protect private property but to terrorise the nascent proletariat into accepting what Marx calls 'the discipline necessary for the system of wage labour'[22] – for example, forms of forced labour such as houses of correction, deportation, the workhouse, as well as flogging, imprisonment, the stocks, etc. The problem of creating labour discipline was also apparent in the periodic occurrences of local labour shortage. Various statutes, such as the Statute of

Labourers (1349) and the Statute of Artificers (1563), permitted the setting of local wage ceilings, and later versions allowed for the control of wages according to local prices of the means of subsistence (an early example of prices and incomes policy!), combined with the subsidisation of low wages from the poor rate. The Laws of Settlement restricted labour mobility in order to enforce local availability of cheap wage labour. Combination of workers in nascent trade unions was of course severely repressed. In these measures state policy fortified the forcible separation of production and consumption and hastened the creation of a class of formally free wage labourers willing to work for subsistence wages. One must not overemphasise the importance of these measures, however, since up to the mid-sixteenth century at least the proletariat was but a small part of the population, while the implementation of statutes was left in the hands of local justices of the peace, who enforced only those parts of the law which might suit their parochial interests and inclinations.

In the second period, the era of competitive capitalism or liberal accumulation, factory machinofacture or what Marx calls 'large-scale industry' begins to predominate. In the period of primitive accumulation the state assisted in forcibly creating capitalist social relations, but by the early 1800s 'concessions' such as the factory acts signalled a change in the role of the state. The measures of the previous period began to hinder the development of free exchange, particularly the free exchange of labour power, and they began to fall into obsolescence. In the period of competitive capitalism the state regulates the free exchange of commodities, including labour power, to ensure that the 'sheer force of economic relations' secures, amongst other things, the supply of cheap and minimally protected labour power. This period is sometimes called the era of 'laissez-faire', but this does not mean that the authority of the state was residual. The authority of the law was central to the establishment of the 'free' exchange of commodities and land, and the 'free' movement of population and wages. By the end of this period there had emerged the basis of a central government bureaucracy tentatively involved in the reproduction of labour power through the factory, education, poor law and public health legislation. The significance of these developments is perhaps that they laid the basis for future state administration rather than their effectiveness in the period in question. The emerging urban proletariat exerted their pressure on Parliament and local authorities from outside. Hence, although Parliament felt obliged to pass an enormous amount of social legislation in this period, particularly concerning housing, neither the central nor local government apparatuses were equipped financially or administratively to enforce it.

The period of classical imperialism sees the accelerated centralisation and concentration of large-scale industry and the spread of capitalist social relations, accompanied by a whole series of changes in the structure of the working class and the state. All historians of welfare have noted the close relationship between imperialism and state welfare expansion. The rivalry with Bismarck's Germany, the poor health of Boer War recruits, the decline in the birth rate, high rates of infant and maternal mortality, alongside working-class pressure pushed governments forward into piecemeal welfare activity with the emphasis on social insurance rather than the provision of services. Labour and social historians have described the emergence of new divisions and strata within the working class in the 1880s and 1890s as the trade union movement spread beyond the artisanal 'labour aristocracy' in the movement of New Unionism. In addition 'new groups of "labour aristocrats" had arisen in the managerial, technical and white-collar grades . . . the real "bourgeois proletariat" of imperialism',[23] while at the other end of the working class the distinction between the 'pauper residuum' and the organised working class was forged more precisely.[24] This was accompanied by developments in bourgeois political economy which celebrated working-class citizenship and a new 'moralised' capitalism. This aggregation of socio-economic changes engendered a significant if gradual reorientation of the domestic as well as the international role of the state *vis-à-vis* the reproduction of labour power and capital. This period therefore sees the emergence of the European working classes organised both at the point of production and in the political sphere. The threat of militant trade unionism and socialist politics required the integration of the organised working class as enfranchised citizens and 'responsible people' with social rights and obligations. A particularly important development in the administrative structure of the state was the restructuring of local government in 1889-90 on a more democratic and rationalised basis under explicit central government regulation. This provided the administrative context for the development of state welfare in the areas of housing, education, town planning, public health, etc. It was accompanied by a professionalisation of government at both local and central levels, and virtually the emergence of a state bureaucracy, staffed by members of a new social stratum, many of whom identified with the Fabian vision of social reform.

In the years before the First World War the rate of profit and rate of surplus value increased dramatically, but during and after the war this situation was reversed. The recession struck earlier in Britain than elsewhere. After the immediate post-war crisis, in which concessions were made in housing and social security policy, governments became intimately concerned less with the reproduction of labour power than in the reconstruction of capital and labour, and the marshalling of the counter-tendencies to the falling rate of profit. A gradual increase in the rate of surplus value was achieved in the 1930s in Britain in the wake of the political defeat of the Labour movement, crystallised in the General Strike and the debacle of the 1931 Labour government. In the inter-war years the permanent existence of an inflated labour reserve army, now closely supervised by the state, performed the classic function of holding down wages and dividing the working class. There was considerable political struggle over state welfare, particularly the level and administration of unemployment benefit, and this hastened the restructuring of the state welfare apparatus along more centralised and bureaucratic lines. This is described in some detail in the following chapter. The extent to which the standard of living and the welfare of the working class was unimproved in the inter-war years is indicated by the fact that state welfare expenditures as a percentage of gross national product only rose from 10.1 per cent in 1921 to 10.7 per cent in 1937, while total state expenditure dropped as a percentage of gross national product from 29.4 per cent to 25.7 per cent over the same period.

Finally, we turn to the present period of advanced or monopoly capitalism, which dates from the late 1930s or the Second World War. This period may once again be divided roughly into an earlier phase of 'boom', continuing until the mid/late 1960s, followed by a phase of stagnation and deepening crisis in the 1970s. Following the defeats of the European working class, rearmament and the Second World War gradually and hesitantly revived the process of capital accumulation, and the rate of surplus value and rate of profit began to increase in the 1940s. The post-war upswing in the rate of profit was seriously mitigated in Britain by the relative strength of the working class, which retained and developed strong shop-floor organisation and was 'the only major proletariat in the world which suffered no serious defeat for the thirty years from 1936 to 1966'.[25] Nevertheless, with the stimulating effect of the international expansion of trade and Britain's highly successful transition to neo-colonialism, the post-war period saw a rise in working-class incomes and an expansion of the value of labour power and state welfare benefits and services. Expenditure on state social services rose from 10.9 per cent of gross national product in 1937 to 28.8 per cent of gross national product in 1975; while state expenditure as a whole rose from 25.7 per cent of GNP in 1937 to 57.9 per cent of GNP in 1975. This more central role of the state in the economy reflected the fruits of the Keynesian 'revolution' in economic thought, which suggested that by manipulation of aggregate demand in the economy (that is intervention in the sphere of consumption but *not* direct intervention into production) governments could stimulate capital accumulation and prevent stagnation and high levels of unemployment. Essentially governments could achieve this firstly by encouraging and regulating working-class consumption by cash welfare payments and fiscal measures and the management of credit expansion, and secondly by promoting public works such as house building and road construction. In these ways government action could produce a 'multiplier effect' on the private sector, that is it would spark off consumer demand and hence capital accumulation by putting money in the pockets of consumers and by the 'pump-priming' effect of public capital projects. however much emphasis one puts on Keynesianism as the progenitor of the 'long boom', clearly the expansion of the welfare state in the post-1945 period derived a crucial part of its legitimacy from Keynesian economics.[26]

By the mid-1960s large cracks were appearing in the economic orthodoxy which oversaw the post-war boom. The rate of profit began to fall sharply and Keynesian remedies, immortalised in the phrase 'stop-go', gradually gave way to direct attempts to limit wage increases in the form of incomes policy and more peremptory interventions in the restructuring of capital. The mid-1960s also saw 'the rediscovery of poverty' under a Labour government in various exposés of the failings of the post-war reforms. This added to the pressures for increased welfare expenditure, which continued to grow as a proportion of gross national product until the mid-1970s. There has been a significant restructuring of welfare administration since the 1960s with a view not only to achieving greater 'efficiency' but also to relieving the pressure on the services (and thus on expenditure) generated by the growing militancy of working-class consumers of welfare and their success in redeeming the welfare rights of citizenship.

This administrative restructuring has created a deeper bureaucratic buffer between individual consumers and the state apparatus. This acts firstly as a surreptitious means of rationing services and benefits, and secondly ensures that the parameters of welfare policy, ultimately drawn by the pressures of the law of value, are not distorted beyond redemption by the participation of welfare state consumers and employees in management and policy making. A crucial mediating role in rationing and the retention of state control is played by apparently neutral bodies of technocratic and professional knowledge, which are inaccessible to consumers and employees. Examples of administrative restructuring include the centralisation of local government finance and structure, local authority structure planning and corporate management, public expenditure planning, social security administrative review, the Fulton review of civil service structure, local Housing Investment Programmes under Whitehall control, the new 'autonomous' water and health authorities and even the 'Great Debate' on education. Under increasing pressure from below, Parliament and local council chambers are no longer (even if they ever were) suitable arenas for the articulation and reconciliation of competing capital interests. The management of the conflicts of interest between capitals over the reproduction of capital and labour power by the state occurs increasingly in bureaucratic extra-Parliamentary spheres, and thus 'the structure of the bourgeois State is determined by the principles of the separation of powers and of a professional bureaucracy – in other words the permanent prevention of any direct exercise of power (self administration) by the mass of the working class'.[27]

IDEOLOGY

Marx's works on economics are written as a critique of the classical political economy of people such as Adam Smith and David Ricardo, and hence of much of modern bourgeois economic and sociological thought. Marx tried to show that the economic or market relations between commodities (including labour power) are only the apparent forms in bourgeois thought of the truly social relations between capital and labour. The classical political economists whom Marx was criticising saw the realm of production in technical terms as 'the realm in which labour sets to work means of production to make products' and therefore in which 'relations of *distribution* [my emphasis] determine the transformation of the product into revenues according to the various classes'.[28] What interested the classical political economists was the distribution and consumption of the social product, not its origins in the nature of value production. For Marx the production of value makes manifest the social relations of capitalism, while in the bourgeois conception production itself is not seen as a social process. The technical conception of production in classical political economy is a fundamental element of bourgeois ideology, since it presumes capitalist relations of production to be eternal and therefore unchangeable. According to Marx, on the contrary, surplus value is not just a 'share of the cake' which accrues to a distributive class. It conveys the essence of the antagonistic social relationship between capital and labour as a relationship of value appropriation. Class inequality begins therefore with the social relations of production, which predicate inequalities in the sphere of distribution and consumption.

Ideology therefore presents the commodity as reflecting

> . . . the social characteristics of men's own labour as objective characteristics of the products of labour themselves, as the socio-natural properties of these things. Hence it also reflects the social relation of the producers to the sum total of labour as a social relation between objects, a relation which exists apart from and outside the producers.[29]

This is exemplified in the nature of the stock and commodity markets of the capitalist world. In Marx's conception

> . . . the commodity-form and the value-relation of the products of labour within which it appears, have absolutely no connection with the physical nature of the commodity and the material relations arising out of this. It is nothing but the definitive social relation between men themselves which assumes here, for them, the fantastic form of a relation between things.[30]

The process whereby the social relations between producers appear as social relations between commodities in the market is called the fetishism of the commodity. Fetishism of the commodity arises from the fact that, under capitalist social relations, the individual producers of commodities 'do not come into social contact until they exchange the products of their labour',[31] and this exchange remains a private 'material' relation between individual worker and individual capitalist, rather than a relationship to the class of producers or society as a whole. The mediation of the private exchange relationship between capital and labour reproduces commodity fetishism, and the eternisation of the capital–labour relation. The state obviously plays a central role in maintaining this fetishism, and following Hirsch it has been argued that[32] the form of the state may be conceived as a fetishised form generated by the fetishised form of the capital–labour relation.

It has already been noted that the existence of the capitalist mode of production is predicated on the availability of labour power as a 'freely exchangeable' commodity, while the fetishism of the commodity derives from the fact that this relationship of appropriation is mediated through the material and individual relations of the labour market. Thus 'the worker is not directly subject to the capitalist, his subjection is mediated through the sale of his labour power on the market'.[33] The domination of capital is maintained through the 'dull compulsion' of the worker to sell his/her labour power rather than through the use of overt physical repression, although the monopoly over the means of forcible repression lies with the state. This maintains the appearance of the class neutrality of the state while guaranteeing and regulating the private exchange of commodities not least, as we shall see, in the form of welfare policies. The social security system assists in the exchange of the commodity labour power, ensuring that it is available as an exchange value. Housing policy regulates the predominantly private production, consumption and exchange of the commodity housing.

The form of the state is a fetishised form because it maintains and reproduces the separation between the economic, apparently merely technical, relations of production and the 'public' political relations of the democratic process. This separation is manifest in the division of members of the working class into, on the one hand, workers at the point of production and, on the other hand, citizens in the political sphere. Hence 'the essential inequality of the capital relation is transformed in the political sphere into the fantastic (i.e., fetishised, elusive) form of equality before the state'.[34] The capitalist welfare state is one of the clearest examples of the fetishised form of the state, embodying as it does the notion of the working–class citizenship in the legislative achievement of universal rights and benefits. Yet this has not posed the remotest threat to the continued existence of the capital–labour relation. Indeed the implementation of this legislation has directly assisted in the maintenance and reproduction of capitalist social relations, while failing to achieve in practice equal and universal access to those rights and benefits permitted by legislation.

In a justly famous essay[35] the liberal sociologist T. H. Marshall traced the origins of the welfare state to the evolution of individual citizenship for workers in the shape of civil, political and social rights, the latter having emerged in the twentieth century as the welfare state. Marshall notes that in the nineteenth century access to social rights (basically the poor law) was conditional on the loss of male civil and political rights; poor law beneficiaries were not accorded the vote until 1929. The widening concept of citizenship and the emergence of social rights has deepened the separation of the political rights of the worker as citizen from his/her rights as a worker at the point of production. In the latter sphere the trade union movement has of course resisted the domination of capital, particularly at shop-floor level, but the achievements of struggle have not by and large been converted into effective legislation. Trade unionists have remained somewhat dubious about the benefits of legislation over the shop floor, preferring to establish workers' rights through collective bargaining. Outside the point of production, however, the concept of citizenship and the emergence of social rights act as a powerful legitimation of the state, creating a kind of unwritten social contract between the individual and the state, exemplified in social insurance, and reinforcing the apparent neutrality of the state as the repository and guardian of the equal rights of all citizens. Marshall postulates 'that there is a kind of basic human quality associated with the concept of full membership of a community – or, as I should say, citizenship – which is not inconsistent with the inequalities which distinguish the various economic levels in the society'.[36] In other words, the existence of the rights of citizenship does not threaten the structure of ownership and control of the forces of production nor does it free the wage labourer from the 'dull compulsion' to offer his/her labour power as an exchange value. Indeed the social rights of citizenship can be forfeited if labour power is not offered as an exchange value in some circumstances. In many areas the definition of the rights of welfare consumers is left to the discretion of the administrators or professionals, and the actual encashment of social rights is sometimes made very difficult or conditional on submissive forms of behaviour. The numerous conditions and pitfalls attached to claiming social security benefits has generated in recent years virtually a welfare rights industry.

In the housing field the rights of citizenship are particularly unclear. Governments consistently strive to achieve 'freedom of choice' in the consumption of this commodity and keenly encourage its free circulation as a directly purchasable commodity in the private market for the working class, but the notion of decent housing 'as of right' is not even translated into legislation, let alone reality.

A more general aspect of the ideology of citizenship, suggested by Marshall, concerns the importance attached to the integration of the citizen into the nation state and the consequent erosion of class differences and class conflict. This has been expanded upon by Boulding, Nobel Prize winner and American economist, who considers that 'if there is one common thread that unites all aspects of social policy and distinguishes them from merely economic policy, it is the thread of what has elsewhere been called the "integrative system"'.[37] The integrative system is that aspect of social relations beyond the strictly economic in the fetishised separation of worker and citizen. Hence 'it is an objective of social policy to build the identity of a person around some community with which he is associated';[38] in other words, to integrate the citizen, the alienated worker, into society. Richard Titmuss, following the same thesis, suggests that the 'fundamental and dominating historical processes' which led to Labour's post-1945 welfare reforms 'were connected with the demand for one society; for non-discriminatory services for all without distinction of class, income or race; for services and relations which would deepen and enlarge self-respect; for services which would manifestly encourage social integration'.[39]

The welfare state is thus conceived as the crucial apparatus, though incomplete, for putting individual citizenship and the unity of the nation before class loyalty and organisation, and therefore mitigating the effects of class conflict and inequality. This is clearly an expression of the now predominant tendency within the ideology of British Labourism that has sought to establish the Labour Party as capable of offering national leadership and promoting class harmony not least through welfare reform. The welfare state tempers the disquieting effects of inequalities and 'diswelfares' amongst citizens, setting aside the fundamental class inequality inherent in the capital–labour relation. The fear of failure in the task of social integration which has fallen to the welfare state is expressed by Roy Jenkins. In the context of his argument (in the early 1970s when Labour was in opposition) for increased transfer payments to the poor to integrate them into the consumer society and against the provision of services by the state, he says that 'the main danger is that our society will become increasingly divided between the affluent and the less well off. On the one side will be the world of youth and opportunities [sic] – on the other the poor, with an increasing sense of deprivation and shut-off-ness from the affluent world about them'.[40]

Hence the welfare state is conceived within the predominant ideo-logy as a historic act of collective altruism, which serves to integrate the citizen into society and to meet his/her needs as they are recognised by the collectivity. As such it is a powerful example of the fetishised form of the capitalist state, which disguises both its origins in the class struggle and the pressure of the law of value, and its functions in the reproduction of labour power and capitalist social relations. Finally in this chapter we shall examine the way in which ideology has influenced the study of social policy and administration.

A NOTE ON SOCIAL THEORY AND THE STUDY OF WELFARE

The sparsity of analyses of welfare policy and administration which go beyond empirical presentations will probably be manifest already to the reader. This reflects in large measure the empiricist tradition in the field of social policy and administration within which most studies of the British welfare state have roughly been situated. Both the originators and the contemporary exponents of social administ-ration have been closely identified with the development of the welfare state, and hence their overriding concern with discrete empiricist investigation and appraisal of welfare needs and policy on behalf of governments and students who mostly become professional practi-tioners within the welfare state. Standard texts offer students a run-down of welfare policy issues and developments concentrating on the question of the mitigation of poverty and the distinct categories of the so-called deprived. Hence they tend only to consider particular policy reforms in a taken-for-granted and hence unquestioned social context. The exponents of social administration have, in a sense, acted as the organic intellectuals for the liberal bourgeoisie, guiding the welfare state and developing its ideology and practice to meet new problems. Nevertheless, most writing and teaching on British welfare is dependent on the social administration tradition, which has ensured the existence of an unrivalled wealth of empirical information and materials for the study of the welfare state. To a considerable extent it will be impossible to escape this influence in what follows, since it is, for example, even written into the form of government statistics.

When students of welfare turn to considering the history of the British welfare state they are again confronted by texts reflecting an empiricist intellectual tradition in the study of history which often amounts to a useful but sterile collection of legislative and political 'facts'. Such histories emphasise the role of great people such as Chadwick, Lloyd George and Beveridge in the formation of the welfare state and are written 'from a centralist, establishment and civil service perspective, concentrating on the role of experts in the process of reform'.[41] The socio-economic forces and the working-class organisations and pressures which have shaped welfare policy and administration are only referred to in the most superficial terms, such as 'the struggle for social justice' or 'the practical problems thrown up by an industrialised society'.

Although the study of social policy history and social administration has not developed an explicit theoretical framework, underlying the literature there are latent theoretical assumptions and forms, which have been identified by radical critics. As George and Wilding[42] have argued, beneath the value-free, common-sense empiricism of social administration, there lies a 'consensus' or 'order' model of society – in other words, an implicit sociological orientation associated with Durkheim, Parsons and others. Titmuss has acknowledged a theoretical debt to Durkheim in his famous essay on 'the social division of welfare',[43] where he suggests that the welfare state has the role of supporting the complex division of labour and hence the complex division of social needs generated by an industrial society. The welfare state thus becomes a vital institution in the maintenance and reproduction of the organic solidarity which binds society together: 'All collectively provided services are deliberately designed to meet certain socially recognised "needs"; they are manifestations first of society's will to survive as an organic whole and secondly of the expressed wish of all the people to assist the survival of some people.'[44]

This is another expression of the ideology of welfare citizenship and integration already referred to, although it is rarely articulated within social policy writing. Such a perspective projects a cohesiveness of norms or values in society, which implies that the welfare state is a neutral product of class consensus designed in the 'national interest' for the 'public good'. The extent of theory development within social policy history and social administration remains eclectic and largely unconscious or implicit, so that as Mishra puts it, 'social administration is unable or unwilling to go beyond a critical and refutational stance largely based on data. What it lacks is any explicit theoretical concern . . . there is little by way of a theoretical (as distinct from normative) debate in the field'.[45]

Recently there have been attempts to meet the criticism that social administration overemphasises consensus in policy formation. Hall et al and Heclo,[46] for example, have used pluralist models of institutionalised conflict (as opposed to class conflict) developed by political scientists to describe policy development. Some historians have also begun to adopt a more radical pluralist methodology. Both these approaches have the great virtue of bringing working-class organisations such as the trade unions and the Labour Party more centrally into accounts of policy formation. Such a method, however, tends to be limited to very useful case studies, and the influence of wider socio-economic and ideological forces is not critically analysed.

Pinker has argued that social administration developed an empiricist and atheoretical methodology in the mid-nineteenth century in an 'arduous campaign against the social consequences of theory and especially the normative theory of political economy'.[47] This is a reference to the classical political economists, such as Smith, Ricardo and Malthus, whose views shaped much nineteenth-century legislation and ideology, concerning amongst other things the obligations of the state to the worker. These obligations in welfare terms were minimal. The role of the state was to guarantee free exchange of commodities to allow the 'hidden hand' or technical forces of the market and the pressure of population to do their work in enforcing the wage relation. To a considerable extent the ideology of the classical political economists concerning the form of the state still holds sway, as we have already discussed. Pinker has marshalled considerable evidence of significant struggle by the advocates of empirical investigation and rational administration to counter the worst excesses of 'laissez-faire' anti-collectivism, but there is no evidence that this went fundamentally beyond the tenets of classical political economy and possessive individualism. On the contrary, social investigation and rational administration were also employed to further the notions of individual self-help and moral responsibility amongst the poor. This articulated a developed form of 'laissez-faire' ideology influenced by social Darwinist and Spencerian sociological models, exemplified in the work of the Charity Organisation Society, which was a stalwart opponent of state welfare provision. This strand in the social administration tradition was influential in the establishment of the various schools of social work and social administration in the first decade of the twentieth century. Pinker suggests that these different origins of social administration present something of a paradox. However, if one observes the relatively happy coexistence over this century of individual and community 'pathology' models of social work theory and practice, together with the empiricist and fragmentary approach to the plight of the poor within the social administration tradition, it seems probable that they reinforced each other quite compatibly.

We would prefer to suggest that the social administration tradition emerged *alongside* and as part of the modified versions of political economy which developed within the period of competitive capitalism. Such modifications were forced upon the predominant ideology by the changes in the structure and requirements of capital and by the struggle and resistance of the working class. The classical political economists considered that 'working class advancement was limited by shortage of capital and threatened by Malthusian pressures; combinations of workers were pointless, if not destructive, because at most they could only affect the mode of distribution of a previously allocated wages fund'.[48] Towards the end of the period of competitive capitalism, more optimistic views on expansion of capital accumulation and the condition of the working class began to take hold. It was gradually acknowledged that the working class could not and would not be confined to pauperism, and hence that the state had a more central role to play in reproducing labour power for a new 'moralised' capitalism. Individualism became enshrined in the notions of free, equal and universal male citizenship and hence social and political rights for the male working class. Clearly the techniques of social administration had an important part to play in the development of the new liberal state in which the 'appeal to facts has a ring of political neutrality and impartiality'.[49] The social administration tradition has also played a significant part in forming and articulating working-class attitudes to poverty and welfare reform, particularly within the Labour movement itself. The coincidence between the interests of capital in general and the functioning of the welfare state is obscured in the contemporary social administration orthodoxy. This orthodoxy is bound by the fetishised form of the state, emphasising the separation between 'laissez-faire' individualism in the private market and state collectivism, in which the latter is conceived in valiant struggle with the former on behalf of the poor and the working class. This encourages the belief that bureaucratic regulation of the private sector and further welfare reform can either eradicate class inequality or make it acceptable.

The study of social policy and administration, inasmuch as it exists as a distinct discipline, is one of the clearest examples of the empiricist and atheoretical tradition in British intellectual culture which has flourished within an intellectual terrain whose foundations have never required fundamental questioning with the continuing triumph of the basic elements of classical political economy. As E. P. Thompson suggests, the theoretical construction of Adam Smith and his colleagues

> . . . was a system of thought so comprehensive and yet so flexible that it formed the structure within which the social sciences and political thought of Victorian England were still framed; it underwrote commercial imperialism; it conquered the intelligence of the bourgeoisie throughout the world; and after a sharp-fought and impressive resistance . . . the English working-class movement capitulated before it and regrouped in order to maximise its rewards within the framework which it dictated. Finally it has survived, less in sophisticated theory than in popular myth, until this day. It is in the name of some 'natural' law of a free economy that the public tolerates its unfreedom in the face of the monopolists, the land-speculators, the controllers of the media of communication.[50]

It is no wonder, therefore, that Marx constructed his greatest work explicitly as a critique of classical political economy.

The background to this book is necessarily an implicit critique of social administration. This is unavoidable in approaching some of the critical welfare issues of the day from a Marxist perspective. The brief accounts of housing and social security policy which follow are obviously very dependent on the empiricist tradition, and the assumptions woven into it. It would otherwise be impossible to write one word about the detailed working of the welfare state. Until recently Marxists have paid little attention to the analysis of the welfare state, tending to write it off as a side issue or a reformist diversion from industrial and seemingly truly political struggles. This book is written under the influence of the revival of Marxist political economy since the late 1960s. The marriage between the concepts developing within that movement of ideas and our knowledge of the welfare state as refracted through the social administration prism is not a very happy one. In the end the intellectual virtue of a Marxist approach is that it should permit the weaving of particular historical and policy developments into a systematic and dynamic conception of the nature and reproduction of social relations in capitalist societies. Hopefully, also, it can serve to demystify the widespread illusions about the nature of the welfare state and raise the question of its fundamental change.

3

Social Security, Class Struggle and the Reproduction of Capital

In this and the following chapter we shall examine aspects of poor relief and social security administration and policy in England and Wales since the early nineteenth century. The terms poor relief and social security are generic terms, neither of which are really adequate, but we shall be concentrating here on cash payments by the parish or the state to those people variously defined as 'in need'. Clearly such payments are a central pillar of the welfare state, which have saved many people from destitution and starvation. As long ago as 1921 social security expenditure formed 4.7 per cent of the gross national product, rising to 6.7 per cent in 1931 amidst mass unemployment. Such proportions were not reached again until the 1960s, but by 1975 it had reached 9.5 per cent. Social security has provided essential material support to working-class people who fall on hard times in a whole variety of circumstances. The growth in the level and coverage of benefits has been linked to the growth of working-class strength and organisation in the struggle towards the improvement of their living conditions. In that sense the social security system is a product of class struggle. It is unlikely that drastic cuts in the level of and eligibility for benefits would be possible aside from a general context of a massive defeat of the working class as a whole. However, the form in which social security benefits are delivered (or not delivered) to working-class people has not been neutral with respect to the class struggle.

The social security system has been a focus of working-class struggle for local democratic control of the state apparatus, particularly from the late nineteenth century until the 1930s, when centralised bureaucratic control was finally established. In the post-war period the struggle has been confined largely to administrative reform and improved take-up and levels of benefit, with a tacit acceptance of the overall policy and administrative structure. The latter is, however, not adapted to serve the interests of the working class, nor is it something over which there is active working-class democratic control. In fact the social security system is concerned with the reproduction of capitalist social relations. This is apparent in the general sense in which it represents and maintains an image of the benevolence of capitalist society, cushioning individual members of the working class from the worst consequences of unemployment, sickness, disability, family break-up and so on. However, the social security system also reproduces capitalist social relations in more particular and direct ways through a variety of discretionary powers and bureaucratic devices, as well as in its policy fundamentals. These policies and practices have always been the subject of many forms of class struggle, which have mitigated their effects but have not altered the fundamental fact that the system continues to function relatively compatibly within capitalist social relations and a capitalist state.

Social security or poor relief attempts to reproduce the immediate capital–labour relation in a number of ways. Above all it is concerned with the reproduction and maintenance of the industrial reserve army of labour, hereafter referred to as the labour reserve army. As Mandel has emphasised, one of the mechanisms

> . . . inherent in the capitalist mode of production which normally keep the increase in the value and the price of wages within bounds is the expansion or reconstruction of the industrial reserve army induced by the accumulation of capital itself, i.e. by the inevitable appearance, in periods of rising wages, of attempts to replace living labour by machines on a vast scale.[2]

Firstly, therefore, the levels of social security benefit may act to keep down the local or national price of labour power (i.e. wages) by establishing an official subsistence minimum which is well below the existing value of labour power, that is the average standard of living achieved by the working class at a particular point in history. This maintains work incentive, or, in other words, the pressure to offer labour power as an exchange value. It may include attempts to maintain differences in the price of labour power between localities or occupations through discretionary powers, or the enforcement of more uniform regional and national prices of labour power to facilitate labour mobility and the reconstruction of capital.

The changing requirements for capital of labour power generate the continual movement of labour and the need for retraining, and the maintenance of a pool of discarded labour in reserve. It is common for the provision of retraining, menial work or the eventual acceptance of less skilled or attractive employment to be made a condition for the receipt of relief. Secondly, therefore, social security policy tries to ensure that the labour reserve army's front line, usually those men considered to be able-bodied, preserve their labour power as a potential exchange value. This means that they must be 'genuinely seeking work' and that married men must be responsible for keeping their families, too, although the married woman's (or even children's) earnings may serve to shift the burden on to the family.

Thirdly, social security is also concerned with those sections of the labour reserve army that are not customarily maintained in immediate readiness for wage work, in the twentieth century at least. This includes the elderly, the disabled, students, single parents, married women and so on, who are nevertheless brought into wage work, but can be repelled from the labour market more quickly and firmly than the front line, if necessary. In many such cases social security policy attempts to shift dependence from the state or parish on to the family. A particularly important example is the case of married women whose dependence on the male wage-earner or male welfare beneficiary has been strongly reinforced. In such cases the absence of statutory regulation or relief maintains the availability of a pool of cheap and unprotected labour power. This is not to argue that we can understand the relationship between these groups and the welfare state solely in terms of their position in the labour reserve army, for clearly they require a more specific and sensitive analysis.

Finally, the social security system seeks to impose forms of discipline and restraint on wage labour in general. For example, it acts as a means of countering the effectiveness of strikes, and, by making benefit conditional on the circumstances in which an unemployed person lost his/her job, it tries to ensure that the intransigent worker cannot so easily turn to the welfare state for support. In certain circumstances work incentive may be encouraged by parish/state subsidisation of low wages – for example, in the present Family Income Supplement. The labelling, by both social security administrators and many others, of the long-term unemployed and other claimants as undeserving or scroungers assists in the preservation of work incentive by rendering claimants socially as well as economically less eligible.

The operation of the system confirms the individuating experience of unemployment, sickness, disability, desertion and so on, militating against collective resistance and struggle on such questions by the working class as a whole. It is made clear that the working class must sell its labour power in order to survive under the command of capital, and in the case of married men that they have responsibility for maintaining their wives and families.

Possibly the most important change in the social security system since the early nineteenth century has been the introduction of National Insurance in 1911 and its gradual extension since then, so that it now dominates state social security provision. In 1977–8 74 per cent of UK social security expenditure was devoted to National Insurance benefits, while supplementary benefit only accounted for 15 per cent, child benefit for 5 per cent and other non-contributory benefits for 6 per cent.[3] The National Insurance system embodies the conservative and individuating notions of self-support and individual/family responsibility inherited from the private and friendly society insurance. It is based on the principle of an individual contract between the worker, the state and the employer, in which each party makes contributions and draws benefits.[4] The actuarial basis is largely fictitious[5] but the importance of the principle that benefits must be strictly related to contributions (the contribution principle) lies elsewhere. For workers it improved and extended the benefits and coverage offered by employers' and friendly society insurance.[6] It rescued many people from having to resort to meagre savings or the hated poor law in hard times, and it also established relatively clear rights to state benefits. For individual employers it helped to create a sense of security amongst workers, raising morale and helping to enforce discipline.[7] For governments it succeeded in containing working-class pressure to improve their living standards and cushion the experience of old age and hard times. The contribution principle bound wage-earners more closely to the state itself, creating a 'direct worker interest in the state'.[8] Simultaneously it divided the army of claimants between the relatively deserving and respectable, who were insured, and the somewhat less deserving uninsured or under-insured groups, who still had to resort to means-tested non-contributory benefits. Above all, as Neville Chamberlain argued in 1925,[9] when he introduced the National Insurance old age pension, National Insurance has assisted in removing some social security questions from the political arena.

Our discussion of social security must, however, begin with the

situation which faced the parishes and the government at the beginning
of the period of competitive capitalism in the early nineteenth century.

THE NINETEENTH–CENTURY POOR LAW

By the early nineteenth century this legislation was beginning to
fetter the development of competitive capitalism, and the emergence
of a free market in labour power in particular. This was exacerbated
by the decentralised form of administration, which concentrated power
in the hands of the local gentry. Hence the reform of the poor
law in the nineteenth century sought to sweep away both subsidies
to the able-bodied independent labourer and the highly discretionary
system of local administration. This provoked a considerable rearguard
struggle by both gentry and common people to preserve 'the older
moral economy as against the economy of the free market'[10] and
'the labourer's last "inheritance"',[11] that is his right to poor relief
in the community of his settlement.

In 1795 the magistrates at Speenhamland, Berkshire, decided to
use the poor rates to subsidise low wages 'in cases where the labourer's
family income fell below the subsistence level, either because the
price of bread was too high or the number of children too large'.[12]
This system was subsequently adopted in most areas of the country,
particularly where enclosure of the commons had denied the labourer
independent access to the means of subsistence and where, for example,
industrialisation had pauperised the hand-loom weaver.[13] The Speenhamland system in fact increased the pauperisation of the agricultural
labourer in the early nineteenth century by keeping wages down
and encouraging underemployment. In one sense Speenhamland
pointed to the future: it was an attempt to create a labour reserve
which would function to keep wages down. It 'failed' in the long
term because it did not create sufficient separation and competition
between the employed and the unemployed. It also directly opposed
the interests of urban capital by attempting to 'maintain a labour
reserve in the countryside and to restrict its movement into the
towns'.[14] The effects of enclosure, pauperisation, underemployment
and the general capitalisation of agriculture evoked persistent and
violent resistance from the agricultural labourers, culminating in the
'Captain Swing' revolts of 1830–2, and thence in poor law reform
and the anti-poor-law movement.

It was the agitation by the agricultural labourers that prompted the appointment in 1832 of a royal commission, which produced the famous Poor Law Report of 1834 and led to the passing of the 1834 Poor Law Amendment Act. The report was not therefore directly concerned with the industrial proletariat, but a general theme throughout[15] was the need, as the commissioners saw it, to create an 'independent class of labourers' – independent that is from paternalist employers and the poor law authorities, a class of labourers which would be forced to sell its labour power as a pure exchange value in exchange for the means of subsistence. Hence, in effect, the 1834 Poor Law was a major enactment designed to assist in the creation of a 'free' market in labour power. It sought to end the paternalistic system of poor relief and replace it with a centrally regulated administration, which would end wage subsidisation out of the poor rates and cut back, if not eliminate, out-relief (that is relief in cash or kind outside the workhouse) to the 'able-bodied' poor. People were to be more actively deterred from applying for relief by the reinforced threat and stigma of incarceration in the workhouse, which would label the pauper as 'less eligible' and undeserving. Amongst the most significant effects of the implementation of the 1834 Poor Law was, firstly, the rationalisation of the local poor law authorities: 15,000 poor law parishes were eventually replaced by 600 poor law unions, employing relieving officers (instead of using volunteers) under more regularly elected boards of guardians. Secondly, a central inspectorate and independent auditing were introduced to oversee the work of the unions. Between 1834 and 1870 the inspectors were subject to the control of semi-autonomous government advisory boards, and after 1870 the inspectorate became part of the Local Government Board, a new government department of the modern variety. Thirdly, a significant reduction in expenditure on out-relief was achieved, at least in the first decade after 1834, though this was not a period of economic depression.[16] Fourthly, a more stringent administration of out-relief to those judged to be able-bodied emerged, while a more rigid discipline was imposed on workhouse inmates, who remained largely the sick, aged and orphans. Despite the avowed intention to suppress pauperism, in 1841, for example, more than 8 per cent of the population of England and Wales were classified as paupers, either in the workhouse or mostly receiving out-relief.

The 1834 Poor Law sought to impose the free exchange of labour power by disciplining and containing the demands of the labour reserve army, establishing a local relief system which did not interfere with wage levels, and ensuring that workers would compete against each other to restrain the price of labour power. There can be no doubt that the deterrent effect of the poor law was very strong,[17] and pushed people into work at subsistence and below-subsistence wages, even when in some cases conditions in the workhouse were materially better than living conditions outside.[18] Nevertheless, in the northern industrial towns labour shortages occurred in boom periods and the poor law commissioners used their powers to actively facilitate migration of agricultural labourers from the south to the north, and they set up actual markets in labour power for manufacturers in Manchester and Leeds.[19] In slump conditions, on the other hand, orphans and others were offered assisted passage out of the country.

In discussing the origins of the 1834 Poor Law historians commonly emphasise two important factors. First was the outcry amongst ratepayers over the cost of relief, which gained in strength with the rise of industrial capitalists and petit-bourgeois to positions of local and Parliamentary power. Secondly, accompanying these changes in political and economic relations, ideological developments were clearly very significant – the shift, that is, from the customary moral economy of agrarian capitalism in the period of primitive accumulation to the political economy of competitive industrial capitalism. Hence the 1834 Poor Law reflected more clearly than ever before the intellectual influence of men such as Malthus, Bentham and Chadwick. It may be described both as 'the most sustained attempt to impose an ideological dogma in defiance of the evidence of human need in English history'[20] and as an 'ethical compromise'[21] between Malthus's proposal to starve the labour reserve army and the Bentham/Chadwick model of collectivised discipline but not starvation of that army. While these ideological aspects are clearly essential to an adequate account of the 1834 Poor Law, rather more importance is perhaps ascribed to the role of ideology rather than the civil disorder and struggles of the decades preceding the passing of the act. In the years after 1834 resistance continued to shape poor law policy, this time directed against the increased power of central government and the restrictions on relief, so that the principles of 1834 were never fully implemented, particularly in the industrial north.

Popular resistance in the rural south, while certainly strong, was put down fairly easily in the mid-1830s and almost all of southern

and central rural England was under the aegis of the new poor
law by 1836. In the north the poor law commissioners came up
against 'a curious blend of parochial defensiveness, Whig theory,
and popular resistance',[22] and many of the newly elected guardians
rejected the commissioners' attempts to impose the principles of 1834.
In some places the anti-poor-law coalition of Radical and Tory forces
boycotted the new unions, thereby effectively neutralising them.[23]
The anti-poor-law movement to a considerable extent formed the
organisational and class basis for the Chartist movement.

The poor relief system advocated in 1834 with rural areas in
mind was not well adapted to the fluctuations of labour supply and
demand in the industrial areas, and probably not in agricultural areas
either for that matter. The deterrent principles of 1834 certainly
helped to keep workers in employment in times of labour shortage,
but in periods of slump it was impossible to deny people out-relief,
since it was impracticable and expensive to commit masses of people
to the workhouse. Hence in the early months of depressions in the
Lancashire cotton towns 'operatives lived mainly off their own
resources and those of their friends, neighbours and kin', but as
the slump wore on, 'more and more were forced to go on to poor
relief and to seek assistance from the charitable funds which gradually
took over the major burden of relief'.[24] Thus the guardians and
relieving officers adapted the principles of 1834 to local requirements
and political situations. Discrepancies between strict theory and more
liberal practice occurred over such issues as the appointment of salaried
personnel, workhouse management, the development of medical relief
(which emerged from indoor relief) and poor law education. Although
the complete prohibition of out-relief for the able-bodied was abandoned, labour yards were established at the workhouses where able-
bodied claimants did menial work such as stone-breaking in exchange
for their out-relief, sometimes called the labour test. Such attempts
to keep the unemployed in readiness for work continued into the
1930s and have recently reappeared in the less punitive form of the
job creation programme.

After the reforming enthusiasm of the 1830s died down 'the working membership of nearly all the Boards settled down to a farmer
from each of the numerous parishes in the rural Unions and to
little groups of retail shopkeepers in the Unions of the Metropolitan
area and the large towns'.[25] While the central authority could and
did issue circulars having the force of law, which regulated all aspects

of poor law administration and finance, the force of law could rarely be called upon, precisely because of the strength of parochial power. Sidney and Beatrice Webb commented somewhat ruefully that 'the inefficiency, parsimony and petty corruption at the base of the Administrative Hierarchy must inevitably have gone far to nullify any superiority in science and statesmanship that may have been manifested in the guidance and control from the top'.[26] The central authority had to come to terms with local labour market and political conditions, particularly since poor relief remained locally financed.

Between 1871 and 1886 a new school of poor law orthodoxy emerged, particularly at central government level after the integration of the poor law administration into the new Local Government Board. There began a new attack on the granting of out-relief to those identified as the 'undeserving' poor. This came partly in response to the depression of the late 1860s, which put greatly increased pressure on the poor law unions, particularly from the urban casual poor. The so-called demoralisation of the casual poor was, in the view of the authorities and many reformers, worsened by indiscriminate charity on a large scale, which tided the poor over the inevitable seasonal unemployment and supplemented earnings and poor relief.[27] In order to stem this demoralisation, out-relief was once again made more restrictive, and in addition the poor law and charitable organisations began to cooperate in the investigation and remoralisation of the poor. Thus in the 1870s and 1880s 'we watch the Inspectors by precept and circular, exhortation and criticism, constantly admonishing the Boards of Guardians that the grant of outdoor relief was dangerous, pernicious and blameworthy'.[28]

Increased use was made of local bye-laws and codes making the grant of out-relief dependent on the character and conduct of the applicant. The major recipients were the aged poor, widows and deserted mothers, who became subject to a test of deservingness applied with a stringency not seen before, even in the 1830s. There was increased use of the labour test for the able-bodied poor, including women. It is perhaps possible to see in this renewal of 1834 orthodoxy a reorientation towards the labour reserve army and the casual poor, as a more rigorous attempt to impose work discipline and to influence workers' character and attitudes while reinforcing the principle of deterrence.

In the period of competitive capitalism the poor law assisted in the creation of a free market in labour power by disciplining and relieving as a last resort the labour reserve army and deterring workers from securing the means of subsistence by any means other than the wage, more often than not a subsistence wage. The implementation of these policies required a degree of centralisation and buraucratisation of poor law administration which was muted and shaped by considerable local resistance, above all from the emergent working-class movement. The state administration in the shape of the central inspectorate and the local officers appear to have waged an administrative war of attrition which slowly achieved greater national uniformity while retaining sufficient discretion to meet local political and labour market conditions.

POOR RELIEF AND THE UNEMPLOYED FROM THE 1880S TO 1918

In the period of classical imperialism the development of poor relief is dominated much less by the question of pauperisation, identified as an inevitable condition of the masses necessitated by the short-term trade cycle and the role of the labour reserve army in keeping wages down. In the context of the changes in the structure of capital and class relations discussed in Chapters 1 and 2, particularly the lengthening of the trade cycle and greater working-class organisation, policy becomes shaped by the more focused and newly identified phenomena of male unemployment and the unfitness of the working population of the world's greatest imperial power. Distinct strata of the labour reserve army and the non-able-bodied become codified within state policy – for example, the distinction between the insured and the uninsured workers, and that between the deserving elderly or widows and the undeserving, so-called feckless or malingering, paupers. Here we shall concentrate on the relationship between the male unemployed and the emerging social security system.

The period begins with what was both a hangover from the earlier period and an indication of new realms of class struggle to come. In February 1886 unemployed dock and building workers rioted in the West End of London, and this appears to have provoked widespread fear and discussion about unemployment amongst the London bourgeoisie. The immediate response was a circular of March 1886 from Joseph Chamberlain, the President of the Local Government Board, urging Boards of Guardians and local authorities to establish public works relief programmes for the 'exceptional' unemployed, which would 'help the workman without subjecting him to the processes of pauperism'.[29] The significance of the circular lies less in what it immediately achieved, which was next to nothing, and more in the change of thought amongst politicians – it marked the end of the era of the reassertion of 1834 poor law orthodoxy. Several demonstrations urging the state to take greater responsibility for the unemployed took place between 1892 and 1895, often organised by the Marxist Social Democratic Federation (SDF). This pressure paid off at the local level to some extent; after the reorganisation of local government in 1889 there was a significant increase in the direct representation of the organised working class and, combined with pressure from the streets, over 100 local authorities undertook relief works in the early 1890s.[30] The local authorities could of course achieve little without central government financial assistance, and they too began to pressurise the government for funds, which were not forthcoming. The revival of trade between 1896 and 1902 appears to have removed the issue from the political scene, including the TUC's agenda.

The slump of 1903–8 produced more insistent pressure from the unemployed on the streets and the Labour movement in general.[31] The variety of demands and proposed policies on unemployment was very great amongst working-class organisations. In the 1880s and 1890s the demand for an 8-hour working day had been championed by Tom Mann as a means of reducing unemployment; many trade unionists sought the limitation of hours and overtime as a solution to the crisis of 1904–8.[32] Others put the emphasis on local relief works without the stigma of pauperisation. The Independent Labour Party (ILP) and the TUC suggested that unemployment might be mitigated 'by a redistribution of consuming power within capitalism',[33] while the SDF and others advocated more radical changes in the control of capital and labour.

These developments in the articulation of working-class political demands are extremely important. On the one hand, they show the increasing influence of a more structural analysis of the questions of poverty and unemployment, while, on the other hand, largely submerging these questions within the immediate trade union concern of mitigating unemployment, and preventing 'respectable' workers from slipping into pauperism. From the late nineteenth century onwards a more significant distinction was recognised by the middle classes and organised workers alike between the respectable organised working class and the residuum of the casual poor. The former had legitimate claims, which would have to be met by negotiation; the latter no longer presented even a remote political threat, they were only a 'social problem'.[34] While this was not a new distinction,[35] the proportion of the working class included in the organised, relatively secure and predominantly male stratum had greatly expanded as the slump cycle no longer hit so hard. While earlier in the century almost all workers experienced cyclical unemployment, from the 1880s onwards they might experience it only once or twice, or maybe never, in a lifetime. In a sense the distinction between the deserving and the undeserving poor was being reproduced in a modernised, more class-conscious form, and although it has been brought under severe pressure in periods of high unemployment, it still remains widespread today. Welfare policy succeeds in reproducing and deepening the real divisions within the working class.

The government response to the class struggle over unemployment in the first decade of the century was experimental and small-scale. The Unemployed Workers Act, 1903, required the formation of distress committees in every large local authority area, using the combined forces of the local authority, the poor law union and the charities. These committees tried to separate the 'worthy unemployed' from 'the loafer', using the casework methods of the Charity Organisation Society and dealing with the former through local authority relief works and the latter through the poor law.[36] Hence there was great antagonism between the unemployed and these committees. The 1903 act also permitted the establishment of labour exchanges by the distress committees, which were taken over by Beveridge at the Board of Trade in 1909. Their success in any terms has always appeared limited, though hard to evaluate.[37] National unemployment insurance was introduced for a limited group of workers in 1912, and its coverage has gradually been extended ever since. While unemployment benefit was granted as an apparent right of the insured worker in exchange for his/her contributions and the compulsion to register at the labour exchange, it was hedged with various qualifications as 'to the diligence and good time-keeping' of the claimant.[38] Throughout its history unemployment benefit has been used in a variety of ways to enforce discipline amongst workers, as we shall see. The Labour movement was extremely suspicious of these pieces of legislation and played no direct part in their framing. There was evidence that the labour exchanges were used to recruit black-leg labour, and compulsory registration was viewed by the *Daily Herald* as 'the beginning of the process of registering and numbering all workers, of keeping complete work records ultimately for use against them'.[39] There was sporadic local resistance to the introduction of national unemployment insurance, but the appointment of trade unionists to directorships of labour exchanges and local insurance committees ensured tacit acceptance.

THE STRUGGLE OVER ADMINISTRATION IN THE INTER-WAR PERIOD

The mass unemployment of the inter-war years overwhelmed the poor law authorities and the National Insurance scheme. There was intense class struggle over benefits and relief for the unemployed. On the one hand, the working class attempted to use its power to protect and improve the living standards of the unemployed, particularly through the boards of guardians and the effects of the hunger marches. On the other hand, state policy sought to prevent benefits threatening wage levels, through the means test, benefit cuts and disqualifications. Policy also sought to enhance the divisions amongst the working class and the unemployed by a series of administrative manoeuvres which, for example, shored up the insurance principle and distinguished between the 'genuinely unemployed' and the 'malingerer'. We begin with the political struggle over the control of the poor law guardians.

The poor law boards of guardians were locally elected bodies, and after the Local Government Act, 1894, many working class guardians were elected, although recipients of poor relief were excluded from the electorate until 1918. Labour guardians were usually outnumbered but their influence was considerable, particularly in places where they worked with the support of local demonstrations by the unemployed. Labour guardians were placed in a difficult position: while they often opposed subsidising sweated wages, the labour test, and the use of relief applicants as cheap labour in the workhouse, they were also concerned with the immediate relief of poverty. The Social Democratic Federation recognised that while the basic objective of the poor law 'was to keep the working people in the labour market, local control made it a potentially more democratic instrument'.[40] Even before the First World War several boards had dropped the labour test and were paying relief comparable to the lowest wages locally, despite government attempts to thwart them.

The first major post-war confrontation occurred in Poplar in 1921 over the refusal of the Labour guardians to levy rates on behalf of other bodies such as the London County Council. This was a protest against the unequal burden of poor relief expenditure and local rate income between rich and poor boroughs; essentially it was a demand for increased subsidisation of the poor rates. The Poplar guardians went to gaol for 6 weeks as martyrs, and eventually the government conceded the issue of rate equalisation. Also in 1921 the National Unemployed Workers Movement was founded, and it first directed its attention to the poor law authorities, bringing considerable pressure to bear on guardians to provide 'work or maintenance' by such tactics as mass applications to the workhouse or occupying the workhouse and the guardians' offices. But the government then started to plan for national uniformity of poor relief rates in order to prevent labour guardians paying relief at levels which threatened local wages. Relieving officers began to adopt fixed scales of relief, varying usually according to family size; they were no longer able to investigate every applicant in the traditional manner, so that the more bureaucratic means test procedure was developed. In 1922 the government prescribed maxima for these scales related to, but below, the local authority manual wage levels determined by the new Whitley councils. For several years these scales were largely unenforceable, and local diversity and discretion remained very marked, varying from blank refusal of relief to the able-bodied to what became known as Poplarism. Poplar and several other labour boards of guardians in East London, South Wales and the North of England paid relief in excess of the government rates, refused to implement a family means test and granted relief to strikers and low-paid workers. Possibly 200 boards, covering half the population, were granting relief which in some way broke with 'poor law principles'.[41] In the years before the General Strike of 1926 it was simply impossible for the government to crack down on these boards, because of the resistance which this would have provoked locally, reminiscent in some ways of the late 1830s.

The behaviour of the boards of guardians during and after the General Strike perhaps marks the climax of working-class resistance to the poor law and the beginnings of more emphatic counter-offensives. State policy on the question of relief of strikers was clarified in 1900, when the appeal courts restrained the Merthyr Tydfil guardians from granting relief to striking miners.[42] Subsequently relief could only be given to support strikers' dependants, and single strikers were formally excluded from obtaining relief. During the General Strike the number of successful applicants for relief reached almost 2½ million, which included single strikers in Poplarist areas at least. The government issued a circular during the strike reiterating the principles of the Merthyr Tydfil judgement and giving a relief scale for strikers' families, which was much lower than that in use in many places. Some boards seem to have exceeded the 'minister's scale', but others paid relief well below the scale levels or none at all. With the continuation of the miners' strike after the collapse of the General Strike in May 1926, various struggles continued in the mining areas over such issues as relief to single strikers, relief of the pit-boys, school meals relief and the family means test. In many Midlands mining areas relief rates were very low, and after the General Strike a policy backlash occurred, with reduced scales and eventually the withdrawal of out-relief altogether for miners' families in the autumn of 1926.[43]

After the General Strike the government seized the opportunity to oust the rebellious boards that still defied poor law principles. Because of the heavy expenditure of 1926, most of these boards were in considerable debt, and the government refused to sanction their borrowing until they toed the line. The boards of guardians in West Ham, Chester-le-Street and Bedwellty were eventually suspended and replaced by government-appointed boards. By early 1927 the central government was in a situation of unprecedented control over the local administration of poor relief. Some of the principles of 1834 were implemented with a vigour reminiscent of the 1870s, which included rigorous investigation of suspected malingerers, stringent control of out-relief at uniform scale rates, labour tests and a more searching means test. In 1927 the powers to surcharge and disqualify offending locally elected guardians and councillors were strengthened, and in 1929 the 635 boards of guardians were replaced by 146 Public Assistance Committees (PACs) of the upper-tier local authorities. Hence direct election of the boards of guardians ceased and poor relief became part of a more centralised and remote local government system.

So far our attention has been focused on the struggles over the poor law, but, as Table 3.1 shows, most unemployed workers were receiving benefit through the National Insurance system, administered

TABLE 3.1 Numbers of people (in thousands) receiving either National Insurance benefit or out-relief on account of unemployment on a particular day of the year, excluding dependants, Great Britain, 1922–39

Date	Poor relief recipients	National Insurance beneficiaries	Total registered unemployed
Jun 1922	356	690	1504
Jun 1923	205	1061 (Apr)	1256
Jun 1924	141	1035 (Dec)	1099
Jun 1925	117	992	1388
Jun 1926	452	1475	1743
Jun 1927	157	825	1091
Jun 1928	120	1057	1285
Mar 1929	113	952	1235
Mar 1930	92	1534	1710
Mar 1931	69	2338	2679
Mar 1932	124	2112	2715
Mar 1933	180	2252	2889
Mar 1934	219	1763	2291
Mar 1935	197	1721	2245
Mar 1936	171	1513	1968
Mar 1937	139	1285	1671
Mar 1938	29	1544	1824
Mar 1939	28	1530	1809

SOURCE E. M. Burns, *British Unemployment Programs, 1920–1938* (Washington, DC: Committee on Social Security, Social Science Research Council, 1941) Tables II, VI, I.

NOTE According to Burns (pp. 106–7), the overlap between poor relief recipients and National Insurance beneficiaries was small, particularly after 1927.

by the Ministry of Labour at the Labour Exchanges. In the crisis period after the sudden ending of the First World War, amidst deep social and industrial conflict and both fears and hopes of Bolshevism, the government immediately introduced what they hoped would be a temporary non-contributory unemployment benefit for demobilised workers, called the 'out-of-work donation' or dole. The National Insurance coverage was greatly extended in 1920, but in order to prevent the 'insured' and demobilised unemployed from resorting to the poor law, strict contributory principles were permanently suspended in 1921 with the introduction of uncovenanted benefit, that is benefit not covered by contributions. This was accompanied by administrative devices designed to ration benefits more strictly and to discipline the employed and unemployed worker alike. The most important of these devices were the household means test and the disqualification of those 'not genuinely seeking work' (the NGSW clause). The means test ensured that earnings by any member of the family were taken into account in calculating entitlement, which led to the departure of many sons, daughters and even grandparents from the 'family home'. In particular it disqualified many women applicants,[44] and in other cases made families totally dependent on the woman's wage. Applicants for benefit had to prove that they were 'genuinely seeking work', which allowed for very harsh interpretations concerning attitudes and reasons for previous job loss. In 1927 10 per cent of all claims for National Insurance unemployment benefit were disallowed 'on the grounds that the claimant either had not done enough work in the past two years or was not making sufficient effort to secure it at the time'.[45]

Clearly the NGSW clause implicitly regulated the behaviour of those in employment in deterring them from leaving their job with the expectation of an automatic right to the dole. The local administration of these discretionary powers was left to the local employment committees, an early example of the form of three-person tribunal now common throughout the welfare state. It was above all more autonomous from local pressure than the boards of guardians; the chairmen were nominated by the local civil servants 'after thoroughly sounding out local opinion'.[46] There was a striking contrast between the close control which the Ministry of Labour exercised over the membership of these local committees and the inability of the Ministry of Health to control the poor law guardians before 1927. In 1928 the local Ministry of Labour officers took full administrative control of unemployment benefit, and the employment committees became appellate 'courts of referees'.

The means test and the NGSW clause were strongly resisted by the Labour movement, particularly the NUWM, and local pressure no doubt mitigated some of the worst effects in particular places. The hunger marches of February 1929 and February 1930 were directed against the NGSW clause, which was officially relaxed by the Labour government following the 1930 march, by which time, however, the high level of unemployment had reduced the measure's effectiveness.

As Table 3.2 shows, during the 1920s expenditure on relief and benefits to the unemployed was confined to about £50 million per

TABLE 3.2 Expenditure (in £ millions) on National Insurance unemployment benefits, supplementary payments and poor relief in cash and kind to the unemployed and their dependants, Great Britain 1920–1 to 1938–9

Fiscal year	National Insurance	Supplementary systems*	Poor relief	Total
1920–21	34.1	–	not available	–
1921–22	52.9	–	not available	–
1922–23	41.9	–	11.1	53.0
1923–24	36.0	–	7.6	43.6
1924–25	44.6	–	4.9	49.5
1925–26	43.7	–	6.4	50.1
1926–27	38.7	–	12.6	51.3
1927–28	36.5	–	7.2	43.7
1928–29	46.8	–	5.2	52.0
1929–30	42.3	3.7	4.3	50.3
1930–31	73.0	19.2	2.3	94.5
1931–32	80.2	30.7	3.6	114.5
1932–33	54.2	50.4	5.9	110.5
1933–34	40.2	48.4	7.4	96.0
1934–35	43.8	42.2	8.9	94.9
1935–36	42.7	42.4	8.8	93.9
1936–37	35.3	37.4	7.5	80.2
1937–38	36.7	36.7	2.2	75.6
1938–39	55.1	35.3	2.2	92.6

* Covers transitional benefits, transitional payments and unemployment assistance allowances.

SOURCE E. M. Burns, *British Unemployment Programs, 1920–1938* (Washington, DC: Committee on Social Security, Social Science Research Council, 1941) Tables VII, X.

year, while the numbers of unemployed in receipt of such support was about 1 million at any given time (see Table 3.1). From early 1930, however, both the numbers assisted and the cost of support more than doubled in a few months, and only began to fall back slowly in 1936. This explosion in unemployment must be partly attributed to the policies of the 1929–31 minority Labour government, as well as the general world trade depression. Government policy

... was based on the belief that any substantial reduction in the number of unemployed depended solely upon the ability of British imperialism to defeat its rivals in the struggle for world markets; therefore the government devoted itself openly to help the recovery of British capitalist industry. Secondly it believed that, in order to effect this recovery, there must be an intensive drive for improving the organisation and equipment of British industry and for lowering the cost of production.[47]

The government, therefore, encouraged industrial rationalisation by securing loans and the cooperation of the trade unions, which harmonised with TUC policy since the General Strike.[48] Hence

> . . . in the drive for rationalisation the employers broke long-standing protective practices; this involved the intensive application of schemes for the sub-division of labour and simplification of productive methods, eliminating more and more the need for craft and skill . . . It led to a greater displacement of workers who had formerly been almost indispensable because of their technical knowledge. The whole policy led to a rapid increase in the number of unemployed.[49]

Not surprisingly, therefore, in August 1931 the Labour government split and McDonald formed a national government, which immediately embarked on more stringent control of government spending that did not contribute to industrial growth, as they saw it. The Treasury limited the increasing expenditure on unemployment benefit in several ways. Firstly, there was an immediate cut in the level of National Insurance unemployment benefit from 17s. to 15s. 3d. Secondly, there was a reassertion of the contributory principle, so that National Insurance benefit proper could only be claimed for 26 weeks by those eligible. The extension of uncovenanted benefit beyond 26 weeks was now to be much more closely controlled by the means test and was renamed 'transitional payments' – transitional, that is, between insurance and the poor law. The transitional payments were to be financed under the direct scrutiny of the Treasury. Finally, the means test was to be used more strictly under the administration of the Public Assistance Committees (PACs, virtually the old poor law authorities) instead of the labour exchanges. This measure cut off 270,000 people from insurance and transitional benefits in the first 3 months of the new policy.[50] Table 3.1 indicates that an increasing proportion of the unemployed had to turn to poor relief from mid-1931 onwards, and presumably many others were either refused relief or could not bear the stigma of applying for it. Table 3.2 indicates that, despite the record level of unemployment in 1933, a fall in the total expenditure on relief and benefits was achieved. The 1931 policies pushed the long-term unemployed towards the deterrent and stigmatised poor law, and away from any notions of benefit as a right of citizenship beyond 26 weeks. This separated the labour reserve army into several camps – the short-term insured unemployed, the long-term ex-insured on transitional benefits, and the uninsured dependent on poor relief or charity.

Once again the government came into confrontation with local working-class resistance and the national struggle of the unemployed. In 1932 government commissioners had to be sent in to replace the Public Assistance Committees in Rotherham and Durham in order to implement the new policies, particularly the means test. The hunger marches of October 1932 and February 1934 were the largest and the most violently attacked by the police. The government also devised various administrative and legal devices for undermining the marchers' strength.[51] Nevertheless, after the 1934 march the government restored the cuts in benefit made in 1931.

The final twist in the long saga of struggle between the government and the unemployed was provided by the Unemployment Act, 1934. Ever since the nineteenth century governments had attempted to create a uniform, centralised social security system which would assist labour mobility and the creation of a national labour market, but would be, above all, immune from local working-class pressure. Throughout the inter-war years the unemployed and local labour movements brought insistent pressure to bear on local employment committees, boards of guardians and PACs, which in many cases broke with strict capitalist social security principles. The 1934 Act, however, transferred responsibility to the Ministry of Labour for assisting *all* those required to register as unemployed. Henceforward the uninsured (those applying for transitional benefit or poor relief) had to apply for means-tested benefit from the new Unemployment Assistance Board (UAB) within the Ministry of Labour, which would use nationally uniform means tests and scale rates with its finances under close Treasury inspection. Local political responsibility for the unemployed was eventually swept away despite another 3 years of local resistance.[52] The Minister of Labour became responsible to Parliament for general policy, but he was immune from questioning on the day-to-day discretionary administration of the scheme.[53] As a sop to local representation a three-person local appeal tribunal was introduced, which is the origin of the Supplementary Benefits Appeal Tribunal of today. The question of unemployment relief was effectively 'depoliticised' by these measures, and the contribution principle was fully restored after the aberrations since 1919. People on transitional benefits were finally reduced to the status of the undeserving, since the UAB inherited much of the poor law administrative philosophy and stigma. The local authority PACs were left with those sick, aged, disabled and women who were not required to register for employment, but the assistance board took over responsibility for many of them during the Second World War. By 1948 all local political control of out-relief was at an end, and its administration was centralised in a great and relatively autonomous bureaucracy called the National Assistance Board.

The governments of the inter-war years were able to achieve the restructuring of the relief system and the containment of the labour reserve army largely because of the political and social isolation of the unemployed from the trade union movement. This was compounded by the tacit acceptance by the Labour movement, particularly after 1926, that the working class would confine itself to exercising its power at the work place and *within* the institutions of the state rather than through any major confrontations with the state. The results for the working class were of course ambiguous; the loss of local power also meant the disappearance of the long-hated poor law structure and the establishment of more clear and uniform welfare rights. On the other hand, state policy and administration had enhanced the divisions within the working class and continued to ensure that, at relatively low cost, the unemployed were kept in readiness for work at low wages, despite the size of the reserve army. The terrain of struggle for relief now began to shift towards the take-up and extension of these welfare rights of the individual citizen, while there have been few fundamental changes in the administrative structure since the 1930s.

SOCIAL SECURITY AND THE MAINTENANCE OF LABOUR POWER SINCE 1939

From the beginning of the Second World War until the mid-1960s governments faced a situation in which the front line of the labour reserve army, that is the registered unemployed, remained small compared to the inter-war years, varying between 200,000 and half a million. There was a relative shortage of labour power and more married women and immigrant workers were recruited into low-status, low-wage employment. Instead of containing the demands of a massive army of registered unemployed, the social security system seemed to be largely concerned with those who were not usually required to register for employment, such as widows, single mothers, pensioners, the sick and disabled. Nevertheless, throughout the post-war period the social security system has continued to enforce labour discipline, push people into low-wage work and maintain the new reserve army of labour in readiness for wage work. From the mid-1960s to the early 1970s the number of registered unemployed steadily rose to over 800,000, and then in the mid-1970s took a great leap towards 1½ million. This latter period has been accompanied by various social security policy adjustments which have sought to soften the immediate effects of unemployment on the individual, subsidise low wages and contain the militancy of the Labour movement and the unemployed over the unemployment question.

One of the most important developments was the introduction in 1966 of the earnings related supplement (ERS) to National Insurance unemployment and sickness benefits, which is paid to workers with full contributions records for up to 6 months. At the same time the period for which flat rate unemployment benefit is payable was extended from 6 months to 1 year. These measures, alongside redundancy payments, were designed to cushion immediate resistance to unemployment as industrial 'rationalisation' gathered pace, and the policy was initiated by the National Economic Development Council in 1963 for precisely this reason.[54] The threat which higher benefits might pose to the incentive to find another job was mitigated by the rule that ERS would not be paid if it brought a person's income in benefits above 85 per cent of his/her normal income in employment.[55] The introduction of ERS, following the introduction of the graduated pension in 1961, further reinforced the structure of inequality amongst the working class and strengthened the individuating effects of the contribution principle.

Table 3.3 shows the ways in which benefit entitlements divide up the registered unemployed, depending on their contribution record and length of unemployment. The large numbers of registered unemployed dependent on non-contributory benefits is striking, particularly in the mid-1970s, as more long-term unemployment and intermittent

TABLE 3.3   Percentage of registered unemployed by benefit entitlement on one day, Great Britain

Date	Flat-rate NI + ERS	Flat-rate NI only	NI plus NA/SB	NA/SB only	No NI or SB entitle-ment	Total registered unemployed (thousands)
Feb 1962	——47.9——		9.9	19.7	22.5	426
May 1965	——42.4——		7.3	22.2	28.1	317
May 1968	17.9	25.7	11.1	24.1	21.3	560
May 1970	18.9	23.6	9.8	24.3	23.3	576
May 1972	19.0	21.9	11.5	19.2	18.3	872
May 1974	17.6	16.5	9.0	34.8	22.2	546
May 1976	20.4	19.4	9.2	34.3	16.7	1200
Feb 1978	——35.2——		9.5	38.8	18.5	1446

NA   National assistance
SB   Supplementary benefit
NI   National Insurance unemployment benefit
ERS   Earnings related supplement

SOURCES   V. George, *Social Security: Beveridge and After* (London: Routledge, 1968) p. 103; *Social Security Statistics 1975* (London: HMSO, 1977) Table 1.32; *Social Security Statistics 1976* (London: HMSO, 1978) Table 1.32; *Ministry of Labour/Department of Employment Gazette*, May 1962, May 1978.

employment reappear. This contrasts with the inter-war years, when the contribution principle was virtually suspended rather than subjecting the unemployed to the poor law; it suggests that much of the stigma of (and resistance to) means-tested relief has disappeared.

The numbers of people registered as unemployed and yet not entitled to any state benefits are surprisingly high. They include many married or cohabiting women, but also many others, such as young people supported by family and those who have been excluded under various discretionary rulings.[56]

LEVELS OF BENEFIT FOR THE UNEMPLOYED

We have suggested that cash benefits for the unemployed help to push down wages and hence the value of labour power by establishing a subsistence minimum which is considerably below the average worker's standard of living historically determined in the class struggle.

In areas and periods of a rising demand for labour power, the level of benefits may fall behind wages as competition amongst employers for labour power pushes the price up. In such a situation the low level of benefit reinforces pressure to find wage work. There is continual pressure from capitalists, particularly in low-wage sectors, to ensure that benefit levels remain low and do not threaten the supply of labour power. In areas and periods of high employment in which living labour is being replaced by machinery, the existence of a large reserve army of labour creates competition amongst workers to offer their labour power as an exchange value. In such a situation the existence of a large reserve army may force down wages and eventually the value of labour power. Benefit levels assist in this by defining a socially acceptable minimum which can be varied by governments according to political and economic conditions. This process occurred very clearly in the inter-war years, notably the cuts in the dole, and there are signs that such cuts in the real level of benefits may be occurring in the 1970s. National Insurance unemployment benefits (including an average amount of ERS) as a proportion of the average take-home pay of male manual workers has varied very considerably over the post-war period. In 1964 this proportion was only 24 per cent for a single worker and 45 per cent for a married man with two children; with the introduction of ERS it rose to record levels of 57 per cent and 78 per cent respectively in 1971, but fell back to 47 per cent and 67 per cent respectively by 1976.[57] These figures suggest that in the last decade National Insurance benefits for the short-term unemployed have probably competed with lower wage levels, this being the price paid for the introduction of ERS.

The level of supplementary benefit for the uninsured and long-term unemployed has kept closely in unison with the gross weekly earnings of male manual workers throughout the post-war period. The Supplementary Benefits Commission (SBC) suggests that this has been deliberate policy, since earnings 'provide a clearer guide to the standards from which claimants must not be excluded'.[58] In other words, benefits are strictly related to (as well as below) average wage levels and hence the value of labour power, rather than retail price levels. Therefore, as working-class living standards drop, claimants' standard of living falls in similar proportions, so that between July 1974 and November 1976 retail prices rose by 68 per cent, supplementary benefit rates by 51 per cent and average gross wages of male manual workers by 55 per cent.[59] The SBC states that very few unemployed claimants 'would be worse off at work than they are on supplementary benefit' and that 'in practice the general level of supplementary benefit is already well below the wages paid even for the least skilled work'.[60] In recent years the levels of both contributory benefits for the deserving (such as pensioners, widows, the industrially injured) have moved ahead of those for the uninsured and long-term unemployed, because the former may exceed wages, as the SBC puts it, 'without provoking . . . hostility'. According to the SBC's interpretation of public opinion, however, 'the British people will not tolerate rates of supplementary benefit for the unemployed which exceed wages on a large scale'.[61] A large number of people eke out their existence below the official subsistence level defined by SBC. In December 1972 the government estimated that 1.78 million people had incomes below the SBC's levels, of whom 55 per cent were pensioners, 14 per cent were normally in full-time work and 11 per cent had been unemployed for over three months.[62]

One of the clearest expressions of the relationship between the social security system and the regulation of wages has been the 'wage stop'. This is a discretionary power to reduce benefit below the prescribed level 'to ensure that an unemployed man's income is no greater than it would be if he were in full-time employment'.[63] This is a modern version of poor law orthodoxy, which insisted that relief should always be less than the lowest local wage rates. The stop level since the late nineteenth century has been determined in relation to the lowest local authority wage rates. In their apologia for the wage stop the SBC argued that the measure was not designed to provide 'work incentive' for the unemployed, but was directed towards low-paid workers whose incentive and discipline would be threatened if others were seen to be receiving more on the dole. In November 1970, before the introduction of Family Income Supplement (FIS), 33,000 people were being wage-stopped, sometimes in tragic personal circumstances.[64] This amounted to 14 per cent of all unemployed supplementary benefit claimants. The wage stop was therefore an important means of adapting benefit levels to local conditions. The regional distribution of wage stop implementation shows by far the highest incidence occurring in Northern Ireland, Scotland and the North West of England, precisely the areas of low-wage employment.[65] The wage stop was suspended for supplementary benefit claimants in 1974, firstly, because it had been rendered obsolete by the introduction of FIS, rising local authority wage levels and high levels of unemployment; secondly, the withdrawal of the wage stop was the successful result of a campaign within the Labour movement coinciding with the election of a minority Labour government. Nevertheless, there is every likelihood that further political changes and the requirement to respond to local labour market conditions will lead to the re-emergence of a wage stop in some form, and it still flourishes in the National Insurance system.[66]

The earnings related supplement to unemployment benefit was introduced in 1966, as already mentioned, in the context of various government measures which 'aimed at securing a greater acceptance by workers of the need for economic and technical change',[67] or, in other words, to assist in the accelerated substitution of living labour by machinery in industry to counteract the falling rate of profit. Another of these measures was the Redundancy Payments Act, 1965, which gave full-time workers employed for over 2 years by the same employer the right to a lump-sum payment related both to length of service and earnings. Redundancy payments thus cushion the effect of industrial 'shake-out' and the concomitant deskilling of labour by countering the most stubborn resistance of workers at the immediate point of redundancy. The experience of redundancy is individuated and the apparent material interests of workers are often set against each other in the pressure of the redundancy situation.

Evaluation of the effectiveness of redundancy payments is complicated by the apparent conviction of many analysts that the act has successfully achieved security, job property rights and adequate compensation for workers, as well as restricting the freedom of employers in pursuing anti-social manpower policies. Such myths surrounding the act have been exposed by Fryer[68] and a government survey of 1969. According to the latter '32% of employers who had experienced redundancies since 1965 thought that the act made it easier to discharge employees, 11% thought it made it more difficult and 52% thought it made no difference'.[69] The conclusion was therefore reached that some improvement in internal manpower flexibility for employers had been achieved by the act, although the act does not appear to have affected general labour mobility.[70] The government survey suggested some success in achieving the cushioning effect by pointing to a decline in the level of strikes over redundancy since the act, despite an increased general level of strike activity. This testifies to the defusing effect of redundancy payments in overcoming trade union resistance to the shedding of labour in industrial rationalisations.

For the redundant worker the Redundancy Payments Act may have softened the immediate blow of redundancy, but it has hardly achieved adequate compensation. According to the government survey, 66 per cent of the paid-redundant who found new jobs preferred their old jobs. The survey also showed the extent of deskilling which takes place in the process of finding a new job after redundancy, although the act itself seems to have had little effect on this.[71] For example, 19 per cent of the skilled paid-redundant only found a semi-skilled or unskilled job subsequently and 42 per cent of the semi-skilled only found unskilled jobs subsequently. The emphasis on length of service in the determination of redundancy pay legitimises the dismissal of older workers, which is often attractive to employers in a shake-out and a drive towards intensification of the labour process. This is in direct contradiction with the usual trade union principle of 'last in, first out', and older workers are often left in a difficult situation, particularly as they will have considerable difficulty in finding another job. The average redundancy payment in 1976 was £615, which is a significant compensation but it is of course only a few weeks' wages. The number of payments has varied considerably from year to year, moving well over 300,000 in 1971 and 1975.[72] It may be significant that these high levels were reached in the years subsequent to general elections, when governments pursued dynamic industrial policies, involving the shake-out of skilled labour. It has been estimated that the total number of unpaid redundancies in 1971 was probably more than 1 million, so that in fact the Redundancy Payments Act only compensates a minority of redundant workers. Very few women have received redundancy payments, since, until recently, they had to work at least a 21-hour week for 2 years to become eligible. These conditions have recently been relaxed to a minimum 16-hour working week, but the casual nature of woman's employment still militates against their eligibility. Nevertheless, expenditure on redundancy payments, which is ultimately borne by employers, was £189 million in 1976, equivalent to about one-third of the total cost of National Insurance unemployment benefits. Hence in a certain sense redundancy payments can be seen as a successful extension of wages struggle, a price extracted from employers in exchange for 'shake-out'.

CREATING INCENTIVE FOR LOW-WAGE WORK AND ENFORCING LABOUR
DISCIPLINE

Poor law authorities have historically used the threat of withdrawal
of relief to bring pressure to bear on the unemployed to find wage
work. Essentially the withdrawal of relief functions as a punishment
for those claimants on the employment register who fail to find
wage work and also serves as a warning to others who might eventually
be in that position. The SBC publicly reiterated the necessity for
such measures, arguing that 'there has to be a certain amount of
pressure on claimants to find work and stay in it and it is a matter
of hard fact that this involves letting it be known that state money
is not there for the asking for anyone who is able to work but
unwilling to do so'.[73] The context of these particular remarks was
the existence of young claimants in tourist areas, who, the SBC
argued, must be pressed into low-wage work; but the argument
is applied far more generally through various discretionary procedures.
Under pressure from the anti-scrounger lobby as well as welfare
rights workers and claimants, in 1968 the SBC made more explicit
its discretionary policy on the withdrawal of benefit to the unemployed. This became known as the 'four-week rule', which officially
operated between October 1968 and December 1973 but has been
part of administrative practice both long before and after these dates.[74]
The rule operates in areas where the Employment Services Agency
(previously the Department of Employment) considers that 'there
are good employment prospects for men seeking unskilled work'.[75]

The four-week rule was conceived to apply differentially to three
groups amongst unemployed claimants. Firstly, unmarried, unskilled men under 45 years old would only be offered four weeks'
supplementary benefit, after which they could only reclaim successfully
if they could convince an unemployment review officer that they
had been 'genuinely seeking work'. Secondly, after 3 months' unemployment, able-bodied skilled men, married men and any women
under 45 years old could become subject to the same procedure.
Thirdly, able-bodied people over 45 years old might have the rule
applied after 6 months' unemployment. These eligibility distinctions
reproduce in a modern form the distinction between the casual residuum, here single unskilled men between 18 and 45, and the slightly
more respectable poor – skilled workers, married men, and women.
People over 45 and the non-able-bodied are ascribed an even greater

degree of eligibility. The implementation of the rule is in fact rather more arbitrary and sometimes punitive for those considered 'workshy' or undeserving by DHSS. It has been suggested that between 1968 and 1973 about 55,000 people actually 'suffering ailments inhibiting a return to work'[76] were deprived of benefit under work incentive discretionary procedures such as the four-week rule. The same survey suggested that roughly half of those to whom the four-week rule was applied still failed to find wage work. On the one hand, this can be interpreted as an extraordinarily high success rate in pushing claimants into work, while, on the other hand, forcing the unsuccessful 50 per cent, who account for some of the least eligible of the labour reserve army, to subsist without state support.

The official suspension of the four-week rule in December 1973, during the 3-day working week and the miners' strike, reflected the record post-war levels of unemployment, which rendered this mechanism for enforcing low-wage work obsolete in many parts of the country. There now operates a more informal procedure whereby the DHSS can withdraw benefit at its discretion if it considers that a claimant is 'not genuinely seeking work'.[77] In 1976 the four-week rule was officially revived to alleviate local and seasonal shortages of cheap labour power.[78]

The question of which claimants should be forced to register for employment is another important area of local administrative discretion which is varied according to labour market and ideological conditions. It has been shown that people who could not be considered fit for work are pressed into finding it, and unsupported mothers have also sometimes been subject to such pressure. More recently, students and those on temporary training or work relief programmes have been removed from the employment register in order to keep the figures down. Pressures on the unemployed to find wage work are not merely exerted on the less eligible, supplementary benefit claimant. The unemployed National Insurance beneficiary who receives benefit 'as of right' is also subject to similar pressures and sanctions. The major difference between the four-week rule and the National Insurance rules is that 'the former is based upon a supposition that a man can get work while the latter is based upon some evidence, however poor in quality, that work has been lost or refused'.[79] In practice this is sometimes a fine distinction, but the difference, such as it is, reflects the identification of the National Insurance beneficiary as being unemployed in the short term. He/she is not therefore expected to have to change occupational status in finding a new job, at least within the first 6 months of unemployment. The short-term unemployed are referred to the new Job Centre services, while the long-term unemployed are referred to the unemployment review officer at the DHSS, who has a more coercive role in directing the claimant to less skilled and lower-status employment. Hence the social security system continues to reinforce divisions between, on the one hand, the short-term 'respectable' unemployed, who receive the benefits of counselling, placing and training, and, on the other hand, the less eligible, long-term or casual unemployed, who may be legitimately deskilled or pushed into low-wage work through the unemployment review procedure. Nevertheless, in 1974 10,000 people had their National Insurance unemployment benefit suspended for 'refusing suitable employment without just cause'.[80] In the same year 27,000 people had their supplementary benefit reduced or withdrawn for similar reasons.

The role of the unemployment review officer (URO) is fundamentally a coercive one, in which the officer can bring sanctions to bear on the claimant as well as rigorously investigating the claimant's circumstances if 'malingering' is suspected. In 1976 almost 150,000 unemployed claimants were called to a URO interview, and 39 per cent of them stopped drawing benefit shortly before or after the interview.[81] Hence SBC can claim success in terms of removing people from the welfare rolls, though how many of them find jobs is unknown. There are two relatively rarely used but important sanctions by which SBC can attempt to maintain the labour power of members of the labour reserve army as a potential exchange value. Firstly, claimants can be prosecuted should they persistently claim benefit 'because they leave, lose or refuse suitable work without good cause'.[82] The basis for prosecution is that the claimant is thereby refusing or neglecting to 'maintain' him/herself or his/her dependants. This sanction therefore draws the limits to the unwritten contract between the unemployed person and the state, which pushes the former into wage work rather than dependence on the state. The number of prosecutions has fallen in recent years, possibly reflecting the high level of unemployment as well as exposure of the Dickensian circumstances in which some prosecutions have been pursued.

Secondly, the SBC runs fifteen re-establishment centres for the long-term unemployed, attendance at which can be made a condition of receiving benefit. An average of 2000 people pass through them each year, where claimants can 'recapture the routine of normal working life'[83] in such activities as woodwork. This long-established service has been dwarfed since 1976 by the great variety of government schemes designed to alleviate the unemployment crisis by various forms of training, employment subsidies and modern versions of work relief such as the job creation programme.[84] Work relief was menial work such as stone-breaking, provided through the poor law, which kept the unemployed in preparedness for wage work. At the moment of course participation in these programmes is not a condition of relief, since they are usually more attractive than subsisting on supplementary benefit, but DHSS encourages claimants to take part.[85]

The introduction of Family Income Supplement (FIS) in 1971 represented a break with the principles of 1834 by providing out-relief to wage workers, and hence a subsidy to low wages, reminiscent of Speenhamland. FIS is a means-tested benefit administered by DHSS on behalf of SBC, which supplements half the difference between a family's income and a prescribed amount (close to the SBC scale). This ensures that the scheme protects the existence of labour power as an exchange value. FIS was introduced in a flurry of Tory paternalism and concern about 'family poverty',[86] but it is certainly not an anachronism, nor something which Labour has sought to abolish. Its introduction in Britain reflected policy developments in the United States, where means-tested welfare has been used to create 'work incentive' for the low paid and unemployed.[87] For example, FIS has assisted in bringing a considerable number of single mothers into wage work; 43 per cent of FIS claimants were single mothers in July 1977, although the average amount of benefit was only £4.78, given to a total of only 84,000 parents.[88] It would clearly be a mistake therefore to overemphasise the significance of FIS in material terms, despite its considerable ideological import.

The social security system also plays a part in the maintenance of labour discipline[89] amongst the employed – for example, through measures to prevent 'voluntary unemployment' (that is, walking off the job) and measures which limit the effectiveness of strikes. Unjustifiable unemployment is identified when the claimant has left a job 'voluntarily without just cause' or has lost a job 'through industrial misconduct'. It may lead to a 6-week suspension of unemployment benefit, known as 'the six-week rule', and a 40 per cent reduction in the claimant's entitlement to supplementary benefit. This acts as a deterrent to workers leaving low-wage work in particular, and as a means, however slight, of enforcing labour discipline or industrial good conduct. This form of disciplining is widely enforced: in 1970 over 18 per cent of National Insurance unemployment benefit claimants (570,000 people) were disqualified under the six-week rule, the percentage falling to 9 (388,000 people) in 1975.[90]

As already discussed, the poor law has been used historically as a means of forcing strikers back to work and preventing 'state subsidisation' of strikers as far as is politically acceptable. National Insurance unemployment benefit is of course not available to strikers, and in some circumstances even those laid off due to an industrial dispute. The principles of the Merthyr Tydfil judgement remain more or less in force today, despite attempts such as the 1972/3 Supplementary Allowances (Non Payment of Strikers) Bill to withdraw even strikers' dependants' rights to benefit.[91] This policy is particularly punitive on single strikers, who have to plead a case of 'urgent need' in order to be granted a small payment, which in October 1973 was up to £5 per week, including rent, when the ordinary supplementary benefit for a single person was £7.15, excluding rent. The increased number of large-scale and long official strikes in the early 1970s led to a dramatic increase in supplementary benefit claims by strikers, largely on behalf of their dependants. In 1972, which saw major strikes by building workers, miners and dock workers, a record number of over three-quarters of a million strikers were involved in disputes long enough to make them eligible for benefit. Only a third of those eligible actually received benefits,[92] amounting to 3.4 per cent of the total expenditure on supplementary benefit in that year. By 1976, with the down-turn in strike activity, only 10,000 strikers claimed benefit, the lowest number for a decade, and this amounted to only 0.02 per cent of the total expenditure on supplementary benefits in that year.[93]

In a recent academic debate on the 'state subsidy' of strikers through the social security system[94] it was argued that the expansion of such payments was not an adequate explanation for the rise in strike activity in the late 1960s and early 1970s, which therefore perhaps obviously had to be explained in terms of other factors. It was thus concluded that the state subsidy notion was unproven and that 'even the abolition of these forms of state benefit to strikers would not make much impact on the overall strike pattern'.[95] This conclusion is ambiguous, since it is not clear what is meant by 'the overall strike pattern', but there would seem to be no doubt that abolition of benefits for strikers' dependants would create great hardship in long strikes and would ultimately weaken workers' resolve and union funds. There is evidence that 'unions are tailoring their actual dispute pay (if any) to the supplementary benefit provisions',[96] and such provision may shape a union's tactics in a dispute.

However, trade unions have yet to effectively organise their members as claimants during a strike. The question of supplementary benefit may not affect the decision to strike, but it may have a decisive effect on the ability of workers to withstand a long strike and also on the tactics and strategy adopted by strikers and trade unions.

In conclusion, we have tried to instance some of the ways in which the social security system has reinforced the capital–labour relation and the compulsion on workers to offer their labour power as an exchange-value. The system has been adapted to the changing demands placed upon it, for example, by the labour shortages during the post-war boom, by the industrial shake-out of labour since the middle 1960s and by the reappearance of large numbers of registered unemployed in the 1970s. This is not of course to argue that measures like earnings related supplements, redundancy payments and benefits for strikers' families do not correspond with working-class interests. Clearly they have emerged in response to working-class strength, and they meet some of the short-term interests of individual members of the working class. In the long term, however, they have contributed in large measure to the considerable acquiescence of the Labour movement in the capital restructuring process. In Chapter 4 we return to the form of the class struggle over social security in the post-war years, after considering the crucial relationship between women, the family and the social security system.

4

Social Security and the Questions
of Women and Bureaucratic Power

1. WOMEN AND SOCIAL SECURITY

So far we have concentrated upon relief and social security for the
unemployed man and his family. The struggles of the unemployed
and workers in general, and the conceptions of unemployment
and poverty which have shaped state policy, have largely been concerned with the unemployment and low income of men, or the
pathological character of individual families. The assumption has
remained since at least the mid-nineteenth century that a woman's
earnings are supplementary to those of a male breadwinner, and
that women (and children) are and should be largely dependent on
the man's income. The social security system not only reflects but
strengthens the subordinate position of women as domestic workers
inside the family and wage workers outside the family. It has, nevertheless, been faced with the pervasive breakdown of women's dependence
on men, brought about by marriage break-up, desertion, widowhood,
unmarried motherhood and so on. Support of these women by the
state has been such as to encourage if possible the renewal of dependence on men and to discourage the break-up of marriage by rendering
single motherhood distinctly less eligible and attractive. It could be
argued that in reality the predominant concern of the social security
system throughout its history has been in relation to such questions
concerning women.

About three-quarters of those adults dependent on non-contributory supplementary benefit are women. Although this is partly attribu-
table to the fact that women live longer, it also reflects women's
economic dependence, which is shifted on to the state when the
man dies or departs or when his contribution record and other income
are insufficient. While poor relief and non-contributory benefit have

been very much directed towards women, paradoxically there is also a sense in which the social security system is deliberately not concerned with women; for the great majority of women have been excluded from any *independent* rights of citizenship to social security simply because they have married and have therefore been assumed to be (in most cases correctly) dependent on their husband's income. Firstly, therefore, the social security system reinforces women's dependence by largely excluding them from independent rights to benefit and providing low levels of benefit to the many women who cannot conform to the norm of dependence on men. The notion that a woman's place is primarily in the home and the ideology of domesticity is implicitly supported by social security policy.

Secondly, social security policy has sustained the position of women, particularly married women, as low-paid, casual wage workers, and as a unique stratum of the reserve army of labour. In a period of labour shortage married women may move into low-paid, short-term employment outside the home, often part-time, and when they are no longer required, they can move quietly back into their families as full-time domestic workers. This has been encouraged by such policies as contracting out of National Insurance, the lack of substantial support in maternity, and the inappropriateness of the contribution principle in the context of women's intermittent employment outside the home. Married women have in fact formed a special category of 'semi-proletarianised' workers, alongside but different from migrant workers.[1]

Here we shall focus on some of the ways in which administration of the poor law, National Insurance and supplementary benefit have contributed to these two aspects of women's subordination in the family and in wage work. Women's dependence on the family and their status as wage workers are of course closely linked, for, without the former, women's semi-proletarian position as casual low-paid workers would be difficult, if not impossible to sustain. Particularly since the second half of the nineteenth century, the man's wage has been widely conceived as a 'family wage',[2] which should cover the cost of maintaining him and his family, while married women's confinement to low-status work for supplementary 'pin money' was confirmed. While this excluded women from the rigours of some forms of wage work, the inadequacy of the so-called family wage contributed to the destitution and undernourishment of many working-class women and children at least until the 1940s.[3] Many families mitigated their poverty by the casual work of mothers and children. In the post-war period married women have made a substantial and relatively permanent contribution to the working-class family income.

Following in the tradition of Engels,[4] socialist feminists have pointed to the various ways in which capitalist development and women's struggles have begun to undermine patriarchy[5] by, for example, bringing more women into permanent wage work, easing the process of domestic labour (housework), increased access to birth control and the general effects of individualism. This is counterbalanced, however, by the realisation that patriarchal social relations have been shaped by and adapted to the requirements of advanced capitalism, and the patriarchal family remains one of its bed-rock institutions. The deep structure of women's subordination is underpinned by the patriarchal family which is '. . . not merely a "hangover" from a pre-industrial stage of capitalism or from pre-capitalist society, nor even of sexist attitudes and prejudices. which can be purged through argument and education, but is of fundamental economic, political and ideological importance to the capitalist mode of production'.[6] Thus 'women's subordination under capitalism lies in the articulation between patriarchal social relations and capitalist development'.[7]

Our understanding of the relationship between patriarchy and capitalism and between women's struggles and the class struggle has been considerably advanced by the analysis of the central contribution of domestic labour to the reproduction of labour power, by the development of socialist feminist history and the analysis of women's wage labour. The particular importance of the welfare state has been recognised in all these areas, on the one hand, in shoring up women's subordination in the family and in wage work, but also in its potential for delivering benefits and services which can contribute to women's liberation. In what follows attention is mostly focused on certain instances of social security policy as it affects women and reproduces their subordination, leaving aside some of the theoretical implications concerning the relation between patriarchy and capitalism.

SINGLE MOTHERS

The treatment of working-class single mothers under the poor law and supplementary benefit administration has ensured that they generally enjoy a lower standard of living and even a lower status than the dependent married woman within the two-parent family. This is as clear from the report of the Finer Committee on one-parent families in 1974 as it is from the 1834 Poor Law report. Thus relief policy has implicitly but consistently strengthened women's economic dependence on men within the family. The working-class woman who is either forced, or possibly chooses, to raise children independently is very often confined to dependence on poor relief or subsistence benefit. On one day in 1976 25 per cent of non-pensioner claimants of supplementary benefit were single mothers (311,000 women), almost all of whom were either unmarried, divorced or separated.[8] In the nineteenth century there were of course many more working-class widows amongst the applicants for poor relief. The treatment of all these women has varied according to their situation, and in the nineteenth century, at least, according to the attitudes of local guardians and relieving officers.[9]

There was little guidance from central government on such questions, with the important exception of unmarried mothers. The latter were considered in the early nineteenth century to be responsible for the multiplication of the impoverished population and the degradation of innocent men. The 1834 Poor Law Amendment Act sought to shift the whole responsibility for illegitimate children from the father and the parish on to the mother, but parish responsibility was restored in 1844 as it became clear that this was driving even more women and children into the workhouse.[10] Under the nineteenth century poor law the unmarried mother was regarded as 'an able-bodied person of demonstrated immorality and relief was accordingly provided on a strictly deterrent basis in the workhouse',[11] and she was forced to abandon her children within it. It seems likely that in order to limit the costs of indoor relief and the rearing of workhouse children some guardians relaxed this code in cases where they considered the mother deserving. By 1914 a government circular was urging 'an earnest effort to discriminate between different classes of unmarried mothers',[12] between the young innocent who needed sensitive help and the depraved or mentally defective who required punishment or incarceration. In general the move away from overtly punitive treatment of the unmarried mother in Britain has been very slow.[13]

Widows, on the other hand, have always been treated as somewhat more deserving cases. The 1834 Poor Law report noted that in many areas widows had established a 'right to public support' (relief outside the workhouse), which unlike any other group of people was indepen-

dent of their 'want of employment' or 'insufficiency of wages'.[14]
Particularly after 1834 this right to support was often conditional
on a wide variety of sanctions designed to cut down relief costs
and encourage fathers generally to protect and insure their families
while still alive. For example, if it was considered that widows could
manage somehow 'with the help of parents, wage-earning children,
charring, letting lodgings etc.', they might be denied out-relief.[15]
Sometimes widows' destitution forced them to send their children
to the workhouse, or their children could be taken away from them
if they were considered inadequate mothers. More often widows
were obliged to foster workhouse children in exchange for relief.
By the early twentieth century the government was urging more
uniform classification of widows' character in order to determine
their deservingness. Widowhood seems to have gained in respectability
after the First World War, not surprisingly, given the enormous
number of young working-class widows created by the war itself.
In 1925 the first contributory pensions act included the provision
of National Insurance benefit for widows and orphans, dependent
of course on male contributions.

   In relation to deserted and separated women and the regulation
of working-class marriage breakdown, the poor law and supplementary benefit authorities have played a specific and central role, despite
increasing working-class access to divorce in the twentieth century.
Three systems of family law have developed in England and Wales
in the divorce court (high court), the summary courts (magistrates'
courts) and the poor law.[16] High court jurisdiction of divorce was
confined to the bourgeoisie in the nineteenth century and today
it has been estimated that 'one half of the complainants who obtain
matrimonial orders in the summary courts never proceed to a divorce,
but remain in a matrimonial limbo',[17] not least because of legal
costs. The jurisdiction of the magistrates' courts and the poor law
authorities together constituted the system of family law which regulated working-class marriage breakdown in the nineteenth century,
and still to a considerable extent today. While acting as a source
of support in the last resort for women left unsupported by their
husbands, the poor law and supplementary benefit authorities have
consistently attempted, however unsuccessfully, to shift the burden
of dependence from the parish or the state by finding a 'liable relative'
who can sustain the woman and her children. In other words an
attempt is made to re-establish a form of economic dependence on

the husband. Where this was unsuccessful, similar sanctions and conditions to those applied to widows under the poor law were employed. The common law obligation on a man to maintain his wife and children became enshrined in statute in 1878, but both before and after that date it has been of little material significance for a host of women. In 1972 liable relatives contributed only about 17 per cent of the net supplementary benefit given to separated wives.[18] The enforcement of this obligation to maintain is obviously viewed with great ambivalence by women, since it is an invitation to re-establish dependence. Hence many such women are, not surprisingly, uncooperative in the attempts to establish paternity or find the husband.

The liable relative obliged by the poor law to support a single or separated woman (with or without children) included, until 1948, grandparents on both sides and adult children, although today it is usually confined to the husband. The Supplementary Benefits Commission (SBC) pursues a policy of 'encouraging' women to obtain maintenance orders and employs liable relative officers to investigate questions of paternity and the financial circumstances of parents and relatives. Clearly their role is often in direct conflict with the desires of women in such situations, and they are sometimes, understandably, regarded with considerable hostility. The Finer report concluded that 'this policy causes great pain and anxiety, for no tangible advantage, to far more claimants than those upon whom it may confer some advantage'.[19]

In 1976 528 convictions against liable relatives were secured by SBC[20] as a sanction against some husbands and a warning to many others. In addition SBC, like its poor law predecessors, is always mindful of a form of abuse called 'collusive desertion', though this is rarely proved.[21] The inadequacy of the system of maintenance payments under separation orders granted by the magistrates' courts is indicated by the fact that 74 per cent of the 129,000 payments ordered by the courts in 1970 were diverted through SBC. In other words, in these cases SBC give the wife maintenance payments regardless of whether they had been paid into court or not. Besides illustrating the poverty of most separated women, it also confirms the difficulty of extracting maintenance from husbands, which, according to Finer, is due not to 'the unwillingness but the inability of men to pay'.[22] It seems therefore that the liable relative measures are in practice now a somewhat cumbersome and inappropriate instrument, yet they do act as a significant legitimation of the obligations of men and the poverty of single motherhood for those couples who are not yet at breaking point.

The post-Beveridge consolidation of the social security system did very little for unsupported mothers,[23] despite considerable pressure on the question from women's organisations. More recently Finer's recommendation of a guaranteed maintenance allowance for unsupported mothers has been ignored. State policy continues to confine an apparently expanding army of these women and their children to the poverty line. Distinctions in eligibility and income remain between unmarried, separated and divorced mothers and widows, although less punitively reinforced by the authorities. Several studies have shown that widows are the least poor amongst single mothers, while unmarried mothers are the poorest. One study of the National Assistance Board in the 1960s noted that, informally, officers used their discretionary powers so that certain women were given low allowances 'and these women tended to be mothers who in any case are held low in public esteem, the mothers of illegitimate children'.[24] Widowed mothers are formally allowed preferential treatment of their pensions in assessment for supplementary benefit.

Another means of shifting the burden of dependence of unsupported mothers and single women from the parish or the state has been the encouragement of them to take employment outside the home, possibly subsidised by out-relief. Despite the strictures from central government against granting out-relief to people in wage work after the Speenhamland experience, many poor law authorities provided relief in aid of wages particularly to single women and unsupported mothers, in part-time and casual employment. Some boards of guardians 'coupled the grant of outdoor relief to single or widowed able-bodied women with the requirement of attendance at the workhouse for so many hours cleaning or washing' and 'there were "needle-rooms" for such women in a few metropolitan unions'.[25] In Nottingham lace-making workshops were established in the workhouse. With the reassertion in the 1870s of the principles of 1834, the government urged the use of a more punitive labour test for single women in particular, using more traditional deterrent and unpleasant tasks. In practice a wide range of policies dependent on local attitudes and employment situations were adopted. As for the contemporary situation, although unsupported women with dependent children are not officially required to register for employment, there is evidence that in some instances DHSS has pressurised them into finding a job.[26]

Many women in that position are anyway keen to get out of the home and the DHSS's pay and into a job. In 1970 more unsupported than married mothers worked full-time outside the home, and their pay and status was lower than that of married women. If part-time employment is included, a slightly lower proportion of single mothers compared to married mothers had a job.[27] This reflects in part the ruling that for separated and unmarried mothers (but not widows) earnings over a small disregard are counted against their supplementary benefit. Unsupported mothers have therefore provided a particularly low-paid supply of labour power, sometimes anxious to keep a job at any price. We have already noted that the introduction of the Family Income Supplement in 1971 revived out-relief in aid of wages, and has particularly been directed towards subsidising the low wages of single mothers.

Nevertheless, the social security system only rather tentatively nudges unsupported mothers into employment. Both in the nineteenth century and today such policies have been tentative because of their dissonance with the notions of motherhood and domestic labour as full-time occupations. The Finer report had little to say about the employment situation of single mothers and was strikingly self-contradictory on the question of whether state policy should encourage single mothers to seek employment outside the home. Embracing the discredited but still powerful ideology of maternal deprivation,[28] Finer suggested that children under five should not spend long periods away from their mothers, thereby implying that mothers of young children should not find employment outside the home. On the other hand, Finer recognised a category of single mother whose hours of work 'or any number of adverse social conditions, such as poor housing, social isolation, a large family or her illness, or sometimes a combination of these circumstances, may . . . make it necessary for the child to be given full-day care'.[29] The implication here is that the children of these poor single mothers will be doubly deprived. The Finer report is the most recent in a long line of post-war policy documents which have reinforced the prejudice against the provision of full-day nurseries for the under-fives for all mothers who choose to take wage work. Hence such provision has largely been confined to meeting the basic needs of single parents who work outside the home.[30] Working-class single mothers are caught in a trap in which they either remain isolated in the home, dependent on supplementary benefit and/or maintenance, or they take low-paid jobs and bear the anxiety of being accused of neglecting and depriving their children.

We have suggested that state policy attempts to shift the burden of single mothers' dependence from the state on to liable relatives or low wages. In a variety of ways policy strengthens the inferior status and position of such women, thereby bolstering the happy norm of the patriarchal family.

COHABITATION

Perhaps the most explicit reinforcement of patriarchy within the social security system is the cohabitation rule. This rule applies to a wide range of private as well as state benefits, but they are not policed as stringently as supplementary benefit claimants. In effect the cohabitation rule attempts to establish a liable relative where none existed before. The rule is based on the principle that 'where a husband and wife are members of the same household their requirements and resources shall be aggregated and shall be treated as the husband's, and similarly . . . as regards two persons cohabiting as man and wife'.[31] This is a simple but admirably clear definition of patriarchy in the ownership of property and the right to benefit. Although cohabitation is officially defined in terms of the man's contribution to the household economy, its implementation suggests the use of the criterion of two or three consecutive nights spent together, or, in other words, a sexual relationship.[32] In the nineteenth century boards of guardians appointed 'cross-visitors', one of whose tasks was to snoop on suspected cohabitees. In 1971 the DHSS was employing 329 special investigators, who spent 38 per cent of their time finding evidence of cohabitation, popularly known as 'sex snooping'. This resulted in 3787 reductions or withdrawals of benefit in that year, which presumably acts as a reasonably explicit warning to others who consider indulging in this so-called abuse.[33]

The cohabitation rule has been attacked by the women's movement because it is the most striking example, and indeed a cornerstone, of the policy of excluding women from independent rights to benefit and the reinforcement of dependence on men. It has also been attacked by claimants' unions, the welfare rights movement, and women on the grounds of the hardships, breaches of privacy and harassment its implementation causes. The SBC has strongly and coherently defended the rule on the basis that its abolition would leave cohabiting couples better off than married couples.[34] In other words, the removal of the rule would reveal rather starkly women's economic dependence and inequality in marriage. Implicitly, as SBC argues, this could be a discouragement to marriage, although this suggests a somewhat cynical view of the reasons for marriage. Paradoxically, far from encouraging marriage, the rule can sometimes prevent a woman creating a relationship with a man, free from the problems and anxieties of immediate dependence. The SBC also suggests that abolition would remove some of the pressure on a man to support his own children. Like the liable relative sanctions, SBC is anxious to retain any measures whereby it can shift dependence from the state on to men, against the wishes of many of the women concerned. Finally SBC argues that the cohabitation rule 'merely gives shape to what remains the desire of society as a whole for fairness and equity in the distribution of the state's financial support to men and women and their families'.[35]

Society's desires on the fairness and equity, in this age of 'equal rights', of denying women independent rights to benefit from the welfare state's safety net have not been fully tested perhaps. Nevertheless, SBC policy does reflect the predominant ideology concerning marriage and women's dependence, and SBC certainly conceives of itself as a stout defender of the 'moral code', with plenty of encouragement from the media and many politicians. As Elizabeth Wilson has suggested, 'in fact, the cohabitation ruling only embodies in slightly more glaring form the innermost assumption of marriage which is still that a man should pay for the sexual and housekeeping services of his wife'.[36]

WOMEN'S WAGE WORK AND NATIONAL INSURANCE

Working-class women in general, and married women in particular, have always been a source of highly exploitable, casual labour power, often on a part-time basis. Social security policy has reinforced this situation in a variety of ways in relation to non-contributory relief, as already discussed. Here we shall concentrate on National Insurance and married women in the post-war period. The Beveridge report and the consolidation of the social security system based upon it sought to strengthen women's dependence and to emphasise their

domestic and maternal 'duties', while at the same time preserving
their availability for wage work.[37] Married women were therefore
encouraged to opt out of most of the National Insurance scheme.
Beveridge assumed, to some extent correctly, that married women's
employment would be intermittent and low paid, and therefore that
National Insurance contributions would be an unnecessary burden
on employers and employees alike. Married women hopefully would
be covered for old age by their husbands' contributions, and would
depend on their husbands for support in sickness or unemployment.
About three-quarters of married women in registered employment
thus chose to pay reduced contributions in the post-war era, thereby
excluding themselves from unemployment and sickness benefits and
from National Insurance pensions in their own right. The minority
who paid full contributions were only entitled to reduced unemployment and sickness benefits, because it was still assumed that their
husbands should contribute some support. Pension rights were subject
to the 'half-test' rule, whereby a married woman was 'entitled to
a pension in her own right only if she has paid contributions for
at least half of the years between the date of her marriage and
the date she reaches retirement age'.[38]

Some of the consequences of the married woman's option emerge
from a study of the 1951–2 slump in the Lancashire textile industry,
where large numbers of married women have always been
employed.[39] It was found that official figures for unemployment
(which reached 34 per cent in April 1952 in one district) underestimated
actual unemployment by about 15 to 20 per cent, since most of
the married women were not registered as unemployed. Having no
entitlement to unemployment benefit and therefore not signing on
at the labour exchange, these women returned to their families, where
in several cases they had to support unemployed husbands and children
out of savings and/or national assistance. Married women who *had*
paid contributions received only 80 per cent of the benefit received
by single people, while widows who had paid full contributions
received much lower benefit, because their widow's pension was
taken into account. A whole series of such 'anomalous' distortions
of the contribution principle have affected women workers, particularly in such sectors as the clothing industry, where short-term and
long-term unemployment were and still are common. The encouragement of married women to opt out of National Insurance therefore
cultivated their particular position as labour power which could be

relatively easily tapped or laid off, and which could also be paid wages below the male 'family wage'.

In the 1970s the government has started to phase out the married woman's option in the context of several interrelated developments. Firstly, women's employment outside the home has become increasingly important, particularly the work of married women. Between 1951 and 1977 the proportion of women in the labour force moved from 32 per cent to 41 per cent, although this expansion has almost been brought to a halt in the present economic crisis. The number of married women as a percentage of the total number of women in the labour force moved from 38.2 per cent in 1951 (2.7 million people) to 63.1 per cent in 1971 (5.8 million people).[40] This army of women workers has become a more central part of the labour force, not merely a reserve army in many sectors, and the women have become more significant within the trade union movement. Secondly, this has been allied with the increasing strength in the women's movement in general, which, alongside EEC entry, prompted governments to pass the Equal Pay Act, 1970, and the Sex Discrimination Act, 1975. While the ineffectiveness of this legislation in guaranteeing equal rights for women is well known,[41] it has positively affected the social security system in a number of ways.

From May 1977 women entering employment outside the home have had to pay full contributions and can receive full benefits, but women already opting out may continue to take the option of reduced contributions and benefits, provided they do not give up paid employment for more than 2 years. This phasing out could therefore take 40 or 50 years to become fully operative, and it was estimated that only 15 per cent of presently married or widowed women would elect to pay full contributions. The government argued that to forcibly increase these women's contributions would cause hardship, but positive discrimination or a break with the contribution principle to overcome this was not considered. The decision about whether to opt in or opt out has been made actuarially extremely complex by these reforms.[42] This applies most of all to pensions. The withdrawal of the half-test rule has been postponed until 1979, but the new state pension scheme which came into operation in April 1978 introduced 'protected' state pension rights for women and *single* men who stay at home to look after one or more children under sixteen, retirement pensioners or invalidity pensioners. To get a full basic state pension in their own right, such people must still have contracted into National Insurance for at least 24 years, but if they do this, their years of 'home responsibility' count as contribution years.[43] This is something of a positive adaptation of the contribution principle which very tentatively recognises women's role as unpaid welfare and domestic workers in the home.

The Employment Protection Act, 1975, introduced new maternity rights for women working more than 16 hours a week for the same employer for at least 2 years. Dismissal on the grounds of pregnancy is now unfair dismissal, mothers have the right to reinstatement into the employer's work force for up to 29 weeks after the birth, and 6 weeks' maternity pay is now mandatory. This is in addition to the already existing maternity allowance and maternity grant. The maternity grant was introduced at the beginning of the National Insurance system in 1911, providing a lump sum to the wife of an insured man or to a woman insured in her own right on the birth of a child. The current maternity grant is only £25. Maternity allowance was introduced in 1948 at the insistent suggestion of Beveridge as an encouragement to increase the birth rate, but it is only available to women with a fully paid up contribution record in their own right and, hence, not to those who have opted out. The rate of maternity benefit in March 1977 was up to £12.90 per week for a maximum of 18 weeks. About 700,000 awards of maternity grant and allowance were made in 1975 at a cost of £47 million, that is about £70 per birth. Hence there now exists a complex maze of entitlements and conditions, which women have to fight their way through in order to gain even these minimal rights, reminiscent of a game of snakes and ladders.[44] It is significant that these maternity rights are mostly conditional on contributions, continuity and hours of employment. The majority of mothers are probably excluded from them (excepting the maternity grant) and they are not therefore sufficient to achieve adequate maternity rights for women. They are primarily employment-related policies and, very much secondarily, family policies, to some extent in contrast to Beveridge's wishes and continental policies.

The positive extension of employment-related social security rights over the past few years, particularly to married women wage workers, has confirmed women's position as a more permanent and enfranchised section of the labour force. This must, however, be qualified in view of several important counter-tendencies. Redundancy payments and the new maternity and employment rights only apply to women

working over 16 hours a week for the same employer for 2 years;
National Insurance rights (unemployment and sickness benefits, maternity allowances, pensions) depend on a full contribution record and
are therefore conditional on similar factors. Effectively many women
working part-time and/or in 'lump' work avoiding National Insurance
(in sweatshops, services and 'home working') are excluded from these
rights. The number of part-time women employees registered with
the Department of Employment increased from 2.8 million in 1972
to 3.5 million in 1975, while the number of full-time women
employees fell in the same period from 5.45 million to 5.42 million.[45]
It can thus be concluded that 'from the point of view of capital
as a whole, part-time work provides the means by which women
can be brought into employment in increasing numbers without
any necessity for the state to provide or extend nursery facilities'[46]
and adequate social security.

WOMEN AND UNEMPLOYMENT

Women are very much under-represented in the unemployment
figures, which cover only those people who register with the Department of Employment (DE). In 1976 the General Household Survey
(GHS) found that, of those people who were actively seeking wage
work, 10 per cent of the men, 63 per cent of the married women
and 21 per cent of the unmarried women were *not* registered as
unemployed.[47] There is therefore a striking amount of hidden unemployment, notably amongst married women. It is not altogether clear
whether this comes about because DE refuses to allow married women
on to the register or because these women do not consider going
on to the register, assuming perhaps wrongly that since they are
not entitled to unemployment benefit, they are not entitled to register.
Certainly DE is unlikely to coax married women on to the register
in an area of high unemployment. Presumably this is a matter left
to discretion in the light of local labour market conditions. It is
well known that the government's job-finding services are not as
effective as private means; only about 10 per cent of jobs are acquired
through government services, so there is not much incentive for
uninsured women to register for employment. Another factor which
discourages women from registering is that, if they do so, they have
to make themselves available for full-time employment, which is

unattractive to many mothers in particular, not least because of the inadequacy of child care facilities.

The annual General Household Surveys have revealed an inverse relationship between the proportion of unregistered unemployed and the general level of unemployment in the 1970s.[48] When the unemployment level has risen, the proportion of unregistered unemployed has fallen. Hence GHSs have suggested that 'among those with no claim to benefit (accounting for most of the unregistered unemployed) there will be a fall in the number actively seeking work during periods of high unemployment because of the belief that there is no suitable work available in their area – ie. "the discouraged workers"'.[49] This applies particularly to married women, who confine themselves to domestic labour and curb their aspirations for wage work as unemployment rises. A readers' survey by *Woman's Own* in spring 1977 suggested that there might be over 1 million women who would like to have employment outside the home, in addition to the 350,000 or so on the unemployment register.

Given these factors and the shortage of labour power in many areas and sectors, registered unemployment amongst women remained much lower than that for men during the post-war boom. While women were equally affected by the industrial shake-out which began in the mid-1960s, those displaced were attracted into the service sector and new light industry. The crisis of the mid-1970s, on the other hand, has affected women's employment particularly badly. Although the registered unemployment rate for women has remained below that for men, between January 1975 and January 1977 (before the withdrawal of the married woman's option) the number of women registered as unemployed rose by 178 per cent, while for men in the same period it rose by 70 per cent.

The administration of unemployment benefit and the unemployment register therefore tends to hide the extent of unemployment amongst women, thereby confirming their role as a relatively invisible and flexible reserve of labour power. The depth of the present crisis and the stronger presence of women within the working population outside the home have begun to puncture this a little.

CONCLUSION

We have briefly described a wide range of instances in which social security policy and administration have reinforced the economic dependence of women upon men within the family. The notion that a woman's place is primarily in the home has thus been strengthened. Social security policy has also encouraged the use of women's labour at low wages often on a casual or part-time basis in a certain sense without threatening the ideologies of domesticity or motherhood. This has been achieved by excluding women from independent rights to social security, and maintaining dependency on male contributions and benefits. Although we have emphasised the predominance of women's dependence on men, which reflects dominant ideology, the reality is that a large and increasing number of households are dependent on a woman's income. In 1971 nearly 2 million women under retirement age were the chief economic supporters in their households, including 300,000 married women, 520,000 single mothers with children and 300,000 single women with elderly or infirm dependents. It has been estimated that 'one in six of all households, excluding pensioner households, are substantially dependent upon a woman's earnings or benefits'.[50] Despite this, women's dependence upon men remains a fundamental pillar of government policy, notwithstanding recent reforms. This is illustrated by the situation of an increasing number of families in which the woman chooses to go out to work full-time while the man stays at home doing the bulk of the domestic labour, although he is capable of 'self-support'. This has thrown up a number of instances in which state policy continues to discriminate actively against women.[51] Such a woman cannot claim Family Income Supplement, unemployment benefit or sickness benefit to support her husband and children, nor can her widower gain access to her pension rights. Here once more the contribution principle gives way and the woman's contributions are devalued. State policy assumes that a married woman is dependent on her husband even if she is the 'breadwinner'. In reply to feminist criticism on this question in 1975 a generally sympathetic minister replied that 'it continues to be a widespread view that a husband who is capable of work has a duty to society as well as to his wife, to provide the primary support for his family'.[52] He concluded that state policy should 'merely provide for the genuine case of *involuntary* role reversal', that is when the man is incapable of 'self-support'. This seems to capture the present state of ideology and policy in relation to women and social security.

2. THE POST-WAR SOCIAL SECURITY BUREAUCRACY

We now turn to consider the general nature of social security administration in the post-war period. The form of administration is clearly
important, since it confronts individual claimants as a structure which
suggests the universality of the welfare rights of citizenship and exudes
rational bureaucratic process. Yet, as we have shown, the payment
of benefits in practice is hedged by various conditions and discretionary
procedures, necessitated by the requirement to maintain and indeed
actively promote capitalist and patriarchal social relations. Here we
shall examine how the system has been adapted to respond to working-
class expectations and challenges to its authority, while preserving
its economic and ideological role.

It is commonly thought that the Beveridge report[53] created the
foundations of the modern social security system. We have already
suggested that in relation to unemployment insurance and national
assistance, the basis had been laid before the Second World War.
Thus the reforms of the 1940s simply improved benefits and rationalised previous policies.[54] Beveridge's more progressive proposals concerning benefit levels and the unlimited extension of the eligibility
period for unemployment benefit were in fact rejected by the 1945
Labour government.[55] The greatest significance of the Beveridge
report lay perhaps in its role in both engineering consent over the
general shape of the welfare state in opposition at the time of its
publication to the war-time government and many of the ruling
class.[56] The report articulated more clearly than ever before the ideology of citizenship, 'universal' welfare rights, women's subordinate
role in the family and the desirability of contributory insurance.
The TUC accepted almost every part of the Beveridge report and
to the surprise of the committee their delegation to it 'were strongly
in favour of contributory insurance . . . contemptuous of "dodgers",
of the "very poor" and "of the type of person who will not join
a Friendly Society" . . . and favoured the withdrawal of public assistance
from wives and children of workers who went on strike'.[57] The
warm reception of the Beveridge report seemed to signify the unambi-
guous acceptance by the working class of capitalist state welfare,
hopefully in exchange for 'full' employment and in preference to
private or trade union insurance or occupational welfare, the only
other alternatives within capitalism.

Beveridge recommended that the administration of insurance and non-contributory benefits should be fully integrated on the assumption that comprehensive National Insurance would eventually reduce non-contributory relief/assistance to insignificance. No doubt with the experience of the 1930s in mind, the post-war Labour government decided on the contrary to strengthen the distinction between the insured and the uninsured by establishing the National Assistance Board (NAB) as a separate administrative unit within the new Ministry of National Insurance; NAB subsequently became the Supplementary Benefits Commission (SBC) within the Department of Health and Social Security (DHSS).[58] The administration of National Insurance unemployment benefit was kept within the Ministry of Labour, subsequently the Department of Employment, as a means of further separating the short-term insured unemployed from the long-term unemployed. There was still the assumption that the former were somewhat more deserving and more easily integrable into the labour market than the latter. The official historian of war-time social policy suggests that there were two main reasons for keeping National Insurance and national assistance separate as far as possible. Firstly, 'it was hoped that the existence of an independent board would keep politics out of national assistance, particularly day-to-day questioning of ministers in the House of Commons',[59] which has worked very successfully.[60] Secondly, the Labour government 'thought it was important to maintain the distinction in the public image between social security as of right and means tested assistance'.[61] In other words, the 'image' of national assistance was to be kept distinctly less attractive and the rights to assistance more hedged by discretionary powers. The division between the respectable and the less eligible claimant was deliberately kept alive in the new administrative forms, as the NAB inherited officials 'steeped in the ways of the poor law', as well as the network of poor law offices, 'most of them small, shoddy and Dickensian'.[62] Today in many DHSS offices a distinct difference in furnishings and ambience is studiously maintained between the National Insurance section and the supplementary benefit section.[63]

The National Insurance scheme proposed by Beveridge was, according to the report, 'designed in itself when in full operation to guarantee the income needed for subsistence in all normal cases'.[64] Beveridge's scheme, of course, has never been fully implemented, but even if it had, it seems unlikely that means-tested assistance or supplementary benefit would have disappeared, given, for example, continuing casual employment, the relation of women to the social security system, the numbers of uninsured sick and disabled, and rising unemployment.

Table 4.1 documents the extent of the failure to realise Beveridge's hopes for the success of the contributory system.[65] It gives a breakdown of the categories of non-contributory benefit claimants, most of whom (between 65 and 77 per cent since 1949) have been having inadequate National Insurance benefits supplemented. The most striking aspect is the overwhelming proportion of people over retirement age who have to claim non-contributory benefit.[66] In 1966 publicity surrounding the creation of SBC and new scale rates unearthed over half a million new claimants, mostly pensioners. Pensioners could from now on claim their National Insurance pension and non-contributory benefit (or supplementary pension as it is sometimes called) all in one weekly payment at the post office rather than going through the DHSS. While this constitutes a reversal of the principles of separating contributory and non-contributory benefit, it does not quite mean that 'the stigma of non-contributory benefits could no longer be distinguished from the prestige of contributory',[67] since the former are means-tested and must be specifically claimed. The declining numbers of old, sick and disabled people resorting to supplementary benefit since the early 1970s indicates the increasing importance of

TABLE 4.1 Percentage of claimants of national assistance/supplementary benefit on one day of the month by type of claimant, Great Britain

Type of claimant	Dec 1949	Dec 1965	Dec 1966	Nov 1972	Dec 1976
Person over retirement age	62.1	68.9	72.9	65.6	57.4
Registered unemployed	5.7	5.6	7.2	13.5	22.2
Sick or disabled			12.0	10.2	8.3
Single parents not included above	32.2	25.5	5.0	7.8	10.3
Others			3.0	2.9	1.8
Total number of non-contributory benefits paid (thousands)	1157	1997	2495	2911	2940

SOURCES V. George, *Social Security: Beveridge and After* (London: Routledge, 1968) Tables 61, 65; *Social Security Statistics 1975* (London: HMSO, 1977) Table 34.30; *Social Security Statistics 1976* (London: HMSO, 1978) Table 34.30.

the state earnings-related pensions and sickness benefits, occupational and private pensions and insurance, and new non-contributory benefits for some of the disabled. However, the number of disabled supplementary benefit claimants with no contributory benefit at all has risen consistently over the post-war period.

The number of registered unemployed receiving supplementary benefit has increased dramatically since the mid-1960s, reflecting the growth of long-term unemployment and intermittent employment. The number of uninsured single-parent claimants has risen by 142 per cent over the last decade. This has not been brought about solely by increased single parenthood or unwillingness of men to pay maintenance. Separated and unmarried mothers have also perhaps shifted from the category of the undeserving to the deserving poor, owing to the efforts of welfare activists and feminists, and thereby improving their eligibility for benefits.

THE SUPPLEMENTARY BENEFITS COMMISSION AND ADMINISTRATIVE DISCRETION

Comparing the figures in Table 4.1 for 1965 with those for later years, one can detect some effects of the creation of SBC and the intensified struggle for benefits in the last decade. The early 1960s saw a splintering of the post-war ideological consensus on the adequacy of the welfare services.[68] This was provoked by the rediscovery of working-class poverty by a new generation of social reformers, who uncovered poverty not only amongst the elderly, but amongst young families and children. This marred the appearance of the affluent classless society which the welfare state was supposed to have helped in creating. The rediscovery of poverty contributed not only to the election of the 1964 and 1966 Labour governments, but to the growth of more assertiveness amongst claimants, more research and action programmes on poverty, and a welfare rights movement.[69] The creation of SBC in 1966 was part of this broader movement of reformist ideas and in particular a response to Labour movement pressure for improved pensions and sickness benefits. Hence, although it ostensibly involved only a change of name and increased benefits backed by more publicity, some significant long-term changes may be identified emerging out of the wider context.

Firstly, the administrative style has changed from one which actively and openly deterred people from claiming to one which, while not exactly encouraging people to claim, accepts that claimants have some rights and status, however ill-defined. Means-tested benefits are now of course widely accepted by the working class and the increased number of claims over the years since 1949 must in part be due to improved take-up, which reached an estimated 75 per cent for supplementary benefit in 1975.[70] Secondly, SBC began to create in 1966 a new division amongst claimants between those on long-term rates and those on ordinary rates of benefit. All claimants of over 2 years' standing, except the unemployed, became eligible for long-term rates of benefit, which by November 1976 were 20 per cent higher than the ordinary rate for married couples and 24 per cent higher for single people. It was considered that long-term claimants had special needs, though more recently SBC declared that it has been having 'some difficulty in finding a convincing rationale for the large gap which is building up'[71] between the two rates. In effect benefits have been differentially raised for those whose income will not affect the incentive to wage work, leaving the unemployed as distinctly less deserving. Finally, SBC has taken more intensive measures against so-called fraud (which includes cohabitation) and 'scrounging' in response to the criticism that it is soft on claimants, and the 'workshy' in particular, which is regularly whipped up by the media and some politicians. This pressure ensures that supplementary benefit does not threaten wages, work incentive, labour discipline or even marriage. The SBC has also responded to the welfare rights and claimants' movements by producing not only handbooks and clarifications of discretionary procedures, but also highly articulate and forthright rationalisations of its policies on such issues as the wage stop, cohabitation, benefit levels and so on. These documents are fine examples of the construction of ideology concerning the welfare rights of citizenship and the role of the social security system, which is often actually legitimated by unsubstantiated references to the views of the 'British people' on various issues.

The structure of SBC remains similar to that of its predecessors, the Unemployment Assistance Board and the National Assistance Board. The commission is a small part-time board of state appointees responsible for management and policy recommendations, while the actual implementation of policy rests with DHSS officers and the formulation of policy with ministers and Parliament. The role of the commission in management appears to be severely limited by its size and its powers of enforcement, since the legislation allows DHSS officers considerable discretion. Policy changes have been rare, and until the present administrative review,[72] seem to have been directly initiated from outside by welfare rights and claimants' organisations, on the one hand, and the hard-line anti-scrounger lobby, on the other. The question of administrative discretion therefore requires some further consideration.

Despite major exceptions, such as the six-week rule and sanctions against voluntary unemployment, the contribution principle seems to establish a relatively clear right to National Insurance benefits, thereby limiting administrative discretion. Even this must be qualified, however, in view of the number of National Insurance appeals which turn on discretionary questions.[73] Supplementary benefit is somewhat different, because it is based on the assessment of an individual's needs as opposed to his/her contribution record. The legislation leaves much of the determination of entitlement to benefit and need in the hands of the civil servants. Hence the system can respond flexibly to local labour market and other conditions, through such measures as the four-week rule, wage stop, unemployment review and so on. The DHSS has established detailed internal guidelines for the administration of supplementary benefit, which are continually revised according to local and national developments. These guidelines amount to an unpublished code of welfare 'rights' and non-rights. They are known as the 'A' and 'AX' codes and are protected by the Official Secrets Act, but even these thick codebooks leave considerable discretion to the local executive officers. The areas of discretion cover such questions as the determination of rent allowance, cohabitation, strikers' benefit, and so on, many of which have already been referred to. One study of the work of the NAB, whose findings still hold good today, showed that discretion was used in a fairly sophisticated way to ration benefits which discriminated against weaker claimants or those considered to be undeserving. Hence

> ... almost all the controversial instructions in the codes were double-edged; all the sections urging repressive action included reminders about the need to take such action with care, reminders about the 'overriding responsibility to meet need'. These escape clauses were used whenever trouble arose over a particular decision. A protest from an applicant tended to be treated as evidence of unmet 'need'.[74]

This is a superb example of the 'Catch 22' situation which faces the claimant and the welfare rights advocate, and which clearly sets severe limits to the overall effectiveness of individual struggle and advocacy, because no clear precedents are set in the exercise of administrative discretion.[75] Apart from the functionality of discretion from the policy point of view already suggested, it seems that the political unacceptability of distinguishing between the deserving and the undeserving poor in legislation and public documents has left the civil servants with the job of interpreting the political and ideological balance of forces in the determination of deservingness. Many studies[76] have found officers using quite explicit and varied subjective criteria of deservingness in the determination of non-contributory benefits.

Over the past decade the welfare rights and claimants' movements have had a very clear impact on certain discretionary areas, particularly on so-called positive discretion, such as one-off exceptional needs payments (ENPs) and regular exceptional circumstances additions (ECAs). The number of ENPs doubled from 1969 to 1.1 million in 1976, the average amount being a mere £21.56.[77] In 1976 about half of all claimants were receiving an ECA, compared to 15 per cent in 1971, the average weekly amount in 1976 being £1.24.[78] ECAs and ENPs now account for about 7 per cent of total supplementary benefit expenditure, and they are extremely expensive to administer. Indeed the whole of the supplementary benefit administration is very labour-intensive. Over the decade since the creation of SBC, the number of local office staff has increased by 150 per cent while the number of claims has only increased by 64 per cent. In 1975 30,000 people were employed in administering supplementary benefit, about half the total staff of the social security system, though they only paid out 13 per cent of all social security benefits.[79]

In the context of increasing cuts in welfare expenditure in 1976 the new chairman of SBC, David Donnison, suggested that the time was ripe for moving to a system with 'more clearly understood civil rights, fewer civil servants and "proportional justice" for large categories of claimant'.[80] This would mean cutting back on the positive discretionary payments and, implicitly, the grounds for appeal. There is no question, however, of cutting back on some of the most labour-intensive, 'negative' discretionary activities, such as those of unemployment review officers, liable relative officers and fraud investigators.[81] Donnison is aiming for 'less centralised decision-making and quicker action – even at the cost of rougher justice and less uniformity in the handling of the discretion which will remain in the system'.[82] This is interestingly at variance with the impression given in the press that *greater* uniformity and *less* discretion is being advocated. Donnison's brisk and businesslike pronouncements may signal the beginnings of a renewed attempt, reminiscent of the 1870s and 1920s, to rigorously separate the deserving and the undeserving. Certainly he is hoping to spike the guns of the claimants' and welfare rights movements by increasing the scope for arbitrary official action, in the attempt to ensure that the SBC can respond flexibly and freely to the situation posed by the expansion of the front line of the labour reserve army.[83]

APPEALS

As already mentioned in Chapter 3, when poor relief for the unemployed was finally centralised and removed from local control in 1934, local appeals tribunals were established to retain some legitimacy and the appearance of an independent check on the administration. In the context of the struggles over unemployment benefit in the interwar years, however,

> ... the creation of the unemployment assistance tribunals was ... a deliberate political act, aimed at making an inherently unpopular reform more acceptable, and at the same time protecting the Minister of Labour from the impact of parliamentary and public criticism of the actions of the board and its officials. It had little to do with any abstract ideas of justice and legal rights.[84]

The operation of the supplementary benefit appeals tribunals (SBATs) has remained more or less unchanged since the 1930s, and they are similar in structure to the National Insurance local tribunals (NILTs) established in 1911. They consist of three people – a chairperson appointed by the secretary of state, a workers' representative nominated by the local trades council and either a local employers' representative or someone from a panel representing the local bourgeoisie. Some striking aspects of tribunals' work and membership emerge from several recent studies.[85] Firstly, the chairperson and the non-worker representative are likely to come from social classes

I and II, while the workers' representative and the appellant are most likely to come from social classes III, IV and V. There is therefore a very distinct class bias in tribunal membership and participation. Secondly, tribunal members are almost invariably men, while in the case of SBATs the appellants are very often women. Thirdly, tribunal members are not usually well versed in the complexities of the system and are very much reliant on the presenting DHSS officer and the tribunal clerk. In many cases trades councils have not realised the importance of educating their panel of representatives in the field of welfare rights. The work of the tribunals is severely circumscribed by the degree of administrative discretion bestowed on the civil servants by the legislation, which is expertly explained and argued for by the officers at the tribunals. Although trade union representation of appellants at NILTs is high and most effective in industrial accident cases, otherwise, at both NILTs and SBATs, appellants' attendance and representation by friends, social workers, solicitors or trade unionists is low. In 1976 0.4 per cent of National Insurance unemployment benefit claims were taken to local appeal, with a 17 per cent success rate, while 1 per cent of supplementary benefit claims were taken to appeal, of which 19 per cent resulted in an increase of benefit.[86] These figures account in part for the low attendance rate, and the low appeal rate, given the very wide areas of discretion. The proportion of supplementary benefit claims taken to appeal has doubled since the mid-1960s, owing to the efforts of claimants' unions and welfare rights workers, although the success rate has not improved.

The appeals machinery can therefore only be a very ineffective check on the state bureaucracy for the claimant. It functions more as a relatively informal test-bed for administrative powers than as a judicial forum,[87] and as a means of strengthening moralistic and prejudicial regulation of the poor. Thus, particularly when the appellant is unrepresented,

... discussion centres around the personal characteristics and psychological make-up of the appellant ... manifesting itself in a central concern with why unemployed appellants do not have jobs and, in appeals for discretionary grants, with the previous history of such grants to assess the appellants' budgeting abilities. The division of the poor into deserving and undeserving groups is a widespread attitude.[88]

While we have been at pains to emphasise some of the changes which have occurred in social security administration, this is a reminder of the extent to which the spirit of the poor law lives on just beneath the surface of the welfare state.

CLASS STRUGGLE AND SOCIAL SECURITY

This aspect of claimants' treatment at appeals is one example of a phenomenon which has been alluded to throughout these two chapters, namely the stigmatisation and pathological labelling of claimants both inside and outside the administration of social security. Such judgements of character and deservingness continue to pervade the system. Although fashions in labelling are constantly shifting with general economic and ideological movements, all claimants and administrators, particularly of supplementary benefit, are conditioned into thinking that they are receiving or giving 'something for nothing'. The exaggerated publicity about fraud and the allegedly workshy carefully nurtures this idea in people's minds. Ostensibly, of course, social security is a basic right of citizenship, as access to the means of subsistence at levels usually below the lowest wages but high enough to prevent begging, destitution or starvation. In fact, however, it is not a gift which is available to all; neither can it be received without strings. We have already considered the limitations and the strings attached to the availability of benefits for the registered unemployed and women. Those who do receive benefit are receiving not so much their rights, but a gift which generates considerable expectations of the beneficiary. Claimants are expected to be 'sensible' in their spending and budgeting, to adjust their standard of living downwards if necessary, to be keen to get a job, anxious to find a husband and so on. In other words they are expected to prove that they are deserving. The undeserving may get a rough time at the hands of civil servants, tribunals, neighbours, etc.

Claimants are subject to expectations which stigmatise them as poor whatever they do, although the stigma is not as strong perhaps as in the days of the poor law. It is not an anachronism nor a vestige of the poor law which can be eradicated by administrative reform and repackaging. The stigma of being a claimant is an essential ingredient in a system designed to discipline claimants and to promote the values of insurance and individual and family self-help. This helps to ensure that expenditure on benefits is rationed by informal means and by claimants themselves, as well as by bureaucratic delay and opacity. The DHSS walk the tightrope of the class struggle over welfare. On the one hand, they are pressed to limit expenditure on benefit, to reinforce their labour market and ideological functions and to strengthen sanctions against claimants. On the other hand, there are pressures to mitigate poverty further, strengthen and improve welfare rights and benefits, and pursue more genuinely the welfare of its clients. This is the terrain on which the class struggle for social security has been fought in the post-war period, and we now turn to considering the pressure for progressive reform of the system.

Continual reference has already been made to the role of the welfare rights and claimants' movements in bringing increasing pressure to bear on the social security system. Their success as a 'poverty lobby' has even been acknowledged by the chairman of SBC.[89] They have helped to increase awareness of welfare rights and they have squeezed a little more for claimants out of the discretionary payments. The formal withdrawal of the four-week rule and the wage stop was due in large measure to their pressure, and with the women's movement they have been pressing hard for an end to the cohabitation rule, so far without success. A whole variety of minor improvements and reforms have been prompted by these groups or movements. It is difficult to isolate the influence of particular groups and sources of pressure on either governments or the Labour movement. Together they form a body of considerable political and ideological strength, although their means of creating pressure and their aims are very varied.

Child Poverty Action Group (CPAG) is a national pressure group formed directly out of the rediscovery of poverty in the early 1960s. It has produced many well-researched and publicised welfare rights guides and exposés of particular failings in the system, believing that 'reform can be achieved by the use of rational argument'.[90] A panoply of particular interest groups such as the Disablement Income Group, Age Concern, National Association of One Parent Families, Women's Liberation Campaign for Financial and Legal Independence, etc., press their claims by research, demonstrations, publicity and lobbying. At the local level a wide variety of legal, welfare rights and social work agencies have emerged in the last decade. They are largely confined to advocacy work, which, when consistently pursued, has achieved some local reforms. Many people, radicalised by the anti-poverty and student movements, have become local authority social workers, energetically advocating clients' welfare rights. The rediscovery of poverty in the 1960s was prompted above all by the work of two academics at the London School of Economics,[91] and since that time the work of countless academic researchers has assisted in making the case for particular reforms and indeed servicing state agencies. All these forces combine to form a somewhat loose and fragmentary welfare rights movement. Many of its members have been active within the Labour movement in pursuing social security reforms, and most of the significant changes have come about with the support of the Labour movement.[92]

The claimants' union movement is possibly even more elusive than the welfare rights movement. It emerged out of the student movement in the late 1960s,[93] and its greatest achievement has probably been in pushing the National Union of Students into becoming an outstandingly successful claimants' union. Claimants' unions have also involved many other people in what are very much local groups, often with a small number of activists and a loose form of membership and organisation. They have sought to resist the individuation and stigmatisation inherent in the system by collective local struggle and confrontation.[94] Understandably their organisation has been volatile and their presence ephemeral, given the forces ranged against them. Their relation to the trade union movement is problematic; some members of claimants' unions see their interests as totally opposed to those of trade unionists,[95] while some trade unionists are openly hostile to what they see as a movement of scroungers. Yet the claimants' movement is based on trade union principles, and the links between the interests of claimants and workers are combined in their common struggle against the interests of capital in general. The particular importance of the claimants' unions and the protests of individuals lies in the threat of their presence and their occasional outbursts of active resistance, such as occupying DHSS offices.

The fundamental contradiction between, on the one hand, the apparent rights of citizenship and, on the other hand, the economic and ideological functions of the social security system has been exposed increasingly effectively by claimants, trade unionists and the welfare rights movement. We have argued that the form of social security administration has helped to confine this class struggle for welfare to the take-up and improvement of particular welfare rights. This has threatened some of the basic functions of the system – for example, by the withdrawal of the wage stop – but bureaucratic adaptations have contained these threats. There remains a widespread view both within the Labour movement and outside it that the social security system is fundamentally fair and reasonable, and only requires fine tuning in order to respond more sensitively to individual needs and to protect the poor. We have argued on the contrary that the working of the system in relation to labour discipline, the labour reserve army, women and so on, protects the interests of capital in general and runs against the collective interests of the working class, while obviously meeting some of the most pressing needs of the poorest section of that class.

5

Private Housing, the State and the Working Class

THE HOUSING QUESTION

Housing is obviously of central importance to the working class
and any consideration of its living conditions and general welfare
under capitalism. It is also of essential importance to 'capital in general',
which requires a supply of labour power housed sufficiently close
to the point of production and housed adequately enough to ensure
reproduction. Working-class housing conditions have been one of
the most crucial material factors pushing forward the class struggle,
both at the level of wages struggle and in other arenas. Housing
expenditure has always taken up a high proportion of working-class
spending; over the post-war period, according to the Family Expenditure Survey, average personal expenditure on housing rose from 9
per cent of total consumer spending in 1953 to 14 per cent in 1973,
and lower income groups spend proportionally more on their housing
than higher income groups.[1] Wage demands are highly sensitive
to working-class housing costs, and hence the cost of housing to
the working class is relevant to the interests of capital in general.
Since the late nineteenth century the state has gradually come to
play a central role both in processing working-class housing pressures
and in ensuring the interests of capital in general in this sphere.
The role of the state has largely been confined to housing consumption
rather than its production; in the shape of central and local government
agencies it has assumed the role of an exchange intermediary and
regulator in the process of consumption. This and the following
chapter offer an analysis of the development of this role, but before
that, a brief discussion of the general nature of the housing question
is necessary.

It almost goes without saying that housing is a commodity like any other, having a dual character as both a use-value and an exchange-value, but it has three particularly important characteristics. Firstly, housing is an essential *use-value* which *must* be consumed by workers to ensure their subsistence and reproduction. Housing is an integral part of the bundle of use-values which, like food, is normally purchased out of wages and contributes to the value of labour power. Secondly, unlike food, the exchange-value of housing is very high, and it is too expensive to be purchased outright by working-class consumers; the high price reflects the high value of housing, that is the large amount of socially necessary labour time required in its production. Hence the working-class consumer becomes engaged in exchange transactions which allow him/her to consume the use-value of housing without immediate ownership – in the UK either by renting from a private or public landlord or by borrowing. Thirdly, since all housing is incorporated into a system of private landed property, the cost or price of housing includes a considerable element of rent, in the specific Marxist sense of the term. These three particular characteristics of the production and consumption of working-class housing immediately raise a number of issues concerning the roots of the 'housing question'.

The most immediate issue is the ever-present housing shortage, which today manifests itself in the phenomena of homelessness, housing waiting lists and the plight of those living in unfit or inadequate housing. This is clearly linked to the high cost of housing, as well as the continued existence of low wages and insecurity of employment for the working class, despite the post-war boom. With loss of employment due to redundancy, illness, victimisation, etc., the individual worker is often forced to adjust his/her standard of living downwards, and this may lead to a move to cheaper and worse accommodation. It is not surprising that housing pressure is the most important factor deterring labour mobility in Britain. The break-up of the family or the loss of the male breadwinner increasingly throws working-class women on to the bottom end of the housing market.[2] There remains a distinct tendency within bourgeois ideology, as Engels observed, to 'explain the housing shortage by moralising that it is the result of the wickedness of man [that is, the unthrifty and immoral working-class consumer], the result of original sin so to speak',[3] exemplified today in aspects of council housing management. The housing shortage in fact reflects both the continued insecurity of working-class living conditions and wages, and the high cost of housing. Ball has placed particular emphasis on the latter, which, he argues, has been exacerbated by the low growth of productivity in the house-building industry. Thus

> . . . the fall in the labour time necessary to produce housing has lagged behind that for other commodities. As a result the value of housing will not have fallen to the same extent as many of the commodities contributing to the reproduction of labour power . . . [This] limits the ability to lower the value of labour power and will therefore act as a restriction on increases in the rate of surplus value.[4]

In other words, the high value of housing may act as a barrier to counter-tendencies to the falling rate of profit, and hence become a problem for capital in general. The empirical basis for this conclusion is still rather meagre, but, if it is true, it is unclear whether this results from the inability of governments to perceive the problem fully or their unwillingness to enter the sphere of housing production. Although during the post-war period governments promoted industrialised building systems[5] and large local authority contracts stimulated the centralisation of capital in the construction industry, housebuilding has not been subject to the restructuring of the labour process aided by the state, as seen in other areas of production. In fact the government initiatives mentioned seem to have failed to increase productivity and have been abandoned. The reasons for this must be related to particular characteristics of the house-building industry and the relative immutability of its labour process. Small and medium capital can still flourish in this sector, which offers a high rate of profit.[6] The relatively low level of fixed capital investment and the notoriously casual labour market allow for great flexibility on the part of the entrepreneur in riding out the peaks and troughs of housing demand. The high bankruptcy rate amongst builders conceals the fact that 'bankruptcies represent more a part of the process of reducing the labour force than a major devalorisation of capital'.[7] The house-building industry has not cried out for state intervention to ensure profitability; recently, however, it has begun to press the government to boost consumer demand through the various means at its disposal.

Ball's thesis has certainly further undermined the popular view that the root of the housing question lies in the 'exploitation' of

housing consumers by loan capital or finance capital. It is true that
various intermediaries, as a direct consequence of the existence of
private property and the high value of housing, appropriate value
from the housing exchange process in the form of interest, professional
charges, housing rent, etc., which are paid out of workers' wages
(variable capital) and state subsidies (surplus value appropriated by
the state). These intermediaries include lending institutions, and
exchange professionals such as surveyors, estate agents, solicitors, landlords and so on, and this appropriation of value even extends into
the public sector. But this is not a relationship of exploitation in
the Marxist sense, since it involves merely a redistribution of value,
which has already been created in the sphere of production. Engels
in *The Housing Question* thus attacks Proudhon's petit-bourgeois socialism, which asserted that 'the tenant is in the same position in relation
to the house owner [that is, landlord] as the wage worker is in
relation to the capitalist'.[8] Proudhon could then argue that the abolition
of private landlordism and its replacement by some form of cooperative working-class owner-occupation, not unlike the housing coopera-
tives promulgated by the present government, is a fundamental part
of a revolutionary socialist programme. Engels refutes this position
on the basis of Marx's value theory:

> The tenant – even if he is a worker – appears as *a man with* money;
> he must already have sold his commodity, a commodity peculiarly
> his own, his labour power, to be able to appear with the proceeds
> as the buyer of the use of a dwelling ... No matter how much
> the landlord may overreach the tenant it is still only a transfer
> of already *existing*, previously *produced* value and the total sum
> of values possessed by the landlord and tenant *together* remains
> the same after as it was before.[9]

Engels therefore concludes that to abolish interest by decree would
simply close off one avenue of investment for money capital but
'the mass of surplus value extracted from the working class would
remain the same; only its distribution would be altered'.[10]

The roots of the housing question cannot simply be located in
the appropriation of value in the exchange system, despite the fact
that we shall concentrate on this process in what follows. This is
just the most immediate and material manifestation of the fundamental
characteristics of the housing commodity already mentioned.

Turning to the third characteristic, the price of housing includes an element of 'rent', a concept which in relation to agricultural production was elaborated upon by Marx with great care and precision.[11] Marx begins from the premise that land in itself cannot be productive of value, since only labour can create value, but he shows that the existence of private landed property does generate forms of super profit or rent. Firstly, the fixed nature of landed property ownership creates continual barriers to capitalist expansion (as well as being necessary to it) and protects its owners from the full force of the law of value, thus creating the possibility of super profits accruing to landed property in the form of what Marx calls absolute rent. Secondly, the existence of differential use-values of different plots of land (due to fertility, location, differences in the amount of capital applied) creates the possibility of super profits, which may again accrue to the landowner in the form of what Marx calls differential rent.

Unfortunately the application of these concepts to the analysis of workers' housing remains somewhat tentative and unquantifiable, but it is clear that the rent element in the cost of housing must at least cover the agricultural rent (both differential and absolute) which could be raised if the land were in agricultural production.[12] In addition it has been suggested that differential rent on urban property may derive from the locational competition amongst land users, particularly in cities; in the case of housing, the distance and cost of transport to and from the work place for the consumer would be an important factor.[13] An element of absolute rent in housing costs derives from the barriers to capital investment on the land created by planning and development controls, as well as the stubborn existence of owner-occupation itself. But how does this rent appear in the cost of owner-occupied housing and council housing? The 'rent' element in owner-occupation is capitalised in the price of the house, and is recouped in an augmented or diminished form when the house is resold. The 'rent' element in council housing is included in the price paid by the local authority for its houses, which is passed on to the tenant and the taxpayer.[14]

In the following we shall examine the consequences of these long-term fundamental forces, which have shaped not only the cost of working-class housing but also the form of its consumption and the political struggles surrounding it. Clearly, too, short-term speculative and other influences will enter into the analysis of particular conjunctures. Here we shall concentrate upon the development of the role of the state in the three major tenure sectors in Britain – private landlordism, owner-occupation, and local authority housing – since tenures provide a convenient means of unravelling state policy. Tenures 'represent the legal recognition of the separate sets of social relations which intervene between the production of housing and its consumption as a use-value'[15] and hence structure both the forms of value appropriation, political struggle and state intervention.

Something of the dramatic changes in working class tenure is conveyed in Table 5.1. While the middle classes have naturally remained in owner-occupied housing by and large, the working class has moved out of private renting into owner-occupation and council housing. The rise of owner-occupation and council housing closely reflects the decline in private renting, but it should be noted that the decline of the latter is exaggerated by the considerable increases in the absolute numbers of dwellings since the First World War. Hence between 1914 and 1976 the actual number of privately rented houses declined by 60 per cent. The doubling of the council housing stock between 1938 and 1951 reflects the oft-belittled achievements of Aneurin Bevan's years as Minister of Health and the post-war

TABLE 5.1 Housing tenure, England and Wales (millions of houses and percentage of stock)

Year	Owner-occupied		Local authority and new towns		Private rented and miscellaneous*		Total number
	Number	%	Number	%	Number	%	
(a) 1914	0.8	10	0.02	0.2	7.1	89.8	7.9
(a) 1938	3.7	32	1.1	10	6.6	58	11.4
(b) 1951	3.9	31	2.2	17	6.4	52	12.5
(a) 1960	6.4	44	3.6	25	4.6	31	14.6
(c) 1966	7.8	49	4.3	27	3.9	24	16.0
(c) 1971	8.9	52	4.9	29	3.3	19	17.1
(c) 1976	10.1	56	5.3	29	2.8	15	18.1

* Includes housing associations.

SOURCES (a) *Housing Policy: Technical Volume 1* (London: HMSO, 1977) p. 38, Table I.23; (b) *Housing Policy: A Consultative Document* (London: HMSO, 1977) p. 14, Fig. 2; (c) *Housing and Construction Statistics* (London: HMSO, 1972, 1978) nos 1 & 22.

controls on private development, and this is the only period in this century in which the rise of owner-occupation has faltered. The most rapid period of decline for private renting took place in the 1950s, largely subsequent to the 1957 Rent Act. The gradual withdrawal of government commitment to council housing, whether Labour or Conservative, is indicated by the fact that its proportion of the stock has only increased by 2 per cent since 1966, and has not increased at all since 1971.

The relationship between tenure and socio-economic class is clearly indicated by Table 5.2.[16] The proportion of owner-occupiers is seen to decline quite regularly and dramatically as one moves down the social scale, while the complete reverse is true of council tenants. The table also confirms that private renting is now very much a residual tenure for all social classes, though higher proportions of the lower social classes remain in this tenure. We now turn to analysing the changes in tenure and the role of state policy in these changes.

TABLE 5.2   Home tenure by social class (Registrar General's socio-economic class 1970 definitions) of head of household, 1971

Social class group	Owner-occupation	Private renting	Council renting
1	85	12	3
2	74	17	10
3	59	22	20
4	45	17	38
5	31	25	44
6	21	23	56

SOURCE   I. Reid, *Social Class Differences In Britain* (London: Open Books, 1977) p. 157, Table 5.26, derived from *General Household Survey: Introductory Report* (London: HMSO, 1973).

THE RISE AND FALL OF PRIVATE LANDLORDISM

Until the Second World War the working class was mostly housed in privately rented accommodation built by small speculative builders for an army of small landlords and 'middlemen', who appropriated value from the provision of this use-value in the form of that part of housing rent which does not cover repairs and other costs. At the outbreak of the Second World War 58 per cent of housing in England and Wales was rented privately, largely by the working class.

Under feudalism and agrarian capitalism, peasants either built their own houses or their accommodation was provided by their employer. In the period of competitive capitalism, with the emergence of factory production and the urban proletariat, 'the towns filled up with country people searching for homes as much as employment'[17] and the notoriously overcrowded and unhealthy ghettoes and slums of Victorian Britain emerged to 'house' the rapidly expanding urban proletariat. The casual and uncertain nature of the nineteenth-century labour market, particularly in London, was reflected in the uncertainties of the housing situation, such as frequent changes of accommodation, eviction, etc.[18] With the establishment of the pure wage contract between capital and labour and the 'free' market in labour power, the vestiges of individual employer interest in the welfare of employees, particularly their housing, all but disappeared. There are some notable exceptions, such as the mining industries, but the housing provided by employers and philanthropists was very much the exception in the nineteenth century, despite the attention that such provision has received from historians.

A market developed to take advantage of the evident need for housing of the cheapest kind for the newly urbanised working class. Our knowledge of how this market worked is very limited; it must have varied considerably from place to place, and little or nothing is known in detail about the role of intermediaries, or the forms of resistance to landlordism. Both the builders and landlords of working-class housing ran essentially small-scale undertakings. Landlordism was one avenue of investment for the small savings of various groups, such as professionals, shopkeepers, artisans and widows with savings, and small businessmen, particularly builders themselves. Just before the First World War those with capitals of between £1000 and £20,000 owned 36.2 per cent of the national wealth, but 53 per cent of the housing property and business premises.[19] In 1840 Thomas Cubitt, the owner of a large firm engaged in building bourgeois villas, remarked that working-class houses 'belong to a little shop-keeping class of persons who have saved a little money in business . . . very few persons of great capital have anything to do with them at all'.[20] It was common for the shopkeeper or publican at the end of the street to be the local landlord also. Frequently of course the working class crowded into the housing vacated by others in the city centres, but the developers and builders of new working-class housing were people with little capital, such as groups of tradesmen, artisans or even lawyers, who for a small outlay could invest in it reasonably profitably.[21] Often large numbers of intermediaries took part in the housing exchange process, particularly in London, where the predominance of leasehold was particularly advantageous to 'middlemen'.[22]

It remains true today that private landlords tend to be individuals with a small number of properties (say 65 per cent of the market), while property companies only account for about 10 per cent of the market and their role seems to be diminishing in the 1970s.[23] Little appears to be known about the workings of the contemporary private renting market beyond rent determination, but Harloe indicates that the role of agents and other intermediaries is very important in the management and development of the sector.

In the second half of the nineteenth century, especially as the period of classical imperialism developed, the beginnings of the decline of private landlordism can be detected. Considerable debate has taken place about the relative importance of pure investment factors, state intervention and tenants' struggle in this decline. Without doubt, the most important factor was the development of more attractive and less troublesome outlets for small capital investment, such as the stock markets, government and municipal debt, building societies and investment in imperialist expansion such as railways and mining. The rate of return on working-class housing investment was severely limited by the wages of prospective tenants; although rents and over-crowding increased in the second half of the nineteenth century, even when the general price trend was downwards, employers were obviously not prepared to raise wages in order to sustain the private landlord.

The gradually increasing importance of public health and sanitary legislation in the second half of the century cannot be ignored, however, in limiting the profit margins of the landlord. The origins of this legislation lie in the cholera epidemics and various other forms of threat presented by the Dickensian slum areas of the cities. Its effectiveness was severely limited, because it merely permitted rather than forced local authorities to act, and the latter were not organised for or capable of the task of enforcement. The town councils were dominated by the same small tradesmen and shopkeepers who were involved in the provision of cheap and unsanitary housing, 'so the wishes of town councillors, builders and owners of house property were often seen to have remarkable agreement'.[24] In the period of classical imperialism from the 1880s onwards the state apparatus was strengthened at both local and national level, not least by the effects of working-class enfranchisement. In towns such as Sheffield in which working-class political pressure was well organised, even before the Reform Acts, housing conditions were considerably better than in other places. Thus, often transmitted and mediated through the state apparatus, pressure from tenants eventually contributed to the decline of the private landlordism; but in the short term at least the implementation of the sanitary legislation exacerbated the pressure on tenants because it further restricted the supply of housing by clearance and closure, and by the imposition of building standards that raised the rent of housing beyond tenants' reach.

RENT CONTROL AND REGULATION

Aside from largely unorganised pressures by tenants,[25] particular significance has been attached to the rent struggles during the First World War, notably in Glasgow, which led to the introduction of rent control. Was this 'the decisive blow to the private landlord?'[26] Evidence suggests that the decline must be traced to the forces emerging in the second half of the nineteenth century already mentioned, but the introduction of rent control in December 1915 was a further nail in the coffin of an apparently terminal case, but a highly symbolic one for the working-class movement and the future shape of state policy. One qualifies this conclusion advisedly, since, if working-class real incomes had risen rapidly after the First World War and if the government had granted reasonable tax concessions to landlords (relief on repairs, depreciation, etc.),[27] there could well have been a revival of private landlordism. In certain senses this is occurring today in the shape of the housing associations in Britain, while private landlordism has continued to flourish in other capitalist countries. In Britain, both before and after the First World War, landlords were not sufficiently organised as a pressure group, and neither capital nor the working class were prepared to defend their interests. The demand for rent control was supported by employers in Glasgow, since they had 'every interest in the stability of rents and therefore of wage demands'.[28] At a theoretical level, the interest of capital in general in this context was to keep rents down, conflicting with particularistic interests of the landlords.

This is not to conclude that the war-time agitation by tenants, which led to swift passage of the rent control legislation, was rather insignificant in the long-term perspective. In fact it placed the housing question firmly into the minds of the government and very much occupied the Reconstruction Committees from early 1916 onwards.[29] This pressure articulated the great working-class grievances against landlordism as a symbol of its immediate oppression, and eventually generated council housing subsidies and the encouragement of owner-occupation. Bierne has suggested that rent control 'marked a clear victory for tenants';[30] this is so, in the sense that it maintained low rents and some security of tenure for the lower income strata of the working class, but it also ensured that these people were confined to very poor accommodation, which landlords could not profitably improve. The blunt nature of anti-landlordism was translated into state policies confined to the periphery of the housing question (i.e. rent control) and a very slow war of attrition in the shape of slum clearance. While many landlords undoubtedly cheated their tenants and took a good profit from their investment, rent control policy merely added to the stagnation of the investments in which most of the working class continued to languish in the inter-war period. Just as nineteenth-century sanitary legislation exacerbated the housing situation for many working-class people by restricting supply, rent control legislation in the twentieth century achieved similar results, while no doubt helping to temper wage demands.

There was not a spectacular absolute decline in private renting in the inter-war period: 900,000 new privately rented dwellings came into the stock, while 1.4 million were lost to owner-occupation, demolition or change of use, a shrinkage of only 7 per cent. Rent control, it should be noted, did not apply to new dwellings, and immediately after the First World War the government instituted 35 per cent increases in private rents (plus more if repairs were done), and later there followed significant decontrol on vacant possession and on higher value property. The 1924 Protection From Eviction Act was passed by the first Labour government, to give some statutory protection to tenants in the face of landlords seeking vacant possession and rent rises. Between 1915 and 1924, therefore, the role of the state as neutral arbiter between landlord and tenant in the shape of the county court was deepened, though there is

little evidence on its effectiveness. The main form of tenants' defence
was the strength of working-class communities in bringing collective
pressure on bailiffs and landlords. There is also evidence of effective
organised resistance by tenants in the years before 1926 and in the
1930s, usually with the active support of the Communist Party and
the antipathy of the Labour Party.[31]

Rent control was uncontroversially reimposed at the beginning
of the Second World War, and in the decade after the war the
private rented sector was more or less ignored in the construction
of the welfare state. An important change in state administration
of the sector was the introduction in the late 1940s of rent tribunals
as a means of adjudication between landlord and tenant, removing
some of the burden from the county courts. A great series of government committees since 1916 had debated on how the state could
institute 'fair rents' while appearing to be impartial and consistent.
Leaving the question in the hands of lawyers and professionals had
not proved very satisfactory on these criteria in the inter-war years,
and in 1945 a rent tribunal was proposed, to be 'composed of members
able to appreciate both the views of owners and tenants and by
their work to inspire confidence in their decisions'.[32] A similar strategy
had already been successfully implemented in the social security appeals
tribunals; both are forms of administration designed to move the
responsibility for adjudication within the welfare state away from
the courts and the state bureaucracy, and on to relatively autonomous
tribunals, apparently independent but state-appointed and fettered
by the regulations imposed by the state. In fact the rent tribunals
were staffed by a lawyer, a valuer and only one lay person.

Between 1938 and 1976 the private rented sector in England and
Wales shrank by 58 per cent or 3.8 million dwellings; it has changed
from being the predominant form of working-class housing consumption to a residual sector still containing the very worst accommodation
and housing migrant and mobile workers, students, poor elderly,
single workers, etc. This loss has undoubtedly been the resultant
of state policy and the forces of the urban property market. The
majority (2.6 million) of these dwellings have been sold for owner-
occupation, which has been made increasingly attractive by state policy
in a variety of ways; 1.2 million have been either cleared, with
tenants rehoused in council housing, or turned over to office use.
Only 300,000 have been bought by local authorities to become part
of the council housing stock, while 400,000 new privately rented

dwellings have been provided, often by flat conversions in the bigger cities.

The most significant form of state intervention in the privately rented sector has remained in the area of rent regulation, and here policy and administration have gone through major changes since the mid-1950s. The 1957 and 1965 Rent Acts and the 1972 Housing Finance Act are the landmarks: the 1957 Act successfully decontrolled the majority of rented property creating insecurity of tenure and opening up the sector to the property speculators; the 1965 Act sought to regulate the sector in such a way as to prevent the worst excesses of the property market while allowing and even encouraging reasonable rent rises; finally, the 1972 Act introduced means-tested rent allowances for 'needy' private tenants, bringing them further into the welfare system.

The 1957 and 1965 Rent Acts sometimes appear as polar opposites, the former representing the actions of a Tory government abandoning social welfare principles and leaving tenants at the mercy of market forces, while the latter is the protective and avuncular achievement of a reforming and anti-landlord Labour government. There is of course a measure of truth in this caricature, but in many ways the two pieces of legislation complemented each other. The 1957 Act was a fairly extraordinary enactment in post-war terms – it was not preceded by a White Paper, it was not based on any research or coherent policy strategy, it went well beyond the dreams of the landed property owners, it is commonly held to have backfired badly, and it contributed to the Tory defeat in 1964. Yet, at the time of its passing, opposition to it was fairly tame. Enoch Powell presented it as a reasonable package designed to prevent under-occupation, help labour mobility, increase repairs and above all implement the apparent consensus on the need for a general rise in rents. The 'analysis' of the Ministry of Housing and the Treasury economists suggested that

> . . . housing was underpriced when they compared the low percentage of income taken by rent by comparison with the large percentage taken up by various 'immoral' expenditures such as drink and tobacco . . . rent increases, the economists concluded would be good things in themselves; they had deflationary characteristics in that they gave to those who would invest, took from those who would spend.[33]

This is a significant reversal of the argument, applied to 1915, that capital in general opposes rent increases; clearly this depends on the historical juncture, and in the midst of the post-war boom the inflationary effect of rent increases was not a predominant concern of capital in general, since the mass of value was increasing and profitability reasonably healthy. On the contrary, a stimulus to investment, a move to encourage labour mobility and the freeing of valuable urban land was closer to the interests of capital in general. Many commentators point to the 1957 Rent Act as a classic failure because it did not revive landlordism and in fact hastened its decline. This is surely to take the packaging of the bill at face value; in fact many of Powell's aims, such as rent rises, encouragement to owner-occupation and even improved labour mobility, were achieved by the act. Jim Callaghan indeed, in concluding a debate on the bill, accepted its principles and aims, but was anxious about the hardship and dislocation that the act might cause. The Labour Party and the working-class movement clearly anticipated some of the adverse consequences, but this was not formed into a coherent oppositional strategy, and the voice of the tenants remained largely unheard in the legislative process. The National Association of Tenants and Residents was mostly refused assistance and support in their campaign against the act by trades councils and local Labour parties, apparently because of their far left and Communist Party support; thus their lobbies and protests were safely ignored.

At the 1956 conference the Labour Party formally adopted the policy of municipalisation, that is the use of local housing authorities to buy out the private landlord. This policy had already been implemented by the Labour council in Birmingham, which at one stroke made the city council the biggest slum landlord in Britain, and this accommodation is now used for Birmingham's 'unsatisfactory' tenants.[34] The economic and political implications of such a policy were gradually realised within the party in the late 1950s, as it also came to terms with the effects of the post-war boom on working-class aspirations; the traditional Labour opposition to landlordism was becoming obsolete in the face of the expansion of owner-occupation and council housing. The municipalisation policy was eventually dropped at the 1961 party conference in favour of a weak pledge to strengthen local authority powers to enforce housing improvements on landlords.[35]

Meanwhile the consequences of the 1957 Rent Act were particularly felt in the inner cities, where many landlords sought vacant possession in order to sell out to property developers for commercial and office development and owner-occupation in the 'property boom', which was now in full swing. Rachmanism[36] became a byword for over-zealous landlords harassing tenants into giving up their tenancies, thus enabling the assembly of highly marketable tracts of land. Homelessness, insecurity of tenure, and Rachmanism were important elements in the so-called rediscovery of poverty, which took place in the early 1960s, and the Labour Party capitalised on the upsurge of protest by condemning the now infamous 'Tory Rent Act'. Richard Crossman's first deed on becoming Minister of Housing in October 1964 was to restore rent control and a measure of security of tenure, with apparently little opposition from the landed property lobby. By this time, 7 years after the 1957 Act, the property developers had assembled their land, so that, to a considerable extent, the stable door was being shut after the horse had bolted.

The 1965 Rent Act instituted the 'fair rent' system under which rent levels on vacant possession or repair by the landlord, can be referred by either landlord or tenant to a local civil servant, the rent officer. He/she, taking into account local rent norms but discounting the effects of scarcity, arrives at a 'fair rent'; if either tenant or landlord object to this assessment, he or she may appeal to a rent assessment committee, drawn from a nominated panel of lawyers, valuers and 'lay people'.[37] This complex and opaque system of rent determination[38] was said to be working well according to a government committee of inquiry in 1971, which presumably means that it receives the consent of tenants and landlords as individuals, although about 7 per cent do object to the rent officer's assessment. There is no valid means of judging the fairness of the system from the published statistics, because there are no criteria in terms of housing standards and state of repair which can be related to rent and cost increases, nor any means of comparability with other tenures. Certainly the fair rent system has secured substantial rent increases for landlords; the average increase in fair rents on re-registration (which happens every 3 or more years) was 47 per cent outside London in 1975.[39] The government suggests that these increases have fallen behind the increase in the cost of living, but it is not clear whether they have fallen behind the increase in real incomes secured by private tenants, which is a more relevant criterion. In 1970 94 per cent of all landlords who applied for an increase were successful, and about 70 per cent

of all applications to the rent officer came from landlords in 1967–72.[40]
One study has described the skilful way in which a London property
company was able to ensure that the free market rent was established
as the registered fair rent on a large number of its properties, thereby
quickly raising the capital value of the properties and increasing their
paper assets.[41]

The state bureaucratic regulation of private rents, therefore, appears
to have protected those tenants who apply to it from the worst
excesses of landlordism, while also guaranteeing and legitimating considerable rent increases. Crossman found that the Labour movement
barely had a policy on landlordism in 1964, but with no apparent
means of consulting the Labour movement, his civil servants and
advisers hatched the fair rent concept.[42] Crossman claims it as 'the
kind of legislation that only a Socialist Minister could produce';[43]
certainly it is a shining example of state bureaucratic administration
in the Fabian tradition, appearing to enforce fair and equal rights
of tenants and landlords, while in fact reproducing a deep structure
of class inequality in housing and the continuing bad state of repair
in this sector. Looking at the sector as a whole in the 1970s, it
is also striking how many tenancies are effectively outside the Rent
Acts – 350,000 tenants of resident landlords, and 700,000 in accommodation tied to their employment or vocation (for example, students
on campus), who are either unable or unlikely to question their
rent levels. In addition there is a considerable but unknown number
of tenants who, either through ignorance or fear of losing the tenancy,
do not take their case to the rent officer.

The ineffectiveness of the state machinery in dealing with the
plight of private tenants is indexed by the very low rates of take-up
for the means-tested rent allowances. These were introduced as part
of the Housing Finance Act, 1972, and are administered by local
housing authorities, in harmony with the general aim of that act
to integrate policy and to change the character of housing subsidisation
towards individual means-tested benefits for the poor, and away from
direct bricks-and-mortar subsidies in the public sector. The government estimated in 1974 an average take-up amongst furnished tenants
of 10–12 per cent and 25 per cent amongst unfurnished tenants.[44]
A second indication of the relative ineffectiveness of policy in its
own terms is the very slow take-up of improvement grants by landlords even in General Improvement Areas and Housing Action Areas,
and local authorities seem reluctant to enforce this. Clearly the expense

for the landlords (and subsequently the tenants) is sometimes an impossible burden, and there is no cash for municipalisation. A study by
community workers in 1975 suggested 'policies centred on voluntary
improvement by landlords continue the mistaken assumption that
the majority are willing to improve'.[45] Rehabilitation policy, which
has replaced clearance, manifestly fails to secure adequate improvements in the private rental sector. Far from challenging or even
directly subsidising the landlord, the Labour government produced
a consultative document in 1977 suggesting the voluntaristic carrot
of more generous fair rent increases as a future policy. The state
has therefore no intention of being drawn into further involvement
in private landlordism, not least because of the public expenditure
implications.

HOUSING ASSOCIATIONS

This statement must be qualified in view of the expansion of housing
associations in recent years. Housing associations offer a variety of
hybrid forms of tenure, but essentially they are a modified form
of private landlordism funded by public and charitable money. At
the end of 1976 there were a quarter of a million housing association
tenancies in England and Wales, only 1.4 per cent of the whole
stock. If one includes housing associations as part of the public sector
as far as finance is concerned, in 1974 they accounted for 7.8 per
cent of public sector housing starts, but by 1976 this had increased
to 16.2 per cent and in 1977 around 23 per cent. Since the early
1960s, the state has promoted housing associations or what is called
'the voluntary housing movement' as an alternative to council housing,
for those who cannot enter full owner-occupation. The great expansion
in their activity since 1974 is due to the Housing Act, 1974, drafted
by the Conservatives but finally passed by Labour, which channelled
large chunks of government money into housing associations via
the Housing Corporation, yet another quasi-non-governmental welfare agency (or *quango*). Housing associations are now largely funded
by the government and the local housing authorities, but, unlike
council housing, this is public money which is spent with little or
no direct public accountability, and is beyond the control of democratic
political bodies. The annual reports of the Housing Corporation do
not allow any cogent analysis of housing associations' rents, cost

and subsidies, and the recent government Green Paper sheds no light on this. According to the 1975–6 Housing Corporation Annual Report

> ... the housing association schemes approved in England during the year will cost a total of £375,464,450 when completed. Of this some 75% or more will be met by public subsidy in the form of the Housing Association Grant, leaving the remainder, financed by Housing Corporation loans, to be serviced by net income from fair rents after management and maintenance have been paid for.

By comparison with council housing this is an extraordinarily high rate of subsidy. In 1976–7 government expenditure cuts threatened a 50 per cent reduction in the housing associations' programme, but this was partially avoided by a £50 million loan secured by the Housing Corporation, with government encouragement, from a consortium of merchant banks.[46] This overt intermeshing of public bodies and private capital is unusual in the welfare field.

Modern housing associations are essentially of two kinds – 'co-ownership' and 'fair rent'. Co-ownership means that tenants' monthly payments include an element of capital going towards partial ownership of the dwelling; however, this half-way house on the way to owner-occupation has not proved very attractive in recent years because of high interest rates and rising costs. Since the Housing Finance Act, 1972, most housing association tenants pay 'fair rents' as determined within the rent officer system, and these rents have proved to be as much as 50 per cent or even 75 per cent higher than comparable council rents, since the application of fair rents in the council sector was abandoned in 1974.[47] Housing associations cannot take advantage of pooled historic costs[48] and their management and building costs are probably higher than the council sector, because they cannot make economies of scale and they are not subject to public scrutiny. Lord Goodman (one of Crossman's advisers on the 1965 Rent Act), as Chairman of the Housing Corporation in 1976, complained that fair rents were a 'legal fiction' which meant a 'hidden subsidy' to private tenants of £1.3 billion per annum.[49] He advocated steep rent rises in order to allow tenants to cover costs more fully, yet the National Association of Housing Associations is said to be 'alarmed' at the high level of fair rents bringing the 'credibility' of the movement into question.[50] The credibility of the movement is certainly constrained by the fact that it has both higher rents and higher levels of subsidy than council housing; yet its ideological strength as an alternative to council housing and even a rung on the ladder to owner-occupation will probably sustain it.

Little is known about the structure of individual associations; a 1971 government report suggested that at that time they were manifestly inefficient and unaccountable organisations. Since then, some have grown into bureaucratic organisations not unlike local housing authorities and some have attracted young radical staff keen to democratise the organisations. In general the degree of tenant control in management and decision-making appears to be very limited. Many associations are controlled by groups of architects, surveyors or builders, fronted by boards of management including local notables, church people, etc. Apart from the nomination of tenants, the role of local housing authorities seems fairly peripheral.

All this is not to deny that, in the face of the obvious inadequacies of council housing, housing associations can provide more flexible and attractive forms of accommodation and meet the needs that councils cannot. But 'the faults of local authority housing, deliberately created as a matter of state policy, are picked out in the housing association ideology as the antitheses of the supposed virtues of housing associations'.[51] The rise of the housing associations is a clear example of the depoliticisation or 'reprivatisation' of the welfare state – it is part of a strategy designed to break up the implicit collective strength of council tenants and the predominance of council housing amongst lower-paid workers, and also to open up new avenues for private appropriation of value (by consortia of merchant banks, exchange professionals, etc.) in the consumption of housing by the working class.

OWNER–OCCUPATION

The great expansion of owner-occupation and its penetration into the working class is apparent from Tables 5.1 and 5.2. State policy has, with the exception of the 1939–51 period, encouraged this trend. The relationship between the state and owner-occupation is not usually treated as part of welfare policy. Unlike rent regulation in the private rented sector and council housing provision, the role of the state in relation to owner-occupation is less visible and not obviously enshrined in statute. But it has in fact become the pillar of state housing policy in Britain to encourage working-class owner-occupation, particularly since the 1930s. Rent decontrol, the deliberate unattractiveness of private landlordism and council housing, and the promotion of housing improvement grants are all policies that implicitly favour the growth of owner-occupation. The Consultative Document on Housing Policy (Green Paper) issued in 1977 looks forward to the favoured expansion of home ownership as opposed to council housing: 'More and more people would like to become home owners ... we should not let our concern for those who are badly housed lead us to overlook the reasonable housing ambitions of the community in general ... public sector housing investment must be directed more selectively.'[52]

In the Green Paper council housing and private renting are presented as tenures for 'the less eligible', while owner-occupation is presented as the aspiration of all rational individuals and families – 'for most people owning one's own home is a basic and natural desire'.[53] This is not merely an ideological statement of the government's hopes; it means that state policy will ensure that owner-occupation remains the most attractive form of housing consumption for those who can afford it, and hence within the current context most consumers will choose owner-occupation. This is a 'choice' which has been structured in advance by state policy, as we hope to show.

Engels, writing in 1872, argued that 'the essence of the big bourgeois and petty-bourgeois solutions to the "housing question" is that the worker could own his own dwelling'.[54] He goes on to show that the housing question cannot be separated from the exigencies of the capital–labour relation (e.g. income and employment insecurity) and hence that owner-occupation itself cannot solve the housing question. However, the ideological significance of owner-occupation is not dismissed by Engels, who attacks the bourgeois social reformer, Herr Sax, quoted as suggesting that the working-class owner-occupier

... has reached the highest conceivable state of economic independence; he has a territory on which he can rule with sovereign power; he is his own master ... he would become a capitalist and be safeguarded against the dangers of unemployment or incapacitation as a result of the credit which his real estate would open to him. He would thus be raised from the ranks of the propertyless into the propertied class.[55]

This is a classical instance of ideological fetishisation, in which capitalism is reduced to the relations of consumption, so that the 'freedom' of the working-class property owner renders him/her economically independent. As Engels points out, in any major slump workers' housing would not command much credit. On the other hand, Herr Sax captures something of the attraction of owner-occupation to the working class and the bourgeoisie alike – it does bring workers into property ownership and the status conveyed thereby, as well as being an individual 'stake in the system', no doubt strengthening acquiescence with capitalist relations of production. These ideological factors help to explain the strong support for owner-occupation amongst many people both within and outside the Labour movement.

In Engels' time owner-occupation was not a possible choice for most workers, because both the level and security of incomes was very low, but in the last 40 years these conditions have changed. It is not impossible that a contraction in real wages and greater insecurity of employment in the current economic down-turn could lead to an enforced withdrawal of workers from owner-occupation, though such a situation could only arise in the midst of a massive political and economic crisis. The advantages of owner-occupation for the working class as individual consumers are quite considerable in the current context – for example, the relative security of tenure, freedom from restrictions on the house's use and alteration, as a form of saving and security for old age and so on. The disadvantages are precisely the other side of the coin of this individuation – it saddles the individual worker with a large long-term debt, it individuates the cost of repairs and maintenance, and any fall in the market value represents a great loss of savings. The burden of owner-occupation is felt much more strongly in a recession, accompanied by a fall in real incomes and house prices. Obviously council housing does not individuate housing costs to the same extent, although here too the loss of a job may lead to arrears and the loss of a tenancy. There is no adequate way of quantitatively comparing the costs and benefits of owner-occupation and council housing, since this depends so much on future house price and interest rate trends as well as state policy.[56]

Unlike private renting and council housing, owner-occupation involves the consumption of housing directly in the commodity form, and the house can be resold at any time. The price of the commodity will be directly related to the value of newly built housing, that is the socially necessary labour time required in its construction, and it will also be affected by short-term gluts and shortages. The movement of house prices in relation to average earnings and general price levels over the past 40 years shows that, ignoring the periods of great shortage (1946–50 and 1972–5), there is a reasonably direct correlation between house prices and average earnings, suggesting that the proportion of the value of labour power devoted to housing has stayed quite stable for owner-occupiers at least.[57] On the other hand, this trend combined with the great increase in the price of housing relative to other consumer commodities indicates the great expansion in working-class consumption and possibly the relatively slow fall in the socially necessary labour time required in the production of housing compared to other consumer commodities.

Because owner-occupation is such a costly investment, and since it also involves legal title to landed property, the market in this commodity requires a large number of intermediaries or exchange professionals – solicitors, estate agents, surveyors, etc. – to facilitate the process of realisation of surplus value for the builder and the process of exchange for the consumer. In these processes the exchange professionals appropriate value via that part of the consumer's wage and the builder's surplus value contributing to their fees. Since housing is an essential use-value, the seller is usually a buyer as well, so that these transactions are continually reproduced. Clearly the state provides the legal framework within which all this takes place, but it is not otherwise concerned in the regulation of these important aspects of the private housing market, which go beyond finance and the effects of clearance and rehabilitation policy.

The great cost of owner-occupied housing makes it necessary for working-class consumers to borrow money capital, and here value is appropriated by the lender in the form of interest payments on these borrowings. In 1975 there were 10.4 million owner-occupied dwellings in the UK, of which 56 per cent were mortgaged. A very substantial number of houses are therefore owned outright, either by people with sufficient money capital to pay cash or by those who have paid off their mortgage, including growing numbers of older workers. The interests of these people are substantially different from those with a large mortgage, since they are not involved with lending institutions and are not directly concerned with interest rates. In what follows we shall, however, be concentrating on the mortgage finance of owner-occupation, because this now closely involves the state and crucially affects the housing market for all consumers. It is important to note that while the media and the government concentrate most attention on the situation of mortgagers, in 1974 the 4.3 million mortgagers in the UK were distinctly outnumbered by the 6.2 million council tenants.

In 1975 the average outstanding debt per building society mortgager was £4262 at an average interest rate of 11.1 per cent, and the total value of all outstanding UK housing loans was £24.4 billion.[58] This £24.4 billion was provided by those who lend their money to building societies (77 per cent of the total), local authorities (11 per cent), banks (5 per cent) and insurance companies (6 per cent). Most of this money is provided by small savers, but a substantial proportion is provided by large investors (i.e. over £5000); in 1974 this proportion amounted to about a quarter of building society investment, according to government estimates,[59] and institutional investment in building societies is increasing in importance. In the UK the building societies are the predominant source of finance for owner-occupation and they enjoy an extraordinary status within British civil society as bastions of security, stability and caution, no matter how often this is punctured by a collapse, fraud, slump or scandal. They have attracted the criticism from social reformers that their lending policies sometimes prohibit the improvement of working-class housing and deny access to housing finance for those in need. One example is the practice of 'red lining', whereby building societies are reticent about lending money to finance house purchase in poorer urban areas, around which they informally draw a red line on the map.[60] Clearly the building societies regard the housing in such areas as a bad investment and the prospective mortgagers as potentially unreliable repayers. The building societies are thus 'encouraging urban decay and dereliction' and 'creating the very uncertainty about property values which makes them reluctant to lend on older properties and areas in the first instance'.[61]

The social 'irresponsibility' of the building societies takes on rather a different aspect if one looks at the nature of their interests. Firstly, the devaluation of inner city older properties further stimulates demand for new suburban houses, which are far more attractive investments. Secondly, the building societies' sole interest is to enhance the investment of those who lend them money, and this does not coincide with making possibly risky advances. Investment in older and cheaper property for lower income groups remains a risky proposition precisely because of continuing insecurity of employment, wages and property values. It is sometimes argued that the building societies are still unnecessarily cautious, and that they are rarely forced to repossess houses. But in fact the building societies' fortunes are becoming increasingly volatile and their fundamental structure necessitates their conservatism. Essentially they borrow short-term money and lend it long term, and they are therefore very vulnerable to changes in short-term lending. In other words there is nothing to stop building society investors trying to withdraw their money virtually on demand, but if this happened, the societies would have to start repossessing owner-occupied property. In order to avoid such a disaster, the societies have to adopt conservative lending policies and promote confidence in themselves as secure and safe havens for 'family savings' and reliable lenders. Building society managers 'are judged by their ability to identify "good payers" and to avoid defaulters'[62] and by the security of the property on which they lend. They are also judged by their ability to create links with local potential investors, builders, and exchange professionals in the promotion of new suburban owner-occupation. Thus 'the key qualities that a manager is expected to have are an ability to forge useful links with the business and professional community'.[63]

The interests of builders, estate agents, surveyors, solicitors and building societies obviously coincide, and this is reflected in the many personal connections, partnerships and common directorships amongst them. There are, for example, four local building societies in North Shields which have a total of thirty directors, including five solicitors, two estate agents, two builders and five accountants.[64] The building societies' policies are shaped by the interests of their investors, and are harnessed with those of the builders and exchange professionals appropriating and extracting value from the exchange and production of housing. By their very nature they are not concerned with those welfare needs of their potential and actual borrowers which do not coincide with their own financial interests. Undoubtedly the societies take great pains to ease the problems of those who fall into arrears on their mortgage, not least to avoid bad publicity. Nevertheless, the number of families made homeless by mortgage arrears is rising; the welfare organisation Shelter estimates[65] that there were over 4000 such families in 1976 (including many with local authority mortgages), and in 1975 about 100,000 households had their mortgage interest repayments met by the Supplementary Benefits Commission. Mortgage insecurity has particularly affected women who have been deserted by their husbands, for they are often kept in ignorance of arrears by husbands and building societies alike.[66]

Many working-class applicants for building society mortgages, particularly those confined to the 'red line areas', resort to the clearing banks, fringe finance or local authority mortgages. In the period October 1972–4 49 per cent of newly purchased owner-occupied dwellings in Saltley, Birmingham, were financed by clearing bank loans at rates of interest considerably in excess of those charged by the building societies, which only provided 7 per cent of the new mortgages.[67] In towns and cities all over the country various back-street sources of housing finance lend at high rates of interest to clients who are either unattractive to the building societies or unaware of their services. Needless to say, fringe financiers borrow their money in turn from clearing banks and finance companies, who thereby extract further absolute rent and value out of the housing market by taking advantage of the immobility of ghetto inhabitants, while disguising the role of respectable financial institutions by the use of intermediaries.

Local authorities can make house purchase loans, and since the 1950s this has facilitated the extension of home-ownership to people beyond the reach of the building societies. The pattern of local authority house purchase lending has, however, been determined more by short-term economic and political factors than as a distinct arm of housing policy. In the early years of the 1974–9 Labour government, local authority lending reached record levels (over 100,000 loans in England and Wales in 1975) as a pragmatic means of injecting some life into the lower reaches of the housing market; 88 per cent of these loans went to first-time purchasers and 34 per cent were for 100 per cent of the valuation of the house. But in 1976 the number of local authority housing loans slumped to only 28,000, as public expenditure cuts began to bite hard. The government has tried to encourage the building societies to fill the gap, but not surprisingly, in view of the above analysis, they have failed to respond very effectively.[68]

An index of the effects of building society policies is suggested by a comparison of the proportions of West Indians, Asians and whites who have mortgages with building societies. In 1974 a survey showed that 73 per cent of white owner-occupiers with mortgages had borrowed from a building society, but the proportions for West

Indians and Asians respectively were 51 per cent and 43 per cent; 39 per cent and 33 per cent of West Indians and Asians mortgagers respectively borrowed from the local authorities compared to only 13 per cent of whites.[69] The building societies clearly regard prospective black borrowers and the property they want to buy as bad investments. This is both a reflection of the employment and housing situation facing black people, and an instance of the institutional racism which pervades the private housing market.

We must conclude that short of a fundamental change in their relationship to investors, borrowers and the state, the building societies will continue to operate more or less completely in the interests of their investors, and it is idle to consider that they have social or welfare responsibilities. The building societies' very positive status as private institutions has been and continues to be actively sanctified by the state. They are ostensibly regulated by the Chief Registrar of Friendly Societies, but 'it is clear that the Registrar feels that the "social role" of the societies and their economic significance are not his concern'.[70] The most important ways in which the state promotes the building society movement is by according them, their borrowers and their investors highly favourable tax and investment status. This is so much the case that the Governor of the Bank of England on behalf of the City has recently expressed concern that the building societies are attracting money capital away from other forms of investment, notably industrial production.[71] Firstly, the state supports the building societies by allowing them to pay a composite rate of income tax on behalf of investors. This arrangement was established in 1894 and 'allows richer investors to get more than the market rate of interest', and also allows the building societies to raise funds more cheaply than other institutions, so that 'effectively half of all building society investors pay tax when they need not and subsidise the rich investor'.[72] This position is legitimated by the building societies' status as 'non-profit-making' organisations, although their 'profits' are manifested in the form of interest payments to investors and their considerable management and advertising expenses.

Secondly, the state underwrites building society risk, most obviously by lending them money in times of difficulty, as in 1974. Paradoxically the 1974 crisis was the indirect result of the introduction of the Competition and Credit Control policy in 1971, which was designed to make British financial institutions competitive within the EEC. This pitched the building societies into a more competitive market for deposits, resulting in the volatile movements of interest rates and building society fortunes of recent times. Thirdly, the state effectively subsidises mortgagers by granting tax relief on their interest repayments, perhaps the most significant example of what Titmuss has called 'fiscal welfare'.[73] In 1976–7 this assistance, as the government prefers to call it, amounted to £205 per mortgaged house in the UK at a total cost of £1.2 billion, while government and rate subsidy to council tenants (excluding rent rebates) was £210 per tenant, costing £1.3 billion. The levels of assistance to the two major tenures have remained roughly comparable for many years when calculated on this basis. Many housing pressure groups, trade unions and various Labour Party branches have emphasised that this form of assistance to mortgagers particularly benefits those with higher incomes and better houses, since they receive relatively greater tax relief.[74] In 1977, however, the Labour government firmly rejected any reforms on the politically sensitive grounds that 'we certainly do not believe that the household budgets of millions of families – which have been planned in good faith in the reasonable expectation that present arrangements would broadly continue – should be overturned in pursuit of some theoretical or academic dogma'.[75] The theoretical or academic dogma referred to is, of course, the idea that the welfare state should not quite so patently redistribute wealth to the advantage of the highly paid and better off.

The building societies continue, therefore, to be given favourable treatment by governments in order to facilitate their pre-eminent role as the promoters of owner-occupation. The building society movement emerged in the late eighteenth century as a means of cooperative self-finance by groups of artisans and skilled workers; it was to some extent designed with the needs of the urban working class in mind. The movement undoubtedly attracted workers' savings, but the incomes and job security of most workers were insufficient to enable them to keep up with a mortgage. In 1920 there were 750,000 building society investors with an average investment of £100, and about 230,000 borrowers. By 1940 there were 2 million share accounts and 1½ million borrowers. The first significant growth of mass owner-occupation took place in the inter-war period, particularly in the 1930s, in the suburbs of the Midlands and the South East, where the new industries of advanced capitalism were developing, and attracting relatively well paid labour, whose housing needs were not met by private or public landlordism. Many of the new owner-occupiers were white-collar workers and state employees whose greater employment security ensured the availability of a mortgage. After the political defeat of the Labour movement in 1931, the National government was free to end subsidies for new council housing with the exception of slum clearance, so that 'the decks were cleared for what was to become the biggest private building boom in British history . . . small houses for sale',[76] bought with a building society mortgage. These houses dominated the building boom.

The building society movement, which had always had official blessings, was publicised and elevated into a sort of crusade for good against evil. Implicitly there was a partnership between the building societies and the National government.[77] After the financial crises of 1929–31 the building societies increasingly attracted large corporate investors looking for relative safety at low rates of interest. This fuelled the boom in new owner-occupation, which played a major part in the revival of capital accumulation and was possibly 'the symbol and main carrier of British industrial recovery from the Great Depression', with its multiplier effect on consumption and employment.[78]

In the post-war period the building society movement steadily expanded alongside the increase in owner-occupation; between 1950 and 1975 the number of building society mortgages increased from 1.5 million to 4.4 million. This expansion has not been quite so smooth and happy as it might appear, however. We have already noted the effects of competition for investment, and volatile interest rates, as well as the essential vulnerability of the building society operation, which generates conservatism. While the number of out-standing mortgages has increased every year since 1950, the increase has varied very significantly from year to year, slumping to only 41,000 in 1974, for example. This reflects in part the increasing number of mortgages that are coming to an end each year, which means that the building societies are constantly looking for good new business, such as that which might be provided by the sale of certain council houses.

The great post-war expansion of working-class owner-occupation and building society borrowing has gradually drawn governments into a relationship with the building societies which goes beyond fiscal and ideological support. Since the 1960s governments have attempted to limit wage increases and the expansion of the value of labour power through prices and incomes policies. In 1964–5 the Labour government put informal pressure on the building societies not to raise interest rates, and referred the question to the National Board for Prices and Incomes in order to delay the increase.[79] The importance of the building societies in relation to incomes policy has become more obvious in the 1970s, and has been recognised in the Social Contract between the trade unions and the Labour government and in the recent Housing Green Paper. In 1973 the government lent the building societies £15 million to keep mortgage rates down and negotiated a Memorandum of Agreement with the Building Societies Association. This agreement assured continued government support for owner-occupation, and joint attempts to stabilise house prices and to maintain 'an orderly housing market'.[80] Civil servants and the building societies have since been devising all sorts of schemes for encouraging owner-occupation for lower income groups, as well as trying to prevent frequent changes in interest rates, and rationing mortgages in order to prevent a house price boom. The building societies are now partially incorporated into the state apparatus, because of the importance of mortgage costs as a part of workers' spending and hence their effect on wage demands.

It may appear from this analysis and from government pronouncements that working-class owner-occupation is unquestionably the form of tenure which most closely accords with the interests of capital in general, but this is not necessarily the case. On the one hand, owner-occupation reinforces the notion of the worker as property owner and 'capitalist'; it individualises debts and maintenance costs and reproduces consumer status divisions which cut across class divisions, so that owner-occupiers are far less cohesive politically and sociologically than tenants. On the other hand, the volatile forces of the housing market create all kinds of disequilibria, which affect wage demands, labour mobility and even the availability of investment capital. In Western Europe the proportions of owner-occupation are much lower than in Britain, and in Sweden the proportion of owner-occupied households fell from 43.9 per cent in 1945 to 35.2 per cent in 1970.[81] It cannot simply be assumed that owner-occupation is the 'natural' form of tenure according with the interests of capital or indeed labour. Nevertheless, in Britain the encouragement of working-class owner-occupation is the cornerstone of both Labour and Conservative housing policy, which confines the state to the task of relatively covert regulation of housing finance in particular and the housing market in general. The thinly disguised policy of ending further expansion of council housing and the attempts to devalue council tenancy are the fruits of governments' realisation of the political and economic consequences of such direct involvement in working-class housing, to which we now turn.

6

Council Housing

In Britain the most direct involvement of the state in housing is the provision and management of what is popularly known as 'council housing', whereby the local authority under government supervision acts as a major housing developer and landlord. As Table 5.1 indicates, before the First World War there were virtually no council houses in Britain, but today about 30 per cent of the housing stock is occupied by tenants of the local authorities, though it seems that this steady growth over five decades has now reached its peak. The extent of direct government provision of housing in Britain exceeds by far the provision in other capitalist countries. In Western Europe governments fund workers' housing through 'quasi-public bodies' similar to housing associations, while in the USA public housing only accounts for 2 per cent of the housing stock.[1]

As Table 5.2 shows, council tenants tend to be lower-paid and lower-status workers, largely those who cannot afford to enter owner-occupation and for whom private landlordism is increasingly neither attractive nor available. Council housing is a major pillar of the welfare state, alongside state education, the National Health Service (NHS) and the social security system. As Table 6.1 shows, state housing expenditure as a proportion of gross domestic product has varied considerably over the years; the bulk of this expenditure has been devoted to council house building and improvement and the variations reflect changing government commitment to the council housing sector. A great expansion in commitment occurred in the immediate post-war period and to a lesser extent in the early phases of the 1964 and 1974 Labour governments. There was a distinct withdrawal of commitment under the Tory return to the free market in the late 1950s and early 1960s, and also in the second phases of the post-war Labour governments. These policy variations are discussed in more detail in what follows.

TABLE 6.1 Percentage gross domestic product devoted to public housing expenditure (current and capital added)

Year	GDP%	Year	GDP%
1924–26	1.6	1970	2.7
1934–36	1.2	1972	2.2
1938	1.6	1972–3	2.4
1950	3.1	1973–4	3.6
1953	3.7	1974–5	4.9
1960	1.8	1975–6	4.1
1965	2.5	1976–7	3.9
1968	2.9		

SOURCES *Housing Policy: Technical Volume 1* (London: HMSO, 1977) Table I.26; *The Government's Expenditure Plans 1978–79 to 1981–82*, Cmnd. 7049 (London: HMSO, 1978) vol. I, Table 6; vol. II, Table 5.11.

Unlike state provision of health services, social security and education, council housing does not overwhelmingly predominate over private provision (with the possible exception of some places in the North of England and Scotland), nor is it provided free to individual consumers. Council housing has always existed in the interstices of a predominantly private housing market which has directly shaped its whole nature, as a form of public landlordism rather than a more benevolent welfare service. Council housing has filled the gap left by the decline of the private landlord and the growth of owner-occupation and new forms of private landlordism. Like the NHS, state education and the post-Beveridge social security system, council housing has received strong support from the Labour movement and, until recently, this was a fairly solid plank in the political platform of Labourism. Council housing has brought much higher housing standards to many working-class people at significant levels of subsidisation, and represents a very important gain for the working class. This is not, however, to argue that council housing is an outpost of socialism within a capitalist society. In fact it is intimately bound up with loan finance, private landed property and private builders. As in other housing tenures, value is privately appropriated in the consumption of council housing, mostly through the interest payments made to loan capital which covers the cost of council housing; in addition absolute and differential rent may be capitalised in the cost of the land to the local authority, and since most council housing is built by private contractors, they extract surplus value in its production.

Unlike the NHS and the social security system, council housing still remains under local political control, enabling tenants and their representatives to exert some local collective political influence. Hence the forms and levels of subsidisation have traditionally been an area of political class struggle. The extent of local political and tenant control of council housing is severely limited in practice, firstly, by the financial constraints imposed by central government, and, secondly, by the forms of housing management adopted by the councils' officers, which use bureaucratism as a means of rationing expenditure and neutralising conflict and tenants' independent organisation. In what follows we shall try to examine central financial constraints and local management control in the context of the class struggle over council housing.

THE EMERGENCE OF COUNCIL HOUSING

Before 1914 about 20,000 houses and flats had been built for letting by English local authorities without government subsidy but with capital borrowed through the government's Public Works Loan Commissioners. It was not until 1919, with the introduction of government subsidy, that council housing began to make an impact. This significant departure from 'laissez-faire' government cannot simply be traced to the exigencies of the post-war crisis or to inspired changes in attitudes amongst the bourgeoisie.[2] From the 1880s onwards, in the period of classical imperialism, working-class influence on state policy no longer evoked blunt responses, but increasingly provoked more sophisticated intervention, as the class struggle and state policy both became shaped by working-class electoral power. Labour representatives and their Liberal allies on town councils successfully pressed for experiments in building working-class housing. In West Ham in 1898 the first socialist group in local government was elected; it was committed to publicly financed housing, the direct employment of building labour and improved workers' dwellings in its brief 5-year reign. However, council schemes were usually small and experimental, and only attracted better-off tenants.

Considerable local pressure for subsidised municipal housing was generated by trades councils and local tenants' organisations[3] and national conferences of trades councils on housing were held in 1902, 1905, 1907 and 1909. The London Trades Council organised large demonstrations in Hyde Park in order to press the London County Council into activity in developing municipal housing. The Workmen's National Housing Council (WNHC) was formed in 1898 to press for council housing and 'fair rent courts' for private tenants. WNHC got TUC support in 1902 for the proposal of interest-free government loans to local authorities for house-building. WNHC kept the housing question alive as a working-class political issue at the national level both within the Labour movement and in Parliament during the Edwardian period. The more bourgeois-influenced and conservative National Housing Reform Council is sometimes misleadingly portrayed as the most significant pressure group in the achievement of subsidised council housing, although it virtually opposed such a policy until the First World War. It concentrated its energy on the use of local authorities as simply land assemblers for the private sector, and changed its name to the National Housing and Town Planning Council in 1909, after its successful promotion of the first town planning act. In 1909, also, a deputation of Scottish miners pressed for government action on the housing shortage; eventually a royal commission on the Scottish housing question was appointed, concluding in its 1917 report that only local authorities subsidised by the state could provide housing for lower-paid workers. In Scotland today council housing accounts for well over half the housing stock. In 1913 the Conservative party even came out in support of subsidised municipal housing to deal with the housing shortage, but the 1909 Liberal government, so often portrayed as a progressive welfare administration, firmly rejected several bills to this effect. Before the First World War, therefore, working-class pressure in the context of the decline of the private landlord had all but achieved subsidised council housing.

During and immediately after the First World War it became clear to the government that housing reform would be vital in maintaining working-class loyalty and containing any real or imaginary threat of Bolshevism, as expressed in Lloyd George's famous promise of 'homes fit for heroes to live in'. The housing agitation by munitions workers in 1915 put housing firmly on the agenda of the various government reconstruction committees, and in 1917 the Commission of Inquiry into Industrial Unrest reported that housing conditions were a major factor creating unrest, and called for mass provision of cheap housing. With the sudden end of the war, mass demobilisation and general industrial unrest, early in 1919 the government introduced a virtually unlimited subsidy for council housing, which assisted the provision of 170,000 houses. This had the intended effect of cooling out workers' aspirations, though it did not help to soak up unemployment as hoped, because of the building unions' resistance to dilution. By mid-1921 the subsidy was abandoned as the government tightened its grip on state capital expenditure, and the dole took the burden of pacifying the working class.

Exchequer subsidies of a limited amount per house were introduced in 1923, and these also assisted the construction of 430,000 privately built houses in the inter-war period. Perhaps the greatest achievement of the first Labour government of 1924 was Wheatley's increase in the council housing subsidy, which assisted in the construction of over half a million council houses in the 1920s. Dickens has pointed to the ironies of Wheatley's policy which was

> ... proposing to double local authorities' loan debts, reduce housing space standards, allowing the building industry to lay down its own terms and penalise tenants if building costs should rise ... Wheatley was the first to agree that his proposals were 'anything but Socialistic proposals ... I want to get houses'. He saw the state's role largely as one of protecting private enterprise from itself...[4]

The establishment of council housing subsidies in the period 1919–24 came about as a result of working–class pressure and applied considerable state resources to the provision of working-class housing. In that sense it was a victory for the working class, but it was not a victory that industrial capital, and the construction industry in particular, resented. The establishment of a major council housing sector in the 1920s may equally be seen as a victory for the capitalist state, firstly, in meeting the strength of working–class demands with public landlordism in partnership with loan capital and the building industry, and, secondly, in its ability to meet the requirements for the reproduction of labour power in the interests of capital in general without upsetting particular interests. After the defeats of 1926 and 1931 the Labour movement's commitment to council housing waned. In the context of the private building boom of the 1930s, the National government was able to lower council house building standards and confine the role of local authorities to rehousing people affected by slum clearance.

GOVERNMENT CONTROL OF COUNCIL HOUSING

It had been reaffirmed in 1919 that the local authorities were to be the state agency responsible for public housing. During the First World War the government itself erected hostels for munitions workers, and there was some feeling that the government itself should develop public housing. Perhaps in order to diffuse the political responsibility the government gave the local authorities discretionary power to implement the housing acts, which has generated a very significant variation in council house provision amongst local authorities. The notion of establishing a state housing corporation was not closely considered; it was not until the 1930s that centralised bureaucratic administration of welfare emerged out of the poor law crisis. Governments have been able to regulate council housing policies quite effectively by changing subsidy arrangements and by their power to control local authority borrowing.

Every housing scheme or, more recently, programme planned by a local authority has to be submitted to the government for the local authority to obtain permission to borrow money in order to build; this is called loan sanction. Governments control the borrowing activity of the local authorities closely in the attempt to regulate and structure both private and public capital investment. The fluctuations in annual council house completions to some extent, therefore, reflect the 'stop-go' economic policies of the Keynesian era, and housing expenditure like other welfare spending has been used as a short-term Keynesian regulator of the economy. Control of loan sanction allows the government to draw tight parameters around local housing expenditure when this becomes necessary, without explicitly and controversially reducing subsidies. This technique has been resorted to by all Labour governments since the Second World War, notably in the economic crises which emerged in 1947, 1967–8 and 1975–6. Labour's Minister of Housing in 1945, Aneurin Bevan, had hopes for a great council housing drive, but this was substantially undermined by the financial crisis of 1947, when the Treasury imposed cuts and 'it became the main function of the Ministry to stop local authorities building too much'.[5] The failure of Bevan's housing programme contributed much to the defeat of Labour in 1951. When Labour returned to power in 1964, the Minister of Housing was Richard Crossman, who suggests in his diary that he was 'very remote from anything Harold [Wilson] suggested when he talked about organising a housing drive'.[6] Crossman argues that the power over the housing drive lies with the Treasury, which controls the purse strings. The failure of Labour's 1960s housing drive once more turned on the cuts in public spending imposed in the post-1967 crisis years. Again in 1974 Labour expanded council house building, but by 1976 this programme was again foundering as the government imposed severe restraints on local authority spending and borrowing.

Alongside loan sanction, governments have used the Exchequer subsidy to council housing itself as a means of shaping local policy. These subsidies have until recently come in the form of a certain amount of money per annum per council house for the length of the 60-year loan taken out to build the house. The amount of subsidy varies with the act of Parliament under which the house was built, and has in recent years varied with the design and purpose of the house and the local authority's financial situation. Subsidies have thus been used to regulate not only the number of houses built, but also their standards, design and amenities. A most striking example of this form of government control occurred in the early 1950s when the Conservatives, anxious to make political capital over the failure of Labour's post-war housing drive, raised the subsidies and lowered the approved building standards. This resulted in what has become known as the Macmillan boom in council house building (after the minister behind it), which created some of the worst ghetto estates of the 1970s. Later, in 1956, as part of their policy of resurrecting private housing, the Conservatives halved the council housing subsidy and limited council house building to 'special needs' provisions (for the victims of slum clearance, old people, etc.) through the subsidy arrangements. In the mid-1950s the government still faced an acute housing crisis, so that:

> The slum clearance policy, the difficulty of decanting 'overspill' resulting from the clearance schemes and the comparative failure of the New Towns policy to relieve the pressure on the waiting lists led to an increased reliance on high density. In the fifties high density meant high rise ... In 1956 an additional subsidy was provided for flats above six storeys.[7]

Cost consciousness and the emergence of 'mass produced' industrialised building methods also encouraged the government to promote high-rise developments. The council housing subsidy was used to encourage high density high-rise building, and the large building corporations that promoted industrialised building were able to further their domination of the public house-building sector. The high-rise and other high density designs have of course created innumerable social problems for tenants, and are now recognised to have been a disaster inflicted on 3 million tenants for many years to come.

The Labour government increased the number of council houses built between 1964 and 1968 by higher subsidies and more generous rationing of loan sanction. The Housing Subsidies Act, 1967, changed the character of subsidy in favour of compensating local authorities directly for the high interest rates which they were now paying for their loans. In the summer of 1967 the economic crisis had an immediate effect on the housing programme, with the introduction of the cost yardstick, which lays down maximum costs for all the varieties and components of council housing. The yardstick effectively rationed loan sanctions and reduced building standards, particularly in the more recent period of high cost inflation.[8] The cost yardstick is an important example of central bureaucratic control over local housing authorities; its inflexibility and arbitrariness has led to criticism of central bureaucratism by local officers. Once again, however, it is merely a rationing device which operates largely unseen by the public.

The development of the council housing subsidy and government control of council housing has undergone innumerable and complex changes in the 1970s. We shall return to this question after examining council house rents and costs at the local level.

COUNCIL HOUSING COSTS AND RENTS

Loan sanction merely gives the local authorities permission to enter several market places – the housing land market, the house-building market and the money market – and the state has done relatively little directly to limit these costs, with the notable exception of the immediate post-war period, when the building industry was subject to licensing and some price control. Obviously a local authority's capital expenditure on council housing is determined by the size of its programme, and thence by the cost of land, site works and building. In 1974 the average total cost of a council house in England and Wales was £9520, 74 per cent of which was taken up by building costs, 11 per cent by site works and 15 per cent by land costs. There have been enormous local variations in these costs, as well as a great upward movement of prices, particularly in the last decade, with cost inflation and fluctuations of the property market.[9] In relation to building land, local authorities, particularly in the large cities, have suffered from the explosion in property prices and rents. Hence, for example,

> ... the shortage and high price of land affected Lambeth acutely. The clearance of sites for redevelopment to make a 'housing gain' became the main hope of eventually overcoming the housing short-age. This meant that the council had to rehouse more families in the new dwellings on a given site than it displaced when demo-lishing the old.[10]

In London local housing authorities have been excluded from using cheap suburban land zoned for low density housing, and have been forced to confine themselves to 'windfall sites', 'where a change of use has taken place or to sites previously considered unsuitable for human habitation [e.g. Thamesmead, a marshland site in Green-wich]'.[11] They have thus been forced to build on these sites at very high densities. The Poulson affair in the North East of England and the Bryants affair in Birmingham have uncovered a considerable degree of corruption in placing huge council building contracts, which no doubt adds to the cost.

Turning to local authorities' current expenditure on council hous-ing, this is dominated, as Table 6.2 shows, by the debt interest repay-ments incurred in borrowing capital, which have throughout the post-war period accounted for between 60 and 65 per cent of costs. The local authorities have to borrow their money on the open money markets, so that in 1974–5 the average rate of interest for new local authority loans reached a record level of 13.8 per cent. It may seem surprising that the proportion of expenditure devoted to debt redemp-tion and interest repayments has decreased slightly over the past decade. This largely reflects the declining levels of new council house building in this period, and increased concentration on refurbishing old estates. The relative expansion of spending on what is called

TABLE 6.2   Housing revenue account expenditure for all local authorities in England and Wales

Year	Repairs and maintenance		Supervision and management		Capital debt redemption		Debt interest repayments	
	£m	% total	£m	% total	£m	% total	£m	% total
1969–70	101	14.4	56	8.0	76	10.8	451	64.2
1970–71	115	14.7	68	8.7	81	10.3	500	63.8
1971–72	126	14.7	82	9.6	88	10.3	507	59.2
1972–73	183	18.7	106	10.8	93	9.5	556	56.9
1973–74	203	16.8	126	10.4	101	8.4	726	60.1
1974–75	264	16.3	188	11.6	116	7.2	988	61.0
1975–76	340	17.2	254	12.8	137	6.9	1180	59.7

NOTE   Percentages do not add up to 100 per cent because of other minor forms of expenditure.

SOURCE   *Housing Policy: Technical Volume 1* (London: HMSO, 1977) Table IV.9.

'supervision and management', which only accounted for 7 per cent of spending in the 1950s and 1960s, reflects both an improvement in wages for local authority staff and the increasingly labour-intensive nature of local housing administration, with the expansion of rent rebate schemes, advisory services and so on. Above all, in relation to costs, we must note the enormous inflation in the current cost of council housing over the past decade, which has far outstripped the retail price index and the rise in average earnings. Land, building and loan finance costs have all risen dramatically; for example, current costs per council house dwelling tripled between 1967–8 and 1975–6, and virtually doubled between 1972–3 and 1975–6.[12]

Naturally the level of costs largely determines the level of council house rents, and until the mid-1970s rents covered between 60 and 75 per cent of council housing costs. Central government has not tried to lay down fixed rules for setting council rents, with the exception of the brief interlude provided by the 1972 Housing Finance Act, which is considered below. Between 1919 and 1921 local authorities had to obtain ministry approval of rent levels, and if the ministry disagreed, the matter was referred to a tribunal. Since then, local authorities have been 'free' to fix rents for individual houses, although aggregate rents are of course strictly limited by the need to balance the accounts and the strict upper limits to state subsidies. Some local authorities have pursued a high rent/low subsidy policy while others have done the reverse. Until recently there remained great differences between local policies, and the low rent/high subsidy policy was often, but by no means always, pursued by Labour-controlled authorities. In general the fluctuations in building costs and subsidies have been determinants of rents as much as party political conviction.

In the inter-war period council rents were on average 50 per cent higher than working-class-controlled rents in the private sector, so that at least until 1932 'the market for local authority houses was largely confined to a limited range of income groups, that is in practice the better-off semi-skilled workers with small families and fairly safe jobs'.[13] After 1933 slum clearance brought lower quality council housing to poorer working-class people, and in the post-war period increasing uniformity of rent levels and a broad working-class composition of tenants has emerged.

Since 1935 each local authority has kept one current account for all its council houses built or acquired under subsidy. On the expenditure side, as already mentioned, all debt charges, and management and maintenance expenses are aggregated, whilst on the income side all rents and subsidies are aggregated; this is called the Housing Revenue Account (HRA). The establishment of the HRA brought both advantages and disadvantages to council tenants, but at least it focused the financial basis of council housing, so that rents are set on the basis of 'pooled historic costs'. In other words, the rent for a particular council house is not related to its own cost of construction, but is part of a consolidated pool of all council rents, which are in turn directly related to the levels of costs and subsidies incurred by the local authority. In effect tenants in older council houses, usually built and financed at lower cost, 'subsidise' tenants in newer, more expensive houses. The loans on most council houses built before the Second World War have now been paid off, although many of them now require expensive refurbishing, which may require new loans. Nevertheless, these older houses are relatively pure use-values, belonging to the community in the shape of the local authority, and value is not appropriated in their consumption. However, part of the rent paid by tenants of pre-war property contributes to the appropriation of value in the consumption of newer council houses through the pooled historic costs mechanism. Another important feature of council housing is that any capital gains which would have accrued to the local authority if it were a private property owner are in fact socialised and assigned to tenants. Of course the local authority has paid for the land and the building in the first place and still has to pay the costs of finance, but all subsequent gains from property ownership are socialised.[14]

Pooled historic costs and the socialisation of property ownership therefore protect tenants of newer council housing from bearing the full economic cost of its provision, to some extent at the expense of tenants in older property. Hence

> ... the high cost of new council buildings and its concomitant loan costs result in dwellings whose rent levels would make it impossible for working class households to live in them, if the rents were directly based on the costs incurred by the local authority ... The pooling of rents solves the problem without changing the structure of local authority housing provision. The effect of the high cost of new building is resolved at the expense of current tenants in an ideological form which is acceptable, namely rent pooling. In those circumstances, tenants are not subsidising each other but paying the loan charges and building costs imposed on local authority housing.[15]

The protective effect of pooled historic costs has been particularly undermined in recent years by cost inflation and high interest rates, which has meant that the real cost of a local authority housing loan is concentrated in the early repayments. Thus rents and subsidies are increasingly contributing only to the cost of the newest houses. The government has expressed anxiety over this 'front-loading' effect,[16] not least because it has contributed to the great rise in council housing subsidies over recent years. The most striking means of undermining the positive effects of council housing finance as well as reducing the costs incurred by the government is by the sale of council houses to sitting tenants, to which the Labour government is now tacitly committed. Firstly, this accords with the fundamental strategy of encouraging owner–occupation, reducing direct state commitments and leaving council housing as a residual tenure for the poor.[17] Secondly, it rehabilitates council houses as exchange values (particularly pre-war houses) so that value may be privately appropriated in their exchange. Not surprisingly the building societies and the exchange professionals have been very keen to promote council house sales, which open up new opportunities for them. So far tenants have not been attracted to the idea in large numbers. In 1972, the peak year for sales so far, 45,000 council houses were sold in England and Wales, the number falling to only 4582 in 1976. In 1977 sales rose for the first time in 5 years to 11,193, but the future significance of sales will depend on the extent of government financial inducements and tenants' ability to meet the costs of owner-occupation.

Ever since the 1920s there has been government pressure on local authorities to confine subsidisation to 'needy' tenants and to ensure that those who can pay a 'cost rent' or an 'economic rent' do so. The local administrative means of achieving selective subsidisation is a rent rebate scheme, or what is sometimes called a differential rent scheme. Labour's 1930 Housing Act first authorised rent rebate schemes in order to help the poorer tenants who were to be brought into council housing by the slum clearances. In many places the schemes soon spread to cover all tenants, and they were largely financed by rent increases, so that, effectively, better-off tenants were subsidising the slum clearance programme out of their rents. There was therefore considerable resistance to these schemes, led by the Leeds tenants, who brought about the defeat of the Labour council on the issue in 1934.[18] From that time until the 1960s many tenants' organisations and Labour-controlled councils have firmly resisted rent rebate schemes, not only because of the burden on tenants, but because the schemes necessitated a means test – a test of the 'needy' tenant's resources and income. The poor law family means test was notorious in the inter-war period as a means of stigmatising and pauperising the unemployed, so that the application to many of the same people, and with the same effect, of a means test for housing was opposed on a class basis. In Birmingham in 1938, for example, the council announced large rent increases, together with a rent rebate scheme and a means test. After petitions failed to work, a rent strike was called, combined with tenants' meetings and demonstrations. The council responded with evictions, which were prevented by mass demonstrations of tenants. Eventually after over 6 months of struggle the council conceded defeat.[19] In St Pancras in 1959 there was a violent demonstration outside the town hall over rent increases and the introduction of a rebate scheme.

In the 1950s housing was the major local political issue in urban working-class areas, particularly the introduction of rebate schemes, which tended to split local Labour parties.[20] Rent rebate schemes were not resisted solely because of objections to means testing, for 'the primary function of differential rent schemes appears to have been and remains to enable rising costs to be met by rent increases',[21] rather than by subsidy. By the early 1970s most local authorities were operating rent rebate schemes, meeting the cost either from the local rates or by raising the rents, although the value of these rebates was estimated at only £18 million in 1971–2.[22] A statutory rent rebate scheme for all local authorities, with the cost shared by the government and the local rates, was introduced under the Housing Finance Act, 1972. As Table 6.3 shows, rent rebates have now become a major and more permanent feature of welfare spending, despite the repeal of other parts of the act. In 1976 only 56 per cent of council tenants were paying their rents unaided either by rent rebates or supplementary benefits, and the take-up rate is now believed to be between 75 and 80 per cent.[23] This means that about half the 5.3 million council tenants in England and Wales are eligible for a means-tested benefit in aid of their council housing costs. Since

TABLE 6.3   Housing revenue account income for all local authorities in England and Wales

Year	Rents* £m	Rents* % total	Government subsidy £m	Government subsidy % total	Local rates subsidy† £m	Local rates subsidy† % total	Rent rebates‡ £m	Rent rebates‡ % total
1967–68	378	69.7	96	17.7	39	7.2	–	–
1968–69	426	69.4	110	17.9	44	7.2	–	–
1969–70	463	66.3	132	18.9	59	8.5	–	–
1970–71	527	66.6	159	20.1	56	7.1	–	–
1971–72	572	66.6	187	21.8	40	4.7	–	–
1972–73	635	65.1	184	18.9	26	2.7	68	7.0
1973–74	668	55.4	237	19.7	65	5.4	155	12.9
1974–75	726	44.7	485	29.9	136	8.4	193	11.9
1975–76	856	43.1	633	31.9	175	8.8	223	11.2

* Rents of dwellings, net of rebates in 1972–3 and after.
† Excludes rebates in 1972–3 and after.
‡ Met by special combined local and national subsidy in 1972–3 and after.

NOTE   Percentages do not add up to 100 per cent because of other minor forms of expenditure.

SOURCE   *Housing Policy: Technical Volume 1* (London: HMSO, 1977) Table IV.9.

1972–3 rent rebates have accounted for about a quarter of the total subsidies to council housing.

This change in the character of subsidisation was part of the broad strategy behind the Housing Finance Act, 1972, designed to concentrate subsidies on poor tenants rather than generally subsidising the cost of housing construction, thereby also bringing council rents closer to 'market rents'; in other words, raising rents to bring them in line with the rent that they would command in the private rented sector. Subsidising poor tenants was achieved by introducing the statutory rebate system, which divided the interests of better-off tenants from the less well-off; and reducing subsidies on housing construction was attempted by the phased introduction of the 'fair rent' system in use in the private rented sector, as described in Chapter 5.

The Housing Finance Bill was hatched in the early years of the Heath government as part of a renewed attack on working-class organisation and living standards, which included the Industrial Relations Act and disputes in the nationalised industries, notably the Post Office, the mines and docks.[24] The myths that council tenants were pampered and yet undeserving and should be made 'to stand on their own two feet' had been fostered by the media, and government promotion of owner-occupation over many years, even though council housing subsidies remained roughly comparable to mortgage interest tax relief. The Housing Finance Act therefore attempted to reduce subsidies to capital spending on council housing gradually and to increase the burden of cost borne by tenants' rent, thereby discouraging local authorities from building new council houses and increasing the unattractiveness of council tenancy. It was hoped that eventually rent income from better-off tenants would be sufficient to pay for rent rebates for poorer tenants without any other subsidy. Hence in 1972–3 general government subsidies fell both in cash terms and in proportion to other forms of HRA income, for the first time in many years (see Table 6.3). Rents were to be increased by an average of £1 a week in October 1972 and by another 50p. a week at regular intervals until 'fair rent' levels were achieved. The setting of council rents was taken out of the local authorities' hands, not only in order to achieve these rises, but also to create greater national uniformity in rent levels to assist labour mobility and create 'fairness between one citizen and another'.[25] The 'fair rent' system provided an apparently neutral, non-political and technical machinery for legitimating the rent rises. The phased introduction of the rent increases was brought to a halt by the election in February 1974 of a Labour government, which instituted a rent freeze and eventually returned statutory determination of council rents to the local authorities.

The Housing Finance Act provoked the most important heroic working-class resistance to welfare reform since the inter-war years. This undoubtedly contributed to the defeat of the Heath government and brought about the repeal of much of the act, but it also, paradoxically, provides an example of the fragility and weakness of the class struggle within the welfare state. Up to 100,000 council tenants refused at one time or another to pay the rent increases demanded by the act, forty-three Labour-controlled local authorities delayed implementation beyond the statutory date and two Labour councils never implemented – Clay Cross in North Derbyshire and, much less publicised, Bedwas and Machen in Wales.[26] The Labour movement was united in its opposition to the bill; the TUC and the Labour Party conference produced circulars and passed resolutions, even encouraging Labour councils not to implement the act, thus to some extent breaking with the principle of constitutionalism and respect for the law which so often circumscribes and defines Labourism. There was, however, no coordinated attempt to build national, mass opposition by the Labour movement to the act, and it was left to individual Labour councils, trades councils, and tenants' organisations to resist at a local level in isolation from each other. The National Association of Tenants and Residents (NATR) pursued the tactic of supporting Labour MPs and councillors, studiously avoiding the suggestion of a national rent strike. As in 1957 in the struggle against the Rent Act in the private sector, a few thousand turned up to NATR's rally in Trafalgar Square as the culmination of national opposition to the act. At the local level tenants either put their faith in non-implementing councils or attempted rent strikes against implementing councils; the movement was inevitably split, and when the non-implementing councillors changed their minds in the months after the act came into force, they effectively cut the ground from beneath the tenants' feet. The contradiction of being both representatives of tenants (or even tenants themselves) and public landlords was never so drastically exposed.

The localised and fragmentary nature of the struggle as it emerged in late 1972 gradually persuaded most tenants and councillors to accept the act, and strengthened the government's hand in threatening individual councillors, in particular, with surcharges and disqualification from public office. By mid-1973 the struggle was all but finished, and it might have been quietly forgotten, had it not been for the unexpected and close defeat of the Heath government in the wake of the miners' strike and the 3-day working week early in 1974. That conclusion must, nevertheless, be qualified in view of the continued attention paid by the media and the state apparatus to the eleven Labour councillors constituting Clay Cross Urban District Council, who steadfastly refused to implement the act. In October 1973 the government sent in a housing commissioner to take over the administration of council housing in Clay Cross, but by March 1974 he had still not managed to collect the £1 rent increase due in October 1972. In April 1974, however, Clay Cross UDC disappeared in local government organisation and the rent increase was secured by the new council. The Clay Cross councillors were disqualified, surcharged, and generally pilloried unmercifully by the state apparatuses for their defiance, with little effective support from the Labour movement in a situation reminiscent of the Poplar guardians who refused to lower the rates of poor relief in 1921-2.

The achievement of the Clay Cross council was not merely to resist the Housing Finance Act successfully. Like some other Labour councils it had for many years pursued a policy of low council rents and energetic building activity, using a high level of local rate subsidy and exploiting the housing acts to the full. By building up something approaching local mass support for the Labour council in Clay Cross,[27] the councillors were able to clear every slum in the town in a period of 7 years. The effect of such policies cannot be destroyed by the dismantling of the council, simply because the houses cannot be pulled down. The Clay Cross example shows that housing finance administration is not always inevitably a bureaucratic device for rationing housing expenditure and creating 'economically viable' state landlordism – it only becomes so with the tacit consent of local and national politicians.

Since 1974 the power of local authorities to determine council rents has been restored, but this statutory power disguises the strategy of Labour governments since the 1960s, which has sought to integrate council rent policies with overall prices and incomes policy, in parallel with policy *vis-à-vis* the costs of owner-occupation. In 1967 the government referred council rents to the National Board for Prices and Incomes, whose subsequent report showed the importance of council rents in affecting workers' living standards and potential wage demands. The report bolstered the government's successful rescinding of rent increases implemented by Conservative local authorities in 1968. In the 1977 Green Paper on housing policy the government emphasised in three different chapters that 'over a run of years rents should keep broadly in line with changes in money incomes'.[28] During the period 1967–8 to 1975–6 unrebated council rents increased by 137 per cent, compared to a rise of 126 per cent in the retail price index and a 186 per cent rise in average earnings.[29] Unsurprisingly during the years of the Housing Finance Act rent increases moved well ahead of both average price and earnings increases, while between 1974 and 1976 this situation was reversed.

Since Labour's latest prices and incomes policy was launched in mid-1975, the government has put pressure on local authorities to raise rents in line with the wage norm, despite the fact that some local authorities have a surplus of funds. In the Green Paper the government proposed to hold annual negotiations with each local authority over the level of its rents and subsidies in which 'all relevant factors, such as past and expected movements in income, costs and prices would be brought into the reckoning'.[30] Clearly, despite the repeal of the Housing Finance Act, the government is slowly taking further control of council housing finance, confirming the removal of decision-making on rents and subsidies from the sphere of local and Parliamentary politics and into private negotiation between state bureaucrats. The one area still open to local discretion is the subsidy from the local rates, which remains more or less directly related to local Labour strength and the proportion of tenants in the electorate.

To conclude, we have suggested that the Housing Finance Act and subsequent policy have succeeded, firstly, in changing the character of state assistance to council tenants in favour of means-tested benefits and away from subsidies to 'bricks and mortar'. Secondly, policy has achieved more uniform levels of rent and undermined local political control of council housing finance. In one area, however, the Housing Finance Act clearly failed; it did not achieve a major reduction in state subsidies, whose proportion of HRA income rose to unprecedented levels in the mid-1970s, as Table 6.3 indicates. This resulted from the early repeal of the act, and the expansion of the building programme in the initial years of the Labour government, combined with very severe cost inflation and the political necessity of controlling rents. Hence in both 1974–5 and 1975–6 rents covered less than half the current costs of council housing. But in 1977–8 the real level (i.e. at constant prices) of general subsidies (excluding rebates) to council housing fell for the first time since 1972–3[31] and capital expenditure on council housing has been falling in real terms ever since the peak of 1974–5. Gradually in the late 1970s, therefore, the burden of council housing costs is likely to be thrust back further on to tenants as the cuts in public expenditure bite deeper.

MANAGEMENT OF COUNCIL TENANTS

So far we have only considered the broad financial and political relations surrounding the provision of council housing, but now, taking this as given, we turn to examining the administrative relations between the tenant and the public landlord. Having made the commitment to council housing, the state in the shape of the local authority has to continually reproduce the relations of consumption of council housing by collecting rents, safeguarding property, allocating tenancies, dealing with arrears and so on. These are the necessary functions associated with any form of landlordism, and the local housing authority is bound to them by its obligations to its capital financers as well as to the government. Since the payment of council rent involves the appropriation of value by loan finance, there is inevitably a class conflict of interest between tenant and landlord, and although this rarely comes to a head collectively, rent arrears and hostility to rent collectors and council officials are symptomatic. In addition, as part of the welfare state, the local housing authority appears to the consumer as having an obligation to house decently or to provide housing 'as a social service'. Local authorities maintain this appearance in general, while, as far as individual consumers are concerned, strict rationing and limitation of the local authority's powers and resources is exercised by the use of bureaucratism removed from public scrutiny, whose actual obligations are shrouded in considerable administrative discretion. The local housing authority therefore manages tenants in accordance with the dictates of landlordism, and council housing management has acted as a form of social control of the working class in the hope that 'order in the home' will generate social order and respect for property in general, and the prompt payment of rent and respect for the council's property in particular.

The historical roots of these latter aspects of management can be traced to attempts by the model dwelling agencies and other philanthropists to inculcate similar values into the slum dwellers of the latter part of the nineteenth century. Perhaps the most striking example is to be found in the work of Octavia Hill, who, unlike other philanthropists, attempted to provide cheap housing for the casual poor rather than better-off workers. She patched up old houses in a spartan style and attempted to reform her tenants, and, by example, influence other landlords. She believed that the landlord/landlady had a moral obligation to his/her tenants, an obligation to reform them in line with the principles of 'political economy', particularly the principles of thrift, cleanliness and above all the prompt payment of rent. Octavia Hill sought to convince the small landlord that a benevolent, despotic care for tenants and their daily lives would be to their own advantage in achieving regular rent payment and fully let houses. Her ideas did not work out very successfully in practice because, firstly, the employment situation of her prospective tenants meant that they were unable to keep up with regular rent payments and a 'respectable' living style. Secondly, many tenants no doubt rejected her benevolent despotism, for

> . . . in her determination to convert the working-class houses under her care into homes of a bourgeois respectability, and to instil in the working classes a sense of self-respect, independence and pride, above all in her insistence upon the virtues of punctuality, cleanliness, order and discipline, she began to assume the role of an enlightened, all-seeing, but omnipresent ruler.[32]

She apparently intervened in almost all aspects of her tenants' lives. Octavia Hill's ideas were a great influence on the work of the Charity Organisation Society and other charitable, social work agencies and eventually on the form of state welfare administration itself. They exemplify the change in ideology concerning the casual poor which took place in the period of classical imperialism, away from punitiveness combined with indiscriminate charity towards the inculcation of bourgeois values and individual moral reform. However unsuccessfully, such forms of social control contributed something towards the creation of the respectable, organised working class.

Beatrice Webb, later to become an architect of modern welfare administration, described in her diary the emerging moralistic style of housing management. She managed some philanthropically financed buildings in the East End of London which were very basic in their amenities and housed those made homeless by sanitary reform. She records that 'my colleague and I had to learn, by actual experiment, how to choose, from a crowd of applicants, the tenants for 281 separate rooms; how to judge at sight relative sobriety and trustworthiness; how to test the spoken and written word, the worth of references'.[33] The housing manager, usually a lady, combined the roles of rent collector, social worker, allocator of tenancies and so on. The search for respectable tenants was an unending struggle, and Beatrice Webb notes that the tenants were a 'rough lot – the aborigines of the East End', and that there was 'pressure to exclude these and take in only the respectable' or those with regular employment.[34] The dilemmas of combining good management and help to the poor posed such difficult questions as 'are the tenants to be picked and all doubtful or inconvenient persons excluded?'.[35] Beatrice Webb concluded from her experience that there should be an 'association of agencies for the housing of the poor', serving as 'a central office to provide caretakers, superintendents and lady collectors' and to keep records of tenants.[36] Here is a mixture of ideas of charity organisation and the embryonic principles of municipal housing management. This diary entry was written in 1885, just 4 years before the creation of the London County Council (LCC), a body which was to take on precisely this function.

The model dwellings agencies provided purpose-built blocks of flats for workers from the 1840s until the turn of the century, financed by capitalists who were prepared to take a steady 5 per cent return on their investment in exchange for the status of 'philanthropist'. The practical effect of these enterprises on the Victorian housing crisis was small, but the style of both building and management became a model for local authorities to follow in the future. By far the most significant was the Peabody Trust, which invested over £1 million in working-class housing in London at an annual profit of £30,000, housing 19,000 people in over 5000 dwellings by the end of the nineteenth century.[37] The Peabody Trust housed a wide range of workers from those occupations with relatively stable employment, but they were beyond the reach of the majority of workers, confined in London to casual employment.[38] The Trust chose its tenants very carefully and subjected them to a strict code of discipline. Applicants had to have an employer's reference and had to be vaccinated. Rents had to be paid in advance and no arrears were tolerated. Tenants had to wash passages and steps daily before 10 a.m., pay for the cost of many repairs, and were not allowed to keep dogs, hang out washing or decorate rooms; children were not allowed to play on the stairs or in the passages, and at 11 p.m. the gas was turned off and the outer doors locked.[39] These rules were designed to deter the 'destructive classes' and the casual poor and to discipline tenants in accordance with the ideal of responsible landlordism. They were no more severe than those which were later applied to council tenants. The Peabody buildings were barrack-like blocks of spartan flats built at high density and low cost on cleared land bought from the Metropolitan Board of Works. The Peabody Trust borrowed large sums from the state and Rothschilds bank to finance some of its schemes and became a 'quasi-public body', working closely with state agencies. Hence in the second half of the nineteenth century there was considerable financial and administrative involvement of the state in the provision of working-class housing, though for a small group of better-off workers initially.

The barrack-like quality and the management rules associated with the model dwellings were certainly carried over into many of the council-built estates of the twentieth century, particularly those pro-vided for people affected by slum clearance. Each council scheme had to be financially self-supporting, so that the standard of housing and the level of rents varied from one neighbourhood to another. The rules governing LCC tenants varied little from one estate to another and very closely mirrored the Peabody rules.[40] In some areas the LCC was able to house better-off workers in the newer industries and thus built cottages rather than flats, employing more imaginative young architects, who were given scope to develop some attractive schemes – for example, in Acton.[41] In 1912 the LCC noted that 'the occupations in which the largest number of tenants are engaged are those of labourer, clerk, policeman, tailor, porter, sales-man, carman, charwoman, cabinet-maker'.[42] Although the list of occupations included the generic category of 'labourer', it seems that the casual poor, widows, old people, etc., were not included amongst those who were housed by the council. They were expected to 'filter up' into the accommodation vacated by the new council tenants. In London, and elsewhere too, the councils slowly stepped into the shoes of the 5 per cent philanthropists and began to engage successfully in the market for housing the respectable working class from the turn of the century onwards.

Nowhere was the form of state involvement in housing the working class of more acute importance to both the bourgeoisie and the work-ing class than in Glasgow. From its creation the proletariat of that city was closely policed by the forces of the state, not least by the sanitary inspectors, who at the turn of the century were raiding hundreds of houses each night, ostensibly to check on overcrowding. The corporation ran workers' lodging houses, favouring ex-NCOs and ex-detectives as managers, and in the early 1900s was expressing great fear at the consequences of relaxing its self-admitted repressive housing policy in favour of more humane responsibilities. In 1904 the corporation estimated that 64 per cent of the city's slum population were 'respectable', while the rest were 'undesirable' in terms of their alcoholism or criminality, being also those subject to casual employ-ment, irregularity of income and low pay.[43] It eventually developed a management strategy which reproduced these perceived divisions amongst prospective council tenants by providing special, low-cost housing under strict supervision for the so-called undesirables. Hence in the slum clearances of the 1930s, for example, a special category of estates was built with a minimum of amenities and lower rents. People were assigned to estates on the basis of a housing visitor's assessment of their desirability or otherwise. If they were assigned to one of the undesirable estates, as most of the former slum dwellers were, they were met by a 'formidable army of agents of social control' – the Public Health Inspector, the factor 'to ensure that rent was paid on time, that stair-head brawls did not become lethal, and that windows were clean', and 'the dreaded "green lady", who examined bed-clothes, looked at children's hair for nits, and gave instructions on baby-management and domestic science'.[44]

Whatever the real difficulties in the experience of rehousing for both tenants and management, the local authorities in Glasgow and elsewhere clearly imposed their régime of social control 'from above', with little understanding of tenants' poverty, and succeeded in repro-ducing divisions and prejudices amongst tenants and others. These experiences in the inter-war period were repeated in a wider but somewhat less brutal way after the Second World War, with the further expansion of council housing and slum clearance.

The principles of housing management and public landlordism which emerged in the late nineteenth century have therefore been adapted to the needs of the modern welfare state, but they have not altogether been lost, precisely because the public landlord remains primarily concerned with the 'rentability' of council housing and the social control of tenants. Nevertheless, an extreme example of the continuation of the Octavia Hill philosophy was recently uncovered by community workers in Paisley

... where a special area in one housing estate has been set aside for problem families, where they are given daily supervision combined with training and instruction designed to teach them the elements of home craft and mothercraft so that in due course when they have proved they can manage their own affairs, domestic, financial and otherwise, they can return to a better house in a more desirable neighbourhood.[45]

The daily supervision is carried out by a 'lady inspectress', who endeavours 'to persuade tenants to keep their houses, stairs and closets clean, their gardens cultivated and the children cared for', in order to 'help the tenants and their children to become better citizens'.[46] It is interesting to note that the attention of management is so often concentrated on the mother in the family and that the 'problem' is identified as a failure of motherhood in some ill-defined way.[47]

Much of the ideology of efficient and moralistic landlordism remains, but it is now transmitted by a more impersonal bureaucratic local government department as opposed to the lady rent collector, whose personal welfare functions have been taken up by social workers. A study of several local housing authorities in the 1960s conveys the flavour of what is seen as good management:

Councils for the most part are preoccupied with behaving as efficient landlords – balancing the account, furbishing the properties, garnering arrears. They prize above all a good (i.e. solvent, tractable, clean and quiet) tenant and tend to favour him, as any private landlord would. Because he is deemed likely to treat it carefully, he is generally given one of the authority's newest and best homes. That is what is meant by sound management.[48]

Not only do councils prize 'good tenants', in some cases they actively promote their view of decent standards, as in the following extract from a handbook issued by a council to its tenants in the 1950s: 'Keep your home clean and tidy. Endeavour to have some method of cleaning as you go along; do not try to clean the whole house in one day [sic]. Regular bed times for children and adults, except on special occasions. Sit down properly at table. Hang up your pots and pans and put them on a shelf . . .'[49]

The social control of tenants is not so much attempted by face-to-face supervision today. It is achieved by a process of amplifying the division amongst tenants, which stigmatises and punishes the less well-off and those labelled 'less respectable' by assigning them to the worst slum estates. The impression is fostered by the media and the local authority that these slum estates have been created and perpetuated by the people who live on them, which shifts the responsibility away from the local authority and on to the tenants themselves. From the management point of view, in order to keep the property in good order and keep arrears down, the stock of council property has to be matched to the rent-paying capacity of the tenants and prospective tenants, since poor tenants are unlikely to have the resources to keep the property in as satisfactory an order as better-off tenants. Hence there are 'respectable' estates for the better-off at one end of the spectrum and 'disreputable' or 'hard-to-let' estates at the other. One management view of the so-called problem estate is that 'a point is reached in some roads where the only tenants willing to accept a vacant house are those whom the housing authority knows will offer problems to the department, the neighbourhood or both'.[50]

Estates thus become labelled as 'problems' because of the perceived pathology of tenants, sometimes labelled 'problem families', and it is concluded that 'some concentration of socially undesirable tenants is inevitable'.[51] The slum estate is not, however, produced by tenants; on the contrary, 'assignment to a ghetto estate is a punishment',[52] and only the most desperate tenants will accept the slum conditions thereon. 'The offence occasioning that punishment may be obvious, such as rent arrears, or it may be subtly in terms of marital relationships which are not approved of by housing visitors';[53] but, whatever the reason, management logic ensures that the poor or 'less eligible' tenant is often confined to the poor or 'less eligible' estate.

This process is confirmed in another more sophisticated administrative view of 'unsatisfactory tenants':

There is of course a great deal of difference between tenants who are 'simply' unsatisfactory in that they are bad rent-payers and those who have major social, economic [sic] or health problems. The former can be dealt with by good housing management – by such measures as transfer to a cheaper house, a rent rebate scheme or by the normally effective shock procedure of issuing a distress warrant for the recovery of arrears, a 'default summons' or a notice of eviction. But where there are some basic underlying problems the housing authority will need to have the assistance of other agencies.[54]

The implication here is that a distinction can be made between those 'simply' in arrears and those with, amongst other things, 'economic problems', which seems unlikely to occur in reality. It is made clear that such 'simply' unsatisfactory tenants are dealt with by transferring them to worse housing conditions – in other words, a cheaper house where they are more likely to encounter health and social problems. Local authorities appear to be quite successful in keeping arrears down by the use of threats and distress, and if necessary by forcible eviction. Birmingham corporation were evicting an average of two families a day according to a study in 1976,[55] and it is still recognised that council evictions are a common cause of homelessness.[56] By such means the local authorities adjust the distribution of council housing according to tenants' ability to pay and the council's judgement of their eligibility.

It is the so-called problem estates which attract the attention of the police and the media because of vandalism and arrears, but it is also these estates which suffer from a lack of investment by the housing authority in repairs, maintenance and amenities.[57] In Coventry, for example, the 'hard to let' estates were built at a time of a notorious decline in council building standards in the early 1950s, and many of the houses are beyond repair. In Newcastle, North Tyneside, Paisley, London and most other towns, it seems that the slum clearance estates built in the 1930s and since the 1950s have become the slum estates of the 1970s. Many of these estates have been deprived of investment since they were conceived.

The reality of the slum estates and the notion of the respectable and solid tenant reinforces and reproduces real divisions amongst tenants and working-class householders in general. A study in Glasgow has shown how the local press and corporation officials amplify the stigma associated with slum estates, which successfully diverts working-class resentment over the housing question away from politicians and the corporation and on to tenants themselves. It was found that the violence, the criminality and depravity popularly associated with a slum estate was largely a myth, which was nevertheless so powerful and so insistently fostered that even the tenants of the estate believed in it and blamed their own neighbours for their plight.[58] It has been suggested that the slum estates are therefore 'not reflections of "real differences" within the working class, they are the producers of them'.[59] This is to overemphasise the power of local management and to ignore the very real divisions of status and income which exist within the working class, so that pensioners, single mothers, and the unemployed, for example, tend to be concentrated on the worst estates. The slum estates and the ideology surrounding them simply geographically highlight and deepen these divisions, which undoubtedly mitigate against collective action by tenants.

It is in the allocation and selection policies of local authorities that tenants are graded and assigned to their appropriate estates. In the immediate post-war period the social and physical planners hoped to create 'mixed' council estates, with a balance of social classes, children, old people and so on. In 1949 Aneurin Bevan announced that council housing was no longer to be statutorily defined as housing 'for the working classes'; it was to become available to all. Despite these hopes, the allocation of council housing has succeeded in reproducing existing class prejudices and inequalities, and 'most big councils have apparatuses to prevent what they regard as undue social mixing on their estates'.[60] Segregation is structured above all by differences of income, but also by age, colour, religion and life-style. This appears to be essential in the eyes of the public landlord to avoid conflicts between tenants and damage to property, and generally to preserve the rentability of council property. For those who are considered for a tenancy or even a transfer, the visit by a housing official is a crucial determinant in where and when they will be rehoused, and it is here that considerable prejudice has been uncovered. The local authorities either formally or informally *have* to make a judgement on the suitability and rent-paying capacity of its prospective tenants, as demanded by their primary role as property landlords. Nevertheless, the prejudicial basis of these judgements has provoked a considerable degree of criticism; for example, a government report in 1969 commented

> ... there is a danger that applicants are graded according to an interpretation of their deserts. This even extends on occasion to a rejection of some from the council house sector. We were sur-

prised to find some housing authorities who took up a moralistic attitude towards applicants; the underlying philosophy seemed to be that council tenancies were to be given only to those who 'deserved' them and that 'most deserving' should get the best houses. Thus unmarried mothers, cohabitees, 'dirty families' and 'transients' tended to be grouped together as 'undesirable'. Moral rectitude, social conformity, clean living and a 'clear' rent book on occasion seemed to be essential qualifications for eligibility – at least for new houses.[61]

There is now a great store of evidence which shows that the danger feared in this report has been a permanent feature of council housing administration, for the reasons already indicated. Since it is not politically acceptable to enshrine such rules of access in legislation, in the post-war period, a great exercise in the social planning and segregation of the working class has taken place behind closed doors. In Hull 'the quality of property occupied is strongly related to the status of the family as assessed by the local authority'.[62] In Glasgow the corporation grades its estates according to their attractiveness and 'new tenants are deliberately assigned to one or other of these graded estates according to the size of household, their housing history and . . . the general "character" of the person's life-style'.[63] In Tameside the local authority proposed in 1978 to grade every council tenant according to 'their degree of cleanliness, maintenance of payments of rent and general social attitude'.[64] In the early 1970s Birmingham housing department operated a rule 'by which cohabitees with children have to wait two years before being considered for an offer'.[65] More recently Birmingham has announced a ghettoisation policy for so-called problem families.

The most visible aspect of housing allocation policy to the public is the housing waiting list. Position in this queue is to some extent determined by the allocation criteria already mentioned. Priority may be given to 'key workers', medical cases and slum clearance victims. There is a considerable contrast between the accounts of the queue given by its members and those offered by housing officials, for example, in Birmingham, where

. . . public statements by housing managers about the Queue emphasises its 'fairness' and therefore the extent to which people who consciously try to 'jump the queue' is seen as essentially unfair

> ... Managers' statements to individuals in the Queue emphasise its 'routineness' – people apply, their applications are assessed in accordance with well-defined rules of eligibility and they are then assigned to lists for various sized accommodation, their place in the Queue being determined by the points scheme.[66]

Managers therefore suggest that they have a scientific allocation system which allows for very little discretion, but since the details of the system are kept secret, there is no way of verifying this. For the waiting list applicants 'the most important features of the system are its apparent randomness, arbitrariness and "unfairness" or simply that no explanation can be given'.[67] In other words, they experience in a fairly acute form the classic features of bureaucratism: secrecy, impersonal treatment, uncertainty, delay, sanctioned 'rules', informal rules and so on. These features are the necessary means for rationing what remains a somewhat scarce 'commodity' – decent housing which tenants can afford. This rationing is done on the basis of the acceptability or otherwise of the prospective tenant to the authority, rather than according to any meaningful and democratically determined definitions of needs. As we have already suggested, the system in fact allows for very considerable administrative discretion. Hence 'pressure, insistence, general cantankerousness are at times clearly of help in advancing the case of individual applicants';[68] such 'evidence of unmet need' legitimates 'queue jumping'. The authority can apparently reduce the demand for housing altogether by excluding such households from the waiting list as cohabitees, owner-occupiers, newcomers to the area and so on. There is some similarity between housing departments' secret allocation rules and the secret codes used by DHSS officers in rationing benefits and disciplining claimants. Similar forms of prejudice and bias are disguised by both bureaucratic discretionary procedures.

　　Much of the revealing research on council housing management has been inspired by the correct perception that it plays a very important role in shaping many working-class lives, and that therefore housing managers wield considerable power (in the behavioural, face-to-face sense) over working-class people and their life chances. The housing departments are a major element in the corporate management structure of contemporary local government alongside the education, planning and social services departments. It has been suggested that officials in such departments, possibly alongside various 'gatekeepers' in the private sector, such as estate agents and building society managers, are 'urban managers' who 'exert an independent influence on the allocation of scarce urban resources',[69] in a fashion analogous to managers in industry. The urban managerialist thesis has been the subject of considerable debate amongst urban sociologists, but we must note some important qualifications and criticisms of its application to housing managers.[70]

Firstly, the emphasis on the independence or relative autonomy of urban managers suggests that they are the possessors of 'a "third interest", neither that of capital nor labour but of some bureaucratically defined national interest'.[71] The urban managers are thus taken as an example of Weber's bureaucratic form of domination and their relation to class power is obscured. We have argued on the contrary that housing management functions to reproduce labour power in the interests of capital in general by efficient provision of low-cost housing and the social control of tenants, using bureaucratism as a means of securing legitimacy, disguising the effects of policy and individuating tenants. A second feature of urban managerialist ideas is the tendency to concentrate on the managers themselves and their face-to-face interaction with clients as the essence of power relations. While undoubtedly individual interactions are crucial in reproducing ideology and class power, the manager is merely the front-line representative of a management structure over whose functions he/she probably has little control. Like the officer in the DHSS, it is tempting to identify the housing official personally as the oppressor. We have argued here that housing officials in fact operate a system whose fundamentals have been shaped historically by local and national government policy. Officials' powers of discretion are designed to ensure the preservation of rentability, the rationing of resources and the reproduction of ideology, although this allows for significant pressures to be brought to bear by tenants and politicians. Thirdly, the urban managerialist thesis sometimes ignores or devalues the role of politicians in the anxiety to point out the power of managers. In fact local politicians of all parties appear to have taken quite an active part in shaping and approving allocation policies and are clearly responsible for those policies. In this area Labour politicians seem to have been generally slow, if not unwilling, to challenge the class prejudices and poor law practices over which they have been presiding. The whole system of council housing management is of course ultimately sanctioned by Members of Parliament.

In recent years pressure from politicians, community workers and tenants has brought about moves towards reforms of council housing management. The government has proposed that housing departments institute a 'framework of consultation' on local policies and publish allocation criteria. In the context of waning pressure on waiting lists as council housing becomes more unattractive, and given the real divisions amongst tenants and prospective tenants, this may not lead to significant changes. An important reaction to the bureaucratism and social control functions of housing management has been the movement for tenant control and even the break-up of the large housing authorities.[72] In the face of public expenditure cuts, the strength of the anti-council housing lobby, and the grievances of tenants, local and central government have come round to agreeing with the idea of 'tenant control' as a means of saving money and off-loading some of the obligations placed on them. For example, it has been proposed that tenants apply for improvement grants, which effectively off-loads over 50 per cent of the costs of rehabilitation on to tenants. Inevitably the question of tenant control poses great dilemmas for tenants, and often means the incorporation of tenants' organisation into the housing bureaucracy. The government is proposing a tenants' charter which will at last give tenants security of tenure and a written tenancy agreement, rights of citizenship granted to private tenants many years ago.

In conclusion, we have suggested that council housing management has developed from a paternalistic yet puritan philanthropy into a welfare bureaucracy, in a way which has preserved its property land-lord, social control and ideological functions despite political and tenant pressures. It has been further suggested that a greater professionalism of housing management might further 'its role in champion-ing the cause of the disadvantaged'.[73] However, any benevolent welfare aspects of council housing management have been very much secondary to its predominant role as guardian of state property and order in the home,[74] and it is difficult to see how professionalisation in itself can alter such structural constraints. On the other hand, the workers in housing departments must have an important role in changing these constraints, alongside tenants and politicians.

Notes and References

CHAPTER 1

1. D. Thompson, 'Discussion: the Welfare State', *New Reasoner*, no. 4 (1958) pp. 127–8.
2. D. Wedderburn, 'Facts and Theories of the Welfare State', in *The Socialist Register 1965*, eds R. Miliband and J. Saville (London: Merlin, 1965) p. 143.
3. See P. Thompson, *Socialists, Liberals and Labour* (London: Routledge, 1967) pp. 117, 238.
4. See A. Marwick, 'The Labour Party and the Welfare State in Britain 1900–1914', *American Historical Review*, no. 73 (1967) pp. 385–7.
5. R. Miliband, *Parliamentary Socialism* (London: Merlin, 1973) pp. 61–2.
6. Ibid., p. 62.
7. This is documented in considerable detail in P. Addison, *The Road to 1945* (London: Quartet, 1977).
8. H. Heclo, *Modern Social Politics in Britain and Sweden* (New Haven: Yale University Press, 1974) p. 295.
9. Ibid., p. 300.
10. J. Saville, 'The Welfare State: An Historical Approach', *New Reasoner*, no. 3 (1957–8) p. 14.
11. P. Thane, 'The History of Social Welfare', *New Society*, 29 August 1974, p. 541.
12. P. Thane, *The Working Class and the 'Welfare State'*, an unpublished paper given at the British Sociological Association Conference, Sheffield (1977) p. 10.
13. Ibid., p. 29.
14. P. Anderson, 'The Antinomies of Antonio Gramsci', *New Left Review*, no. 100 (1976–7) p. 63.
15. G. Leversha, 'Beyond Spontaneity', in *Class, Hegemony and Party*, ed. J. Bloomfield (London: Lawrence & Wishart, 1977) p. 119.
16. Ibid., p. 122.
17. L. Colletti, *From Rousseau to Lenin* (London: New Left Books, 1972) p. 225.
18. K. Marx, *The First International and After* (Harmondsworth: Penguin, 1974) p. 206.

19. N. Geras, *The Legacy of Rosa Luxemburg* (London: New Left Books, 1976) p. 60.
20. Ibid., p. 60.

CHAPTER 2

1. The following are particularly useful: J. Harrison, *Marxist Economics for Socialists* (London: Pluto, 1978); B. Fine, *Marx's Capital* (London: Macmillan, 1975); P. Sweezy, *The Theory of Capitalist Development* (New York: Monthly Review Press, 1968); E. Mandel, 'Introduction' to Karl Marx, *Capital*, vol. 1 (Harmondsworth: Penguin, 1976).
2. J. Holloway and S. Picciotto, 'Capital, Crisis and the State', *Capital and Class*, no. 2 (1977) pp. 91–2.
3. See E. Mandel, *Late Capitalism* (London: New Left Books, 1975) Ch. 5.
4. See ibid., p. 148.
5. K. Marx, *Capital*, vol. 1 (Harmondsworth: Penguin, 1976) pp. 275–6.
6. Ibid., p. 275.
7. Mandel, *Late Capitalism*, pp. 150–1.
8. Ibid., p. 151. Mandel argues that this is precisely what happened in Nazi Germany in the 1930s.
9. Marx, *Capital*, vol. 1, p. 1069.
10. Ibid., p. 275.
11. Conference of Socialist Economists (CSE) Pamphlet No. 2, *On the Political Economy of Women* (London: Stage 1, 1976) pp. 10–11.
12. Ibid., p. 15.
13. Ibid., p. 13.
14. An important debate on this question has been raised by B. Fine and L. Harris, 'The Debate on State Expenditure', *New Left Review*, no. 98 (1976).
15. For further clarification see J. Holloway and S. Picciotto, 'Introduction: Towards a Materialist Theory of the State' in *State and Capital: a Marxist Debate*, eds J. Holloway and S. Picciotto (London: Edward Arnold, 1978). See also R. Miliband, *Marxism and Politics* (Oxford: Oxford University Press, 1977) Chapter IV.
16. E. Altvater, 'Some Problems of State Interventionism' in *State and Capital*, eds Holloway and Picciotto, p. 41.
17. W. Müller and C. Neusüss, 'The Welfare-State Illusion' in *State and Capital*, eds Holloway and Picciotto, p. 37.
18. J. Hirsch, 'The State and Social Reproduction' in *State and Capital*, eds Holloway and Picciotto.
19. Ibid., p. 64.
20. Marx, *Capital*, vol. 1, p. 875.
21. E. P. Thompson, *Whigs and Hunters* (Harmondsworth: Penguin, 1977) p. 207.
22. Marx, *Capital*, vol. 1, p. 899.
23. E. J. Hobsbawm, *Labouring Men* (London: Weidenfeld, 1968) p. 325.
24. See G. Stedman Jones, *Outcast London* (Harmondsworth: Penguin, 1976) Chapter 18.

25. Mandel, *Late Capitalism*, p. 179.
26. See V. George and P. Wilding, *Ideology and Social Welfare* (London: Routledge, 1976) Chapter 3.
27. Mandel, *Late Capitalism*, p. 495.
28. S. Clarke, 'Marxism, Sociology and Poulantzas' Theory of the State', *Capital and Class*, no. 2 (1977) p. 4.
29. Marx, *Capital*, vol. 1, pp. 164–5.
30. Ibid., p. 165.
31. Ibid., p. 165.
32. Holloway and Picciotto, 'Capital, Crisis and the State'.
33. Ibid., p. 79.
34. Ibid., p. 80.
35. T. H. Marshall, 'Citizenship and Social Class', reprinted in T. H. Marshall, *Sociology at the Crossroads* (London: Heinemann, 1963).
36. Ibid., p. 72.
37. K. Boulding, 'The Boundaries of Social Policy', reprinted in *Social Administration*, eds W. Birrell, P. Hillyard, A. Murie and D. Roche (Harmondsworth: Penguin, 1973) p. 192.
38. Ibid., p. 192.
39. R. Titmuss, *Commitment to Welfare* (London: Allen & Unwin, 1968) p. 191.
40. R. Jenkins, 'Poverty is Preventable', reprinted in *Social Welfare in Modern Britain*, eds E. Butterworth and R. Holman (London: Fontana, 1975) p. 403.
41. J. R. Hay, *The Development of the British Welfare State 1880–1975* (London: Edward Arnold, 1978) p. 104.
42. V. George and P. Wilding, 'Social Values, Social Class and Social Policy', *Social and Economic Administration*, vol. 6, no. 3 (1972).
43. R. Titmuss, *Essays on the Welfare State* (London: Allen & Unwin, 1963) pp. 44 and 54.
44. Ibid., p. 39.
45. R. Mishra, *Society and Social Policy* (London: Macmillan, 1977) p. 7.
46. P. Hall, H. Land, R. Parker and A. Webb, *Change, Choice and Conflict in Social Policy* (London: Heinemann, 1975); and H. Heclo, *Modern Social Politics in Britain and Sweden* (New Haven: Yale University Press, 1974).
47. R. Pinker, *Social Theory and Social Policy* (London: Heinemann, 1971) p. 50.
48. Stedman Jones, *Outcast London*, p. 3.
49. Mishra, *Society and Social Policy*, p. 16.
50. E. P. Thompson, 'The Peculiarities of the English' in *The Socialist Register 1965*, eds R. Miliband and J. Saville (London: Merlin, 1965) p. 336.

CHAPTER 3

1. For further discussion of the shape of welfare expenditures see I. Gough, *The Political Economy of the Welfare State* (London: Macmillan, 1979).
2. E. Mandel, *Late Capitalism* (London: New Left Books, 1975) p. 151.

3. *The Government's Expenditure Plans 1978–79 to 1981–82*, vol. II, Cmnd. 7049–II (London: HMSO, 1978), Table 2.12.
4. The contribution and benefit record of every insured person and recipient of benefit is kept at the Longbenton office of DHSS in Newcastle, which is one of the largest office organisations in Europe, employing over 10,000 people. The contributory principle has thus created a whole army of clerks completely remote from their clientele, performing a highly routinised function in an almost Kafkaesque operation. See R. G. S. Brown, *The Management of Welfare* (London: Fontana, 1975) pp. 84–5.
5. See J. C. Kincaid, *Poverty and Equality in Britain* (Harmondsworth: Penguin, 1973) pp. 214–20; and also V. George, *Social Security & Society* (London: Routledge, 1973) pp. 17–19.
6. In the inter-war years the 'approved societies' (friendly societies and insurance companies) ran many of the welfare insurance schemes on behalf of the government.
7. See J. R. Hay, 'Employers and Social Policy in Britain', *Social History*, no. 4 (1977).
8. G. V. Rimlinger, *Welfare Policy and Industrialisation in Europe, America and Russia* (New York: Wiley, 1971) p. 339. Chapter 4 of this book describes the political origins of social insurance under Bismarck in Germany in the 1870s.
9. B. B. Gilbert, *British Social Policy 1914–1939* (London: Batsford, 1970) p. 236.
10. E. P. Thompson, *The Making of the English Working Class* (Harmondsworth: Penguin, 1968) p. 73.
11. Ibid., p. 247.
12. E. J. Hobsbawm and G. Rudé, *Captain Swing* (Harmondsworth: Penguin, 1973) p. 27.
13. See Thompson, *The Making of the English Working Class*, p. 314.
14. M. Dobb, *Studies in the Development of Capitalism* (London: Routledge, 1963) p. 275.
15. S. G. and E. O. A. Checkland, *The Poor Law Report of 1834* (Harmondsworth: Penguin, 1974).
16. See D. Roberts, *The Victorian Origins of the British Welfare State* (New Haven: Yale University Press, 1960) p. 258.
17. See M. Anderson, *Family Structure in Nineteenth Century Lancashire* (London: Cambridge University Press, 1971) p. 137; and Thompson, *The Making of the English Working Class*, p. 334.
18. See Thompson, *The Making of the English Working Class*, p. 295.
19. See ibid., p. 246, and A. Redford, *Labour Migration in England 1800–1850* (Manchester: Manchester University Press, 1964) Chapter VI.
20. Thompson, *The Making of the English Working Class*, p. 295.
21. R. Pinker, *Social Theory and Social Policy* (London: Heinemann, 1971) p. 57.
22. Thompson, *The Making of the English Working Class*, p. 89.
23. Oldham was a particularly militant example. See J. Foster, *Class Struggle and the Industrial Revolution* (London: Weidenfeld, 1974) Chapter 3.
24. Anderson, *Family Structure in Nineteenth Century Lancashire*, p. 150.

25. S. and B. Webb, *English Poor Law History: Part II – the Last Hundred Years* (London: Frank Cass, 1963), p. 229.
26. Ibid., p. 230.
27. See G. Stedman Jones, *Outcast London* (Harmondsworth: Penguin, 1976) Chapters 14 and 15.
28. Webbs, *English Poor Law History: Part II*, pp. 440–1.
29. Ibid., p. 179.
30. See J. Harris, *Unemployment and Politics: a Study in English Social Policy 1886–1914* (London: Oxford University Press, 1972) p. 149.
31. See P. Ryan, 'Poplarism 1894–1930' in *The Origins of British Social Policy*, ed. P. Thane (London: Croom Helm, 1978) p. 62.
32. See K. D. Brown, *Labour and Unemployment 1900–1914* (Newton Abbot: David & Charles, 1971) which describes the development of the politics of unemployment within the Labour movement.
33. Harris, *Unemployment and Politics*, p. 235.
34. Stedman Jones, *Outcast London*, p. 321.
35. See E. P. Hennock, 'Poverty and Social Theory in England', *Social History*, no. 1 (1976).
36. See B. B. Gilbert, *The Evolution of National Insurance in Great Britain* (London: Michael Joseph, 1966) p. 243.
37. See B. Showler, *The Public Employment Service* (London: Longman, 1976).
38. Harris, *Unemployment and Politics*, p. 364.
39. P. Thane, *The Working Class and the 'Welfare State'*, an unpublished paper given at the British Sociological Association Conference, Sheffield, 1977, p. 27.
40. Ryan, 'Poplarism', p. 58.
41. See ibid., pp. 76–8 and Webbs, *English Poor Law History: Part II*, pp. 846–910.
42. The history of relief for strikers is described by J. Gennard, *Financing Strikers* (London: Macmillan, 1977) Chapter 2.
43. See ibid. and P. Ryan, 'The Poor Law in 1926' in *The General Strike*, ed. M. Morris (Harmondsworth: Penguin, 1976).
44. A. Deacon, 'Concession and Coercion: the Politics of Unemployment Insurance in the 1920's' in *Essays in Labour History*, eds. A. Briggs and J. Saville (London: Croom Helm, 1977) p. 16.
45. E. Briggs and A. Deacon, 'The Creation of the Unemployment Assistance Board', *Policy & Politics*, vol. 2, no. 1 (1974) p. 51. This explains in part the shortfall between the numbers of registered unemployed and the numbers claiming relief and benefits on account of unemployment; see Table 3.1.
46. Ibid., p. 50.
47. W. Hannington, *Unemployed Struggles 1919–1936* (London: Lawrence & Wishart, 1977) p. 211.
48. See M. Jacques, 'Consequences of the General Strike' in *The General Strike 1926*, ed. J. Skelley (London: Lawrence & Wishart, 1976).
49. Hannington, *Unemployed Struggles*, p. 211.
50. Ibid., p. 230.
51. See M. Turnbull, 'Attitude of Government and Administration to the

Hunger Marches of the 1920's and 1930's', *Journal of Social Policy*, vol. 2, no. 1 (1973).

52. See M. Branson and M. Heinemann, *Britain in the Nineteen Thirties* (London: Panther, 1973) pp. 43–54.

53. Briggs and Deacon, 'The Creation of the UAB', p. 61.

54. See H. Heclo, *Modern Social Politics in Britain and Sweden* (New Haven: Yale University Press, 1974) pp. 150–2.

55. See Kincaid, *Poverty and Equality in Britain*, pp. 99–100.

56. See F. Field, 'Making Sense of the Unemployment Figures' in *The Conscript Army*, ed. F. Field (London: Routledge, 1977).

57. *Social Security Statistics 1976* (London: HMSO, 1978) Table 46.05.

58. *Supplementary Benefits Commission Annual Report 1976*, Cmnd. 6910 (London: HMSO, 1977) para. 1.10.

59. *Social Security Statistics 1976*, Table 46.02.

60. *SBC Annual Report 1976*, para. 1.14.

61. Ibid., para. 1.13.

62. See *Penelope Hall's Social Services of England & Wales*, ed. J. B. Mays, ninth edition (London: Routledge, 1975) p. 114.

63. See Supplementary Benefits Commission, *The Administration of the Wage Stop* (London: HMSO, 1967).

64. See L. Elks, *The Wage Stop: Poor By Order*, Poverty Pamphlet No. 17 (London: Child Poverty Action Group, 1974).

65. Ibid., p. 70.

66. On the other hand, it could remain discretionary, although there are pressures from within DHSS to bring it back to improve work incentive. See G. Weightman, 'Under the Grille', *New Society*, 5 January 1978, p. 6.

67. N. D. Ellis and W. E. J. McCarthy, 'Introduction and Interpretation' in S. R. Parker, C. G. Thomas, N. D. Ellis and W. E. J. McCarthy, *The Effects of the Redundancy Payments Act* (London: HMSO, 1971) p. 3.

68. R. H. Fryer, 'The Myths of the Redundancy Payments Act', *Industrial Law Journal*, no. 1 (1973).

69. Parker *et al.*, *The Effects of the Redundancy Payments Act*, p. 62.

70. See R. Martin and R. H. Fryer, *Redundancy and Paternalist Capitalism* (London: Allen & Unwin, 1973) p. 172.

71. See Parker *et al.*, *The Effects of the Redundancy Payments Act*, Table 3.38.

72. Quarterly figures are given in the *Department of Employment Gazette*.

73. *Report of the Committee on Abuse of Social Security Benefits* (Fisher), Cmnd. 5228 (London: HMSO, 1973) p. 109.

74. See M. Meacher, *Scrounging on the Welfare* (London: Arrow, 1974) p. 36.

75. *Supplementary Benefits Handbook* (London: HMSO, 1974) para. 203.

76. Meacher, *Scrounging on the Welfare*, p. 71.

77. See F. Field, 'Fiddlers on the Hoof', *The Guardian*, 26 January 1976.

78. See *Supplementary Benefits Commission Annual Report 1975*, Cmnd. 6615 (London: HMSO, 1976) p. 72.

79. M. J. Hill, *Policies for the Unemployed: Help or Coercion?*, Poverty Pamphlet

The Far Side®

LAST IMPRESSIONS

— 2002 —

November

"Crimony! ... It seems like every summer there's more and more of these things around!"

Tuesday 19

No. 15 (London: Child Poverty Action Group, 1974) p. 6.

80. See Field, 'Fiddlers on the Hoof'.
81. *SBC Annual Report 1976*, p. 153.
82. *Supplementary Benefits Handbook*, para. 211.
83. Ibid. para. 207.
84. See F. Field and S. Winyard, 'Government Action Against Unemployment' in *The Conscript Army*, ed. F. Field (London: Routledge, 1977).
85. *SBC Annual Report 1976*, pp. 58–60.
86. See B. Jordan, *Poor Parents* (London: Routledge, 1974) Chapters 1–4.
87. See M. Rein, 'Work Incentives and Welfare Reform' in *Incentives and Planning in Social Policy*, eds B. Stein and S. M. Miller (Chicago: Aldine, 1973).
88. *Social Security Statistics 1976*, Table 32.10.
89. See Kincaid, *Poverty and Equality in Britain*, Chapter 12.
90. *SBC Annual Report 1975*, p. 69.
91. See Gennard, *Financing Strikers*, p. 148.
92. Ibid., Table 2.1.
93. *SBC Annual Report 1976*, p. 28.
94. See Gennard, *Financing Strikers*, Chapter 7.
95. J. W. Durcan and W. E. J. McCarthy, 'The State Subsidy Theory of Strikes', *British Journal of Industrial Relations*, vol. XXII (1974) p. 45.
96. Gennard, *Financing Strikers*, p. 115.

CHAPTER 4

1. V. Beechey, 'Some Notes on Female Wage Labour in Capitalist Production', *Capital and Class*, no. 3 (1977) pp. 53 and 57.
2. See ibid., pp. 51–4. For further discussion see J. Humphries, 'Class Struggle and the Persistence of the Working Class Family', *Cambridge Journal of Economics*, vol. 1 (1977).
3. See L. Oren, 'The Welfare of Women in Labouring Families: England, 1860–1950' in *Clio's Consciousness Raised*, eds M. S. Hartman and L. Banner (New York: Harper & Row, 1974).
4. F. Engels, 'The Origin of the Family, Private Property and the State' in *Selected Works of Marx and Engels*, one volume (London: Lawrence & Wishart, 1970). Engels considered that the entry of women into wage work prompted by capitalist development would bring about the liberation of women. For recent feminist criticism of Engels see R. Delmar, 'Looking Again at Engels' in *The Rights and Wrongs of Women*, eds J. Mitchell and A. Oakley (Harmondsworth: Penguin, 1976).
5. Patriarchy is used here as a rather loose synonym for women's subordination to men.
6. Beechey, 'Some Notes on Female Wage Labour', p. 47.
7. Women's Studies Group, Centre for Contemporary Cultural Studies, *Women Take Issue* (London: Hutchinson, 1978) p. 48.
8. *Social Security Statistics 1976* (London: HMSO, 1978) Table 34.32.
9. The data on the nineteenth century used here draws substantially upon

P. Thane, 'Women and State Welfare in Victorian and Edwardian England', to be published in *History Workshop Journal* during 1978–9.

10. See U. Henriques, 'Bastardy and the New Poor Law', *Past and Present*, no. 37 (1967).

11. M. Finer and O. McGregor, 'The History of the Obligation to Maintain' in *Report of the Committee on One-Parent Families*, vol. 2, Cmnd. 5629 (London: HMSO, 1974) Appendix 5, para. 64.

12. Local Government Board Circular to Boards of Guardians, *Relief to Widows and Children* (London: HMSO, 1974).

13. See N. Middleton, *When Family Failed* (London: Gollancz, 1971).

14. S. and E. O. A. Checkland, *The Poor Law Report of 1834* (Harmondsworth: Penguin, 1974) pp. 113–14.

15. Middleton, *When Family Failed*, p. 52.

16. For further explanation see Finer and McGregor, 'The History of the Obligation to Maintain'.

17. *Report of the Committee on One-Parent Families* (Finer) vol. 1, Cmnd. 5629 (London: HMSO, 1974) para. 4.67.

18. Ibid., para. 4.215. See also J. C. Kincaid, *Poverty and Equality in Britain* (Harmondsworth: Penguin, 1973) pp. 208–12.

19. *Report of the Committee on One-Parent Families*, vol. 1, para. 4.202. It has been suggested that 'the obligation on men to maintain their wives ... is as much concerned with preserving male work incentive as with the welfare of their families' by H. Land, 'Social Security and the Division of Unpaid Work in the Home and Paid Employment in the Labour Market' in DHSS, *Social Security Research Seminar* (London: HMSO, 1977) p. 50.

20. *Social Security Statistics 1976*, Table 34.93.

21. See *Report of the Committee on Abuse of Social Security Benefits* (Fisher) Cmnd. 5228 (London: HMSO, 1973) p. 148.

22. *Report of the Committee on One-Parent Families*, vol. 1, para. 4.90.

23. See E. Wilson, *Women and the Welfare State* (London: Tavistock, 1977) p. 152, and Kincaid, *Poverty and Equality in Britain*, pp. 207–8.

24. D. Marsden, *Mothers Alone* (Harmondsworth: Penguin, 1969) p. 31.

25. S. and B. Webb, *English Poor Law History: Part II – the Last Hundred Years* (London: Frank Cass, 1963) p. 373.

26. Marsden, *Mothers Alone*, pp. 247–51.

27. A. Hunt, *Families and Their Needs*, Office of Population, Censuses and Surveys (London: HMSO, 1973).

28. See M. Rutter, *Maternal Deprivation Re-assessed* (Harmondsworth: Penguin, 1972).

29. *Report of the Committee on One-Parent Families*, vol. 1, para. 8.128.

30. See J. Tizard, P. Moss and J. Perry, *All Our Children* (London: M. Temple Smith, 1976).

31. *Ministry of Social Security Act 1966*, Schedule 2, para. 3(1).

32. See R. Lister, *As Man and Wife: a Study of the Cohabitation Rule*, Poverty Research Series No. 2 (London: Child Poverty Action Group, 1973).

33. *Report of the Committee on Abuse of Social Security Benefits*, p. 148.

34. See *Cohabitation, a Report by the Supplementary Benefits Commission to the Secretary of State for Social Services* (London: HMSO, 1971).

35. Ibid., p. 4.

36. Wilson, *Women and the Welfare State*, p. 81.

37. Ibid., pp. 149–52.

38. J. Coussins, *The Equality Report* (London: National Council for Civil Liberties, 1977) p. 105.

39. P. Townsend, *The Social Minority* (London: Allen Lane, 1973) Chapter 5.

40. O. Adamson, C. Brown, J. Harrison and J. Price, 'Women's Oppression Under Capitalism', *Revolutionary Communist*, no. 5 (1976) p. 24.

41. See Coussins, *The Equality Report*.

42. See A. Coote and T. Gill, *Women's Rights* (Harmondsworth: Penguin, 1977) pp. 109–13 and 129–42.

43. See ibid., pp. 110–11 and 130–1.

44. See J. Coussins, *Maternity Rights for Working Women* (London: National Council for Civil Liberties, 1976) pp. 12–13.

45. Adamson *et al.*, 'Women's Oppression Under Capitalism', p. 32.

46. Ibid., p. 28.

47. *General Household Survey 1976*, Office of Population, Censuses and Surveys (London: HMSO, 1978) p. 198.

48. See ibid., p. 52. For further discussion see J. Gardiner, 'Women & Unemployment', *Red Rag*, no. 10 (1975).

49. *General Household Survey 1974*, Office of Population, Censuses and Surveys (London: HMSO, 1976) p. 102.

50. H. Land, 'Women: Supporters or Supported?' in *Sexual Divisions and Society*, eds D. L. Barker and S. Allen (London: Tavistock, 1976) p. 119.

51. See R. Lister and L. Wilson, *The Unequal Breadwinner* (London: National Council for Civil Liberties, 1976).

52. Letter from B. O'Malley to the Women's Liberation Campaign for Legal and Financial Independence, 14 May 1975.

53. *Report on the Social Insurance and Allied Services* (Beveridge) Cmd. 6404 (London: HMSO, 1942).

54. See H. Heclo, *Modern Social Politics in Britain and Sweden* (New Haven: Yale University Press, 1974) p. 143.

55. See ibid., pp. 148–9.

56. See P. Addison, *The Road to 1945* (London: Quartet, 1977) Chapter VIII.

57. J. Harris, 'Social Planning in War-time: Some Aspects of the Beveridge Report' in *War and Economic Development*, ed. J. Winter (London: Cambridge University Press, 1975) p. 248.

58. Before the Second World War, National Insurance benefits and contributions (apart from unemployment benefit) were managed by the 'approved societies' under the regulation of the Ministry of Health. After the war the state took over the administration of National Insurance. A Ministry of National Insurance and a Ministry of Pensions were established in 1946, and merged in 1953 to form the Ministry of Pensions and National

Insurance (MPNI). In the context of the creation of the National Health Service the state finally took over much of the working-class friendly society insurances established from the eighteenth century onwards. In 1966 MPNI was renamed the Ministry of Social Security and in 1968 it was integrated with the Ministry of Health to form the giant Department of Health and Social Security (DHSS).

59. R. Titmuss, 'New Guardians of the Poor in Britain' in *Social Security in International Perspective*, ed. S. Jenkins (New York: Columbia University Press, 1969) p. 156.
60. See Kincaid, *Poverty and Equality in Britain*, pp. 41–2.
61. Titmuss, 'New Guardians of the Poor', p. 156.
62. Ibid., p. 157.
63. See G. Weightman, 'Under the Grille', *New Society*, 5 January 1978, p. 5.
64. *Report on Social Insurance and Allied Services*, para 23.
65. The proportion of social security expenditure devoted to National Insurance has, however, increased from around 60 per cent in the 1940s to around 75 per cent in the mid-1970s.
66. Unfortunately there is insufficient space here to enter into the very important questions of pensions, retirement and old age.
67. Titmuss, 'New Guardians of the Poor', p. 167.
68. A detailed account of the context leading to the creation of SBC is provided by A. Webb, 'The Abolition of National Assistance' in *Change, Choice and Conflict in Social Policy*, eds P. Hall, H. Land, R. Parker and A. Webb (London: Heinemann, 1975).
69. See *Gilding the Ghetto*, CDP – Community Development Projects (London: Home Office, 1976).
70. *Social Security Statistics 1976*, Table 34.28.
71. *Supplementary Benefits Commission Annual Report 1976*, Cmnd. 6910 (London: HMSO, 1977) p. 126.
72. This was published on 13 July 1978 after this chapter was completed. It appears to reflect quite closely the proposed shape of reform as discussed here.
73. See K. Bell, P. Collison, S. Turner and S. Webber, 'National Insurance Local Tribunals: a Research Study', Part 1, *Journal of Social Policy*, vol. 3, no. 4 (1974) p. 306.
74. M. J. Hill, 'The Exercise of Discretion in the National Assistance Board', *Public Administration*, vol. 47 (1969) p. 85.
75. *The Limits of the Law*, CDP – Community Development Projects (London: Home Office, 1976) Chapter 7 and pp. 48–52.
76. See ibid., and M. J. Hill, 'Exercise of Discretion in the NAB'.
77. *Social Security Statistics 1976*, Table 34.97.
78. Ibid., Table 34.93.
79. The pay and conditions for work in local DHSS offices. The desk clerks are of course the front line representatives of the state apparatus and, given the functions of the system, it is hardly surprising that officers sometimes abuse claimants and vice versa. Over recent years the Civil and Public Services Association, the officers' union, has successfully cam-

paigned for an easing of their work-load, although it remains heavy, reflecting the low status of the system as a whole.

80. D. Donnison, 'Dear David Bull, Frank Field, Michael Hill and Ruth Lister . . .', *Social Work Today*, vol. 6, no. 20 (1976) p. 623.

81. See D. Donnison, 'Supplementary Benefits: Dilemmas and Priorities', *Journal of Social Policy*, vol. 5, no. 4 (1977) p. 346.

82. Ibid., pp. 354–5.

83. See D. Donnison, 'Against Discretion', *New Society*, 15 September 1977, p. 88.

84. T. Lynes, 'Unemployment Assistance Tribunals in the 1930's' in *Justice, Discretion and Poverty*, eds M. Adler and A. Bradley (London: Professional Books, 1975) p. 7.

85. R. Lister, *Justice for the Claimant*, Poverty Research Series No 4 (London: Child Poverty Action Group, 1974); R. Flockhart, 'Some Aspects of Tribunal Membership' in Adler and Bradley, *Justice, Discretion and Poverty*; K. Bell, *Research Study on Supplementary Benefit Appeal Tribunals* (London: HMSO, 1975).

86. *Social Security Statistics 1976*, Tables 1.20 and 34.20.

87. Lynes, 'Unemployment Assistance Tribunals', p. 8.

88. T. Prosser, 'Poverty, Ideology and Legality: Supplementary Benefit Appeal Tribunals and Their Predecessors', *British Journal of Law and Society*, vol. 4, no. 1 (1977) pp. 46–7.

89. See Donnison, 'Dear David Bull . . .', p. 624.

90. P. Seyd, 'The Child Poverty Action Group', *Political Quarterly*, vol. 47 (1976) p. 190.

91. B. Abel Smith and P. Townsend, *The Poor and the Poorest*, Occasional Papers in Social Administration No. 17 (London: Bell, 1965).

92. This particularly applies to reforms concerning pensioners.

93. See H. Rose, 'Up Against the Welfare State: the Claimant Unions' in *The Socialist Register 1973*, eds R. Miliband and J. Saville (London: Merlin, 1974).

94. See B. Jordan, *Poor Parents* (London: Routledge, 1974) Chapter 5.

95. At least according to B. Jordan, *Paupers* (London: Routledge, 1973).

CHAPTER 5

1. *Roof*, vol. 2, no. 1 (1977) p. 3. Similar proportions obtained in the nineteenth century according to E. Gauldie, *Cruel Habitations* (London: Allen & Unwin, 1974) pp. 164–5.

2. See B. Glastonbury, *Homeless near 1000 Homes* (London: Allen & Unwin, 1971) Chapter 3.

3. F. Engels, *The Housing Question* (Moscow: Progress Publishers, 1970) p. 42.

4. M. Ball, 'British Housing Policy and the House Building Industry', *Capital and Class*, no. 4 (1978) p. 79.

5. R. McCutcheon, 'High Flats in Britain, 1945 to 1971' in *Political Economy and the Housing Question* (London: Conference of Socialist Economists

180 NOTES AND REFERENCES TO PAGES 110–18

Housing Workshop, 1975) Chapter 5.

6. Various authors have pointed to the possibilities of absolute rent or super profits occasioned by the low organic composition of capital and barriers to capital penetration presented by the labour process in the house-building industry. See I. Bruegel, 'The Marxist Theory of Rent and the Contemporary City' in *Political Economy and the Housing Question*, p. 43.
7. M. Ball, *British Housing Policy and the House Building Industry*, Centre for Environmental Studies Conference Paper (London: 1977) p. 12.
8. Engels, *The Housing Question*, p. 19.
9. Ibid., p. 19
10. Ibid., p. 33.
11. K. Marx, *Capital*, vol. III (London: Lawrence & Wishart, 1972) Part IV.
12. See R. Murray, 'Value & Theory of Rent: Part 1', *Capital and Class*, no. 3 (1977) p. 112.
13. See R. Murray, 'Value & Theory of Rent: Part 2', *Capital and Class*, no. 4 (1978) p. 28, and I. Bruegel, 'The Marxist Theory of Rent', p. 43.
14. See Chapter 6 of this book.
15. M. Ball, 'British Housing Policy', p. 85.
16. See also *Housing: A Consultative Document*, Cmnd. 6851 (London: HMSO, 1977) p. 145, Table 7.
17. Gauldie, *Cruel Habitations*, p. 73.
18. See G. Stedman Jones, *Outcast London* (Harmondsworth: Penguin, 1976) Part II.
19. A. K. Cairncross, *Home and Foreign Investment 1870–1913* (Cambridge: Cambridge University Press, 1953), p. 86.
20. Gauldie, *Cruel Habitations*, p. 337.
21. This is documented, for example, in *The History of Working Class Housing*, ed. S. D. Chapman (Newton Abbot: David & Charles, 1971), especially the chapters by M. Beresford on Leeds and J. Treble on Liverpool.
22. Stedman Jones, *Outcast London*, pp. 210–13.
23. See *Housing Policy: Technical Volume 3* (London: HMSO, 1977) p. 74.
24. Gauldie, *Cruel Habitations*, p. 125.
25. D. Englander, *Bulletin for the Study of Labour History* no. 36 (1978) p. 53, points out that 'landlords and bailiffs who overstepped the bounds of propriety could provoke angry crowds; the labouring poor never fully accepted the absolutism of proprietory right', but we know little of this resistance.
26. S. Clarke and N. Ginsburg, 'The Political Economy of Housing' in *Political Economy and the Housing Question*, p. 13.
27. The inequitable tax position of housing landlords is explained by A. A. Nevitt, *Housing Taxation and Subsidies* (London: Nelson, 1966) Chapter 4.
28. P. Dickens, *Social Change, Housing and the State*, Centre for Environmental Studies Conference Paper (London, 1977) p. 4.
29. P. Johnson, *Land Fit for Heroes* (Chicago: Chicago University Press, 1968) p. 18.

30. P. Beirne, *Fair Rent and Legal Fiction* (London: Macmillan, 1977) p. 78.
31. See ibid., p. 86; P. Piratin, *Our Flag Stays Red* (London: Thames Publications, 1948); B. Moorhouse, M. Wilson and P. Chamberlain, 'Rent Strikes – Direct Action and the Working Class' in *The Socialist Register 1972*, eds. R. Miliband and J. Saville (London: Merlin, 1972); P. Corrigan and N. Ginsburg, 'Tenants' Struggle and Class Struggle' in *Political Economy and the Housing Question*, Chapter 9.
32. Beirne, *Fair Rent and Legal Fiction*, p. 221.
33. M. J. Barnett, *The Politics of Legislation: the Rent Act 1957* (London: Weidenfeld, 1969) p. 78.
34. See R. Means, *Social Work and the Undeserving Poor*, Centre for Urban and Regional Studies, University of Birmingham, Occasional Paper no. 37 (1977) Chapter 2.
35. See M. H. Wicks, 'Labour and the Private Landlord', *Social and Economic Administration*, vol. 4 (1970).
36. See *Report of the Committee on Housing in Greater London* (Milner Holland) Cmnd. 2605 (London: HMSO, 1965) Appendix II.
37. See R. Crossman, *The Diaries of a Cabinet Minister*, volume 1, *Minister of Housing 1964–66* (London: Hamish Hamilton and Jonathan Cape, 1975) p. 309.
38. The details of the system in practice are well explained in 'Housing Advice Notes', *Roof*, vol. 1, nos. 4, 5, 6 (1976).
39. *Housing Policy: Technical Volume 1* (London: HMSO, 1977) p. 77.
40. Beirne, *Fair Rent and Legal Fiction*, pp. 137–8.
41. M. Harloe, R. Issacharoff and R. Minns, *The Organisation of Housing* (London: Heinemann, 1974) pp. 114–16.
42. See Crossman, *Diaries of a Cabinet Minister*, vol. 1, p. 28. Crossman's advisers included Harry Hyams, a well-known property speculator, owner of Centre Point, who was also a director of the giant construction corporation G. Wimpey & Co.
43. Ibid., p. 619.
44. See *Roof*, vol. 1, no. 1 (1976) p. 4.
45. *The Poverty of the Improvement Programme*, CDP – Community Development Projects (London: Home Office, 1977).
46. Subsequently the Housing Corporation, as part of this deal, 'signed an agreement with merchant bankers Morgan Grenfell to borrow £35 million from a syndicate of banks at 1¼% above the London interbank rate', according to *Up Against a Brick Wall: the Dead-End in Housing Policy* (London: National Union of Public Employees/Services to Community Action and Tenants, 1978) p. 52.
47. See *Roof*, vol. 1, no. 5 (1976) pp. 130–2.
48. See Chapter 6 of this book for further explanation.
49. See *Annual Report of the Housing Corporation 1975–6* (London: 1976) p. 1.
50. See *Roof*, vol. 1, no. 5 (1976) p. 130.
51. J. Swann, 'Housing Associations: a Socialist Critique' in *Political Economy and the Housing Question*, p. 117.

52. *Housing Policy: a Consultative Document*, p. 8.
53. Ibid., p. 50.
54. Engels, *The Housing Question*, p. 9.
55. Ibid., p. 45.
56. See Clarke and Ginsburg, 'The Political Economy of Housing', p. 18.
57. See *Housing Policy: Technical Volume 2* (London: HMSO, 1977) Table VI.19.
58. See ibid., Table VII.4.
59. Ibid., p. 129.
60. See S. Weir, 'Red Line Districts', *Roof*, vol. 1, no. 4 (1976) pp. 109–14; M. Boddy, 'Building Societies and Owner Occupation' in *Housing and Class in Britain* (London: Conference of Socialist Economists Housing Workshop, 1976) p. 39; S. Duncan, 'The Housing Question and the Structure of the Housing Market', *Journal of Social Policy*, vol. 6, no. 4 (1977) pp. 389–96.
61. Weir, 'Red Line Districts', p. 114.
62. J. Ford, 'Building Society Managers', *Roof*, vol. 1, no. 5 (1976) p. 144.
63. Harloe *et al.*, *The Organisation of Housing*, p. 84.
64. *Profits Against Houses*, CDP – Community Development Projects (London: Home Office, 1976), p. 51.
65. N. Finnis, 'Mortgage Arrears: Tomorrow's Problem', *Roof*, vol. 3, no. 1 (1978) p. 10.
66. J. Tunnard, *No Father No Home?*, Poverty Pamphlet No. 28 (London: Child Poverty Action Group, 1976).
67. *Profits Against Houses*, p. 55.
68. See N. McIntosh, 'Mortgage Support Scheme Holds the Lending Lines', *Roof*, vol. 3, no. 2 (1978) pp. 44–7.
69. D. McKay, *Housing and Race in Industrial Society* (London: Croom Helm, 1977) p. 90.
70. Harloe *et al.*, *The Organisation of Housing*, p. 87.
71. *Sunday Times*, 21 May 1978; see also *Roof*, vol. 3, no. 2 (1978) p. 39.
72. *Profits Against Houses*, p. 38.
73. R. Titmuss, *Essays on the 'Welfare State'* (London: Allen & Unwin, 1963) Chapter 2.
74. S. Clark, *Who Benefits?*, a Study of the Distribution of Public Expenditure on Housing (London: Shelter, 1977) p. 13. In 1966 the Labour government introduced the option mortgage scheme, which assists a small stratum of owner-occupiers who pay little or no income tax. This was the only aspect of housing policy mentioned in Harold Wilson's memoirs of the 1964–70 Labour government.
75. *Housing Policy: a Consultative Document*, p. iv; see also ibid., p. 39.
76. N. Branson and M. Heinemann, *Britain in the Nineteen Thirties* (London: Panter, 1973) p. 205.
77. Dickens, *Social Change, Housing and the State*, p. 19.
78. S. Pollard, *The Development of the British Economy 1914–1967* (London: Edward Arnold, 1969) p. 238.
79. Crossman, *Diaries of a Cabinet Minister*, vol. 1, p. 605.
80. *Housing Policy: Technical Volume 2*, p. 106.

81. Duncan, 'The Housing Question and the Structure of the Housing Market', p. 398.

CHAPTER 6

1. See *Public Housing in Europe and America*, ed. J. S. Fuerst (London: Croom Helm, 1974); and A. Heidenheimer, H. Heclo and C. Teich Adams, *Comparative Public Policy* (London: Macmillan, 1976) Chapter 3.
2. Various interpretations are offered by the following: *Housing Policy: Technical Volume 1* (London: HMSO, 1977), pp. 3–7; P. Wilding, 'Towards Exchequer Subsidies for Housing 1906–1914', *Social and Economic Administration*, vol. 6, no. 1 (1973); B. B. Gilbert, *British Social Policy 1914–1939* (London: Batsford, 1970) Chapter 3.
3. See A. S. Wohl, *The Eternal Slum: Housing and Social Policy in Victorian London* (London: Edward Arnold, 1977) p. 324.
4. P. Dickens, *Social Change, Housing and the State*, Centre for Environmental Studies Conference Paper (London: 1977) p. 16.
5. M. Foot, *Aneurin Bevan: a Biography*, vol. 2 (London: Davis-Poynter, 1973) p. 95.
6. R. Crossman, *The Diaries of a Cabinet Minister*, vol. 1, *Minister of Housing 1964–66* (London: Hamish Hamilton and Jonathan Cape, 1975) p. 43.
7. R. McCutcheon, 'High Flats in Britain, 1945 to 1971' in *Political Economy and the Housing Question* (London: Conference of Socialist Economists Housing Workshop, 1975) p. 97.
8. See F. Berry, *Housing: the Great British Failure* (London: Charles Knight, 1974) p. 249.
9. *Housing Policy: Technical Volume 3* (London: HMSO, 1977) Table VIII. 16.
10. M. Harloe, R. Issacharoff and R. Minns, *The Organisation of Housing in London* (London: Heinemann, 1974) p. 32.
11. J. Swann, 'The Political Economy of Residential Redevelopment in London' in *Political Economy and the Housing Question*, Chapter 6.
12. See *Housing Policy: a Consultative Document*, Cmnd. 6851 (London: HMSO, 1977) p. 152, Table 17.
13. M. Bowley, *Housing and the State 1919–1944* (London: Allen & Unwin, 1945) p. 129.
14. This is explained further in B. Kilroy, 'How a Council Loses on Sales', *Roof*, vol. 2, no. 3 (1977) pp. 76–80.
15. M. Ball, 'British Housing Policy and the House Building Industry', *Capital and Class*, no. 4 (1978) pp. 94–5.
16. See *Housing Policy: Technical Volume 3*, p. 43. For further explanation see D. Webster, 'Council Rents', *New Society*, 23 October 1975, p. 213.
17. See A. Murie, 'Council Sales Mean Poor Law Housing', *Roof*, vol. 2, no. 2 (1977).
18. See S. Schifferes, 'Council Tenants and Housing Policy in the 1930's' in *Housing and Class in Britain* (London: Conference of Socialist Economists Housing Workshop, 1976) p. 67.

19. See ibid., pp. 67–8, and P. Corrigan and N. Ginsburg, 'Tenants' Struggle and Class Struggle' in *Political Economy and the Housing Question*, pp. 138–9.
20. See J. G. Bulpitt, *Party Politics in English Local Government* (London: Longman, 1967).
21. R. Parker, *The Rents of Council Houses*, Occasional Papers in Social Administration no. 22 (London: Bell, 1967), p. 47.
22. *Housing Policy: Technical Volume 3*, p. 40.
23. Ibid., p. 40.
24. See A. Barnett, 'Class Struggle and the Heath Government', *New Left Review*, no. 77 (1973); and R. Blackburn, 'The Heath Government: a New Course for British Capitalism', *New Left Review*, no. 70 (1971).
25. *Fair Deal for Housing*, Cmnd. 4728 (London: HMSO, 1971). This was the White Paper which laid out the principles of the Housing Finance Act, 1972. For further discussion on this act see P. Beirne, *Fair Rent and Legal Fiction* (London: Macmillan, 1977) Chapter 3.
26. See L. Sklair, 'The Struggle Against the Housing Finance Act' in *The Socialist Register 1975*, eds R. Miliband and J. Saville (London: Merlin, 1975).
27. The council's story and the context of the struggle is told in D. Skinner and J. Langdon, *The Clay Cross Story* (Nottingham: Spokesman, 1974).
28. *Housing Policy: a Consultative Document*, para. 9.37.
29. Ibid., p. 152.
30. Ibid., para. 5.29.
31. *The Government's Expenditure Plans 1978–79 to 1981–82*, volume II, Cmnd. 7049-II (London: HMSO, 1978) Table 2.7.
32. Wohl, *The Eternal Slum*, p. 188. See also G. Stedman Jones, *Outcast London* (Harmondsworth: Penguin, 1971) pp. 193–6.
33. B. Webb, *My Apprenticeship* (Harmondsworth: Penguin, 1971) p. 267.
34. Ibid., p. 272.
35. Ibid., p. 273.
36. Ibid., pp. 278–9.
37. Wohl, *The Eternal Slum*, p. 154.
38. Ibid., p. 155–6. See also Stedman Jones, *Outcast London*, pp. 183–8.
39. Wohl, *The Eternal Slum*, pp. 159–60.
40. Ibid., pp. 267–8.
41. See J. Tarn, *Five Per Cent Philanthropy* (London: 1973) Chapter 8.
42. *The Housing of the Working Classes in London* (London: London County Council, 1913) p. 104.
43. S. Damer, *Working Class Housing and Working Class Incorporation: Glasgow 1861–1919*, unpublished paper given to the Conference of Socialist Economists Housing Workshop (1976) pp. 15–23.
44. S. Damer, 'Wine Alley: the Sociology of a Dreadful Enclosure', *Sociological Review*, vol. 22 (1974) p. 225.
45. *Whatever Happened to Council Housing?*, CDP – Community Development Projects (London: Home Office, 1976) p. 82.
46. Ibid., p. 48.
47. In a submission to a government committee in 1938 the Incorporated

Society of Women Housing Managers suggested the further employment of women as managers because of 'the greater facility with which they are able to establish friendly and confidential relations with the housewife, the real manager of the home'. Central Housing Advisory Committee, *Management of Municipal Housing Estates* (London: HMSO, 1938) p. 10.

48. J. Tucker, *Honourable Estates* (London: Gollancz, 1966) p. 11.
49. C. Ward, *Tenants Take Over* (London: Architectural Press, 1974) p. 12.
50. R. Wilson, *Difficult Housing Estates* (London: Tavistock Institute, 1963) p. 14.
51. Ibid., p. 14.
52. D. S. Byrne, *Problem Families – a Housing Lumpenproletariat* (Durham: Durham University Department of Sociology and Social Administration, 1974) p. 12.
53. Ibid., p. 12.
54. Central Housing Advisory Committee, *Council Housing Purposes, Procedures and Priorities*, Cullingworth Report (London: HMSO, 1969) p. 252.
55. D. Evans, *Where Do We Go From Here?: a Study of Eviction From Council Housing in Birmingham*, M. A. Dissertation, Applied Social Studies Department, Warwick University (1976).
56. See B. Glastonbury, *Homeless Near a Thousand Homes* (London: Allen & Unwin, 1971) Chapters 3, 4, 5.
57. See J. Baldwin, 'Problem Housing Estates', *Social and Economic Administration*, vol. 10 (1976) pp. 131–4. See also *Whatever Happened to Council Housing?* and *Coventry's Council Houses: the New Slums* (London: Shelter, 1974).
58. See Damer, 'Wine Alley'.
59. S. Damer, 'A Note on Housing Allocation' in *Housing and Class in Britain*, p. 73.
60. Tucker, *Honourable Estates*, p. 50.
61. *Council Housing Purposes, Procedures and Priorities*, para. 96.
62. F. Gray, 'The Management of Local Authority Housing' in *Housing and Class in Britain*, p. 80.
63. S. Damer and R. Madigan, 'The Housing Investigator', *New Society*, 25 July 1974, p. 226.
64. *Rights* (Bulletin of the National Council for Civil Liberties), vol. 2, no. 3, p. 8.
65. R. Means, *Social Work and the Undeserving Poor*, Centre for Urban and Regional Studies, University of Birmingham, Occasional Paper no. 37 (1977) p. 34.
66. J. Lambert, B. Blackaby and C. Paris, *Neighbourhood Politics and Housing Opportunities*, Centre for Environmental Studies Conference Paper (London: 1975) p. 9.
67. Ibid., p. 9.
68. N. Lewis, 'Council Housing Allocation: Problems of Discretion and Control', *Public Administration*, vol. 54 (1976) p. 155.
69. Gray, 'The Management of Local Authority Housing', p. 76.
70. See the following: M. Harloe (ed.), *Captive Cities* (London: Wiley, 1977) particularly the Introduction and Chapters 1, 2 and 7; R. Pahl, *Whose*

City? (Harmondsworth: Penguin, 1975) Chapter 13; P. Norman, *Managerialism: A Review of Recent Work*, Centre for Environmental Studies Conference Paper (London: 1975).

71. Harloe (ed.), *Captive Cities*, p. 14.
72. Ward, *Tenants Take Over*, for example.
73. V. Karn, 'The Newest Profession', *Roof*, vol. 2, no. 6, p. 178.
74. See J. English, R. Madigan and P. Norman, *Slum Clearance* (London: Croom Helm, 1976) pp. 121–2.

Index

'A' and 'AX' codes   100
Abel Smith, Brian   179
Adamson, Olivia   176
Addison, Paul   169, 177
allocation of council housing   158, 164–7
Altvater, Elmer   28, 170
Anderson, Michael   172
Anderson, Perry   169
appeals   102–4; *see also* Supplementary Benefit Appeals Tribunals

Baldwin, John   185
Ball, Michael   109–10, 179, 183
Barnett, Anthony   184
Barnett, M. J.   181
Beechey, Veronica   175
Beirne, Piers   118, 181, 184
Bell, Kathleen   178, 179
Bentham, Jeremy   52
Beresford, M.   180
Berry, Fred   183
Bevan, Aneurin   113, 143–4, 164, 183
Beveridge, William   41, 57, 91
Beveridge Report   8, 9, 12, 85, 88–9, 95–7, 177, 178
Bismarck, Otto von   12, 32, 172
Blackburn, Robin   184
Boddy, Martin   182
Boulding, Kenneth   39, 171
Bowley, Marion   183
Branson, Noreen   174, 182
Briggs, Eric   173, 174
Brown, K. D.   173

Brown, R. G. S.   172
Bruegel, Irene   180
building societies   116, 130–6, 149
Bulpitt, J. G.   184
bureaucracy   xiii, xiv, xv, 6, 31, 33, 35, 55, 66, 95–107, 119, 123, 143, 154, 155, 161, 167–8
bureaucratism   4, 5, 10, 13, 145, 156, 166, 168
Burns, E. M.   61, 63
Byrne, David S.   185

Cairncross, A. K.   180
Callaghan, Jim   121
Chadwick, Edwin   41, 52
Chamberlain, Joseph   11, 55
Chamberlain, Neville   49
Charity Organisation Society   43, 57, 157
Checkland, S. G. and E. O. A.   172, 176
Child Poverty Action Group   105
citizenship   13, 14, 29, 32, 35, 37, 38, 39, 42, 43, 65, 80, 95, 99, 104, 106, 168
claimants unions   103, 106
Clark, Steve   182
Clarke, Simon   171, 180, 182
class struggle   2, 3, 4, 5–13, 22, 23, 25, 26, 40, 43, 46, 47, 53, 57, 58, 65, 78, 81, 104–7, 108, 117–18, 140, 150, 153–4, 156
Clay Cross   153, 154
cohabitation rule   87–8, 99, 100, 105
Colletti, Lucio   16, 169

Communist Party of Great Britain 119, 121

Community Development Projects (CDPs) xiii, 181, 182, 184

Conservative Party 141

contribution principle 49, 61, 64–5, 67–8, 74, 76–7, 80, 89, 90, 91, 94, 100, 172

Coote, Anna 177

Corrigan, Paul 181, 184

cost yardstick *see* Housing Subsidies Act, 1967

council housing 3, 6, 10, 12, 15, 109, 112, 113–14, 118, 119, 121, 126, 127, 128, 130, 135, 138–68; management 109, 126, 140, 147, 156–68; subsidies and finance 123, 134, 139, 140–56

Coussins, J. 177

Crossman, Richard 9, 122, 123, 144, 181, 182, 183

Cubitt, Thomas 115

cuts in welfare expenditure ix, 4, 54, 60, 64–5, 101, 125, 132, 135, 142, 143, 145, 156, 168

Damer, Sean 184, 185

day nurseries 86–7, 92, 93

Deacon, Alan 173, 174

Delmar, Ros 175

Department of Health and Social Security (DHSS) 74–6, 85, 87, 96–7, 99, 100, 103, 105, 106, 166, 167, 172, 174, 178

Dickens, Peter 142, 180, 182, 183

differential rent schemes *see* rent rebates

Dobb, Maurice 172

domestic labour 24, 25, 79–81, 86, 91, 93

Donnison, David 101–2, 179

Duncan, S. 182, 183

Durcan, J. W. 175

Earnings Related Supplement (ERS) 67–9, 71

Elks, L. 174

Ellis, N. D. 174

Employment Protection Act, 1975 91

Engels, Friedrich 27, 81, 109, 111, 127–8, 175, 179, 180, 182

Englander, D. 180

English, John 186

Equal Pay Act, 1970 90

Evans, David 185

Exceptional Circumstances Additions (ECAs) 101

Exceptional Needs Payments (ENPs) 101

'fair rents' 12, 119, 122–4, 125, 141, 152

family 2, 3, 17, 24–5, 48, 49, 59–60, 62, 68, 77–8, 79–94, 95, 98, 104, 109, 131, 134, 161, 185

Family Income Supplement (FIS) 48, 70–1, 76, 86, 94

family wage 23, 24–5, 80–1, 90

fetishism 17, 36–7, 44, 128

Field, Frank 174, 175

Fine, Ben 170

Finer, M. 176

Finer Report 82, 84, 85, 86, 176

Finnis, Nick 182

Flockhart, R. 179

Foot, Michael 183

Ford, J. 182

Foster, John 172

four-week rule 73–4, 100, 105

friendly societies 11, 49, 95, 172, 177, 178

Fryer, R. H. 71, 174

Fuerst, J. S. 183

Gardiner, Jean 177

Gauldie, Enid 179

General Household Survey (GHS) 92–3, 114, 177

General Strike, 1926 33, 59–60, 64

Gennard, John 173, 175

George, Victor 41, 68, 97, 171, 172

Geras, Norman 18, 170

Gilbert, B. B. 172, 173, 183

Gill, Tess 177